Inside CORBA

Distributed Object Standards and Applications

Thomas J. Mowbray
William A. Ruh

ADDISON-WESLEY

An imprint of Addison Wesley Longman, Inc.

Reading, Massachusetts • Harlow, England • Menlo Park, California
Berkeley, California • Don Mills, Ontario • Sydney
Bonn • Amsterdam • Tokyo • Mexico City

The publisher offers discounts on this book when ordered in quantity for special sales. For more information, please contact:

Corporate & Professional Publishing Group
Addison Wesley Longman, Inc.
One Jacob Way
Reading, Massachusetts 01867

Library of Congress Cataloging-in-Publication Data

Mowbray, Thomas J.
    Inside CORBA : distributed object standards and applications / Thomas J. Mowbray, William A. Ruh.
        p.   cm.
    Includes bibliographical references and index.
    ISBN 0-201-89540-4
    1. Object-oriented programming (Computer science)   2. CORBA (Computer architecture) I. Ruh, William A.
    QA76.64.M695   1997
    005.2'76'0218—dc21   97-16075
                                                                              CIP

Sponsoring Editor: J. Carter Shanklin
Project Manager: Sarah Weaver
Production: Editorial Services of New England, Inc.
Set in 10-point Melior by Circle Graphics

ISBN 0-201-89540-4
Text printed on recycled and acid-free paper.
2 3 4 5 6 7   MA   00 99 98 97

2nd Printing October, 1997

The Addison-Wesley Object Technology Series
Grady Booch, Ivar Jacobson, and James Rumbaugh, Series Editors
[http://www.awl.com/cseng/otseries/]

David Bellin and Susan Suchman Simone, *The CRC Card Book*
0-201-89535-8

Grady Booch, *Object Solutions: Managing the Object-Oriented Project*
0-8053-0594-7

Grady Booch, *Object-Oriented Analysis and Design with Applications*
Second Edition, 0-8053-5340-2

Dave Collins, *Designing Object-Oriented User Interfaces*
0-8053-5350-X

Martin Fowler with Kendall Scott
UML Distilled: Applying the Standard Object Modeling Language
0-201-32563-2

Martin Fowler, *Analysis Patterns: Reusable Object Models*
0-201-89542-0

Ivar Jacobson, Maria Ericsson, and Agenta Jacobson
*The Object Advantage: Business Process Reengineering
with Object Technology*
0-201-42289-1

Ivar Jacobson, Magnus Christerson, Patrik Jonsson, and Gunnar Overgaard
Object-Oriented Software Engineering: A Use Case Driven Approach
0-201-54435-0

Ivar Jacobson, Martin Griss, and Patrik Jonsson
Software Reuse: Architecture, Process and Organization for Business Success
0-201-92476-5

Wilf LaLonde, *Discovering Smalltalk*
0-8053-2720-7

Lockheed Martin Advanced Concepts Center and
Rational Software Corporation
Succeeding with the Booch and OMT Methods: A Practical Approach
0-8053-2279-5

Thomas Mowbray and William Ruh
Inside CORBA: Distributed Object Standards and Applications
0-201-89540-4

Ira Pohl, *Object-Oriented Programming Using C++*
Second Edition, 0-201-89550-1

David N. Smith, *IBM Smalltalk: The Language*
0-8053-0908-X

Daniel Tkach and Richard Puttick, *Object Technology in Application
Development*
Second Edition, 0-201-49833-2

Daniel Tkach, Walter Fang, and Andrew So
Visual Modeling Technique: Object Technology Using Visual Programming
0-8053-2574-3

Forthcoming Titles

Grady Booch, James Rumbaugh, and Ivar Jacobson
Unified Modeling Language User Guide
0-201-57168-4

Ivar Jacobson, Grady Booch, and James Rumbaugh
The Objectory Software Development Process
0-201-57169-2

James Rumbaugh, Ivar Jacobson, and Grady Booch
Unified Modeling Language Reference Manual
0-201-30998-X

This book is dedicated to:

My lovely wife,
Kate Mowbray

My patient and caring wife, Karen, and wonderful children
Kayla, Kristen, Katie, and Colin

Contents

Part 1   **CORBA Basics**

Part 2   **CORBA Standards**

List of Figures and Tables

Foreword

The field of distributed object computing is reaching maturity. Standards have been available for more than five years (the first version of the Common Object Request Broker Architecture, or CORBA, specification appeared in late 1991), and dozens of implementations of both CORBA and layered application development services are available. Distributed object solutions for real business problems are becoming the norm, replacing the experimental vehicles of the early 1990s.

With a crowd of books available to help make this natural software development evolution possible, and more books appearing all the time, the reader may wonder at the value of another book illuminating the CORBA and layered specifications. This book breaks the mold, however. By taking the reader through the entire spectrum of the distributed object approach, from requirements analysis through systems development, with a thorough treatment of relevant standards, Ruh and Mowbray leave one with a firm grounding in the subject. More important, for the first time, management of distributed object systems, including legacy systems integration, is treated on an equal footing. Given the fact that systems maintenance and management occupies far more of the lifecycle of a software system than analysis and development, stressing management requirements is an important component of the book.

When the Object Management Group began its work in 1989, one of the aims was to move software development closer to the age of components. While most engineering fields by the late 1980s had already moved to standard components (from bolt thread sizes to integrated circuits), software has resisted standardization, apparently preferring the "artistic" mode of creation, with each new piece of software hand-crafted by wizards and warlocks. It is particularly important that Ruh and Mowbray emphasize the need to support software reuse in the same way integrated circuit designers reuse cell designs. Furthermore, they illuminate the CORBA approach to building, managing, and composing reusable software components of various sizes.

As more organizations build distributed, object-oriented component software in heterogeneous settings (and all organizational settings are heterogenous), clear approaches to using the relevant standards and tools are needed. Enjoy a straightforward, no-nonsense introduction to the subject!

Richard Mark Soley, Ph.D.
Vice President & Technical Director
Object Management Group, Inc.

Preface

This book is written for people interested in adopting, designing, and developing systems using distributed objects. The common object request broker architecture (CORBA) is a consensus standard from industry that has significantly changed how information system development is accomplished for both achieving a distributed object-oriented system, as well as for migration of legacy systems to modern architectures. In writing this book, it is assumed the reader has a general knowledge of computer science or programming.

In the book, all standard CORBA-related specifications and key upcoming specifications are covered. Examples of the usage of CORBAservices are included. Since CORBA is a system-oriented technology, applications of the standards, including architecture, development, and migration approaches, are also covered. An entire chapter is devoted to a case study providing lessons learned from real experience.

Overview of the Contents

Part 1 provides an introduction to the technology and its benefits and the key motivations and impacts of adoption. Part 1 sets the context for CORBA technology, including addressing the key organizational challenges involved in the adoption of CORBA, as well as the essential management guidance to assure successful adoption and exploitation of the technology.

Part 2 provides a user's guide to the CORBA standards. These chapters provide a useful introduction to the standards with examples of their applications. The book covers detailed techniques for the use of the interface definition language (IDL), the CORBA 2 standard, and the CORBAservices. This coverage includes concepts, definitions, and examples. The new IDL/JAVA language mapping is introduced. In Part II, the first comprehensive model of CORBA components and CORBAservices is provided. This model and associated examples support rapid understanding of complex OMG standards and their interrelationships.

Part 3 addresses the application of CORBA to the definition and development of information systems. Technical guidance on how to apply the standards to create successful systems is provided. In particular, CORBA applications and lessons learned are covered. CORBA is compared with related technologies that will aid in your product selection and justification. Approaches for defining CORBA-based architecture, interfaces, and software are included.

Chapter 10 is a case study of a CORBA-based enterprise migration and the lessons learned in implementation and management of the project.

For readers new to CORBA, the book is intended to be read sequentially. If this book achieves anything, it is expected that the reader will understand IDL, an international standard (ISO DIS 14750) that is quickly becoming the universal notation for application program interfaces. Readers familiar with the CORBA infrastructure should read Chapter 4, covering the CORBAservices. Given the large number of these services, it is rare to encounter anyone with knowledge of them all or even of a significant number. Advanced readers should also read Chapter 7, which sets a context for the definition of CORBA-based software architectures, and Chapters 8 and 9, which define a unique approach for CORBA development and migration.

Relationship of This Book to CORBA Specifications

This book does not replace the CORBA standards documents. Instead, it provides an introduction and guidance to readers and users of the standards. There are several large volumes of CORBA standards, including CORBA, CORBAservices, and CORBAfacilities. Even though CORBA standards are more readable than many other types of standards documents, they are voluminous. In many cases, CORBA standards do not include abstractions and examples that are essential for understanding. Furthermore, the specifications do not deal with the application of CORBA to architecture and development, only to its definition.

The first priority is to provide an insightful summary of the standards. The abstractions and examples should aid the reader's understanding of the technology. The standards chapters do not attempt to address all the needs of knowledgeable CORBA practitioners, only the needs of people who want to learn more about the full range of the technology.

The second priority is to provide guidance on how to use these standards and technologies. The authors have been involved in the technical work and management of CORBA projects since 1991, when the standard was first created. This technology presents some fundamental differences in practices for developers, architects, and managers.

It was learned through reviewing and mentoring numerous CORBA projects that many organizations ignore these essential differences in their use of CORBA. This leads to the creation of systems with brittle architectures and implementations, similar to what was created with precursor technologies. By trial and error, some organizations learn how to use the technology more effectively, but many do not progress much beyond the initial level. A key mission of this book is to shorten the learning curve of those organizations adopting CORBA so that they can adjust the management and technology practices to fully exploit the CORBA technologies. In doing so, they will create and migrate to more-effective information systems.

Supplemental Materials

The CORBA specifications described in this book can be downloaded from the Object Management Group's Web site: `http://www.omg.org`

The specifications and profiles from the case study can be downloaded from `http://www-ismc.itsi.disa.mil/ciiwg/ciiwg.html`. Note that this is an ongoing activity and that document names have changed several times throughout this project.

Updates on the material in this book, news, and comments for the authors can be found on `http://www.serve.com/mowbray/`

Acknowledgments

The authors wish to thank all of the people who made this book possible. It is not possible to enumerate everybody who gave us ideas, review, help, and encouragement, but in particular, we wish to recognize Doug Antoon, Lydia Bennett, Bill Brown, Edna Davis, Vic DeMarines, John Eaton, Marty Faga, Millie Forrest, Julie Gravallese, Dolly Greenwood, Michael Guttman, Jack Hassall, Steve Hirsch, Bill Hoffman, Dr. Barry Horowitz, Joel Jacobs, Michael Josephs, Cliff Kottman, Eric Leach, Dave Lehman, Dr. Chris Lopresti, Frank Maginnis, Dr. Pat Mallett, Raphael Malveau, John Marsh, Jason Matthews, Dr. Mark Maybury, Skip McCormick, Chris Metzger, Kate Mowbray, John Polger, Henry Rothkopf, Karen Ruh, Richard Soley, Shel Sutton, John Tisaranni, Dr. Bhavani Thuraisingham, Pat Townes, Gloria Trumpower, Doug Vandermade, Debra Wittreich, Ron Zahavi, Tony Zawilski.

A special thanks is given to the reviewers of this book whose comments and insights were an invaluable contribution. John M. Anderson, Colm Bergin, IONA Technologies Inc.; Justin Freitag, Department of Software Development, Monash University, Australia; Donald G. Joder, Booz-Allen & Hamilton Inc.; Lloyd W. Taylor, DIGEX, Inc.; and John Weiler, The OBJECTive Technology Group, Ltd.

We would especially like to thank Liz May for coordinating all the editing, graphics, and typing for the manuscript, ensuring a successful completion to a long journey.

CORBA Basics

An Introduction to CORBA

1.1 Information Systems: From the Back Room to the Front Office

It is 1976. John, director of data processing, sits at his desk faced with the challenge of automating the financial management system for a Fortune 500 corporation. His boss, Paul, vice president of operations, has told him to develop a budget and plan. John calls his IBM representative and asks for assistance in the selection of hardware and system software. He estimates the lines of code to be developed and with this information determines the number of programmers. Finally, he lays out the schedule using the state-of-the-art in structured approaches, including a requirements analysis, design, code, test, and operations phase, and extends the schedule to 24 months.

His budget and plan approved by Paul, John sets about developing the system. Software designers are free to create designs based on requirements specifications, and programmers are free to code the designs in any manner they choose. John delivers a capability in 27 months, a little late and without all the envisioned functionality, but operating. Operations are more efficient, but few people in the corporation notice any substantial change. John is commended for his excellent effort and is able to relax as the system goes into operations mode.

In 1996, Karen, the new chief information officer, sits at a chair in the office of Paul, now CEO and president. At the meeting are the chief operations officer, the vice president for sales and marketing, and the general managers of each of the product divisions. The competition has released a new on-line service that allows their customers to easily order, track, and receive bills for goods and services. In addition, they have access to manuals and product literature. The competition's sales are up 40 percent and their customers are raving about the quality of the new service. Paul wants to know how they will respond to this new threat in no more than six months.

Each member of the company's senior management team responds by describing how his or her information system has all the information and functionality needed to support the development of a new service. Karen, whose office was only recently created, is forced to be the bearer of bad news to Paul. First, each of the systems is on a separate network. Second, three different hardware platforms are being used, and even where they are common, the versions of the operating systems are not compatible. Finally, each of the existing applications was built to operate in a stand-alone mode and offers no usable external interfaces. Karen's staff is currently poring over the existing documentation and legacy code to determine the difficulty of developing interfaces and extending functionality. She believes the financial management system, built and extended over the past 20 years, will be the most difficult to interoperate and probably should be replaced.

Karen presents a plan that shows how a new on-line service will be developed for the corporation by integrating the existing applications and replacing the financial management system with a commercial off-the-shelf product that meets 95 percent of their needs. She knows six months is not enough but cannot predict anything without building some of the interfaces. So she pushes the six months to twelve, knowing she can do it if all goes perfectly. The management team grumbles but accepts her proposal.

Her budget and plan approved, Karen sets about developing the system. The software designers are constrained by the existing systems and commercial off-the-shelf applications included in their design. The programmers are constrained by the existing code and application interfaces. Karen delivers a capability in 27 months, very late and without all the envisioned functionality, but operating. Everyone in the corporation is affected by the change as new applications are loaded onto their PCs. Paul continues to press for expansion of the service to keep up with the competition's continually improving capabilities.

1.2 Analyzing the Scenario

The underlying issues Karen confronted were:

- Multiple platforms, languages, and systems
- Mixture of client-server and mainframe-oriented applications built as stand-alone systems
- Lack of a well-defined architecture
- Conflicting data formats and semantic definitions
- Corporate desires to perform integration not planned in the original designs

This scenario is representative of the course of events at companies in recent years. Systems technology has changed from a largely invisible clerical support tool to a highly visible competitive necessity, often at considerable cost in terms of corporate resources and individual careers. The technological changes associated with this transformation of computing technology and business needs are depicted in Figure 1.1.

The first notable aspect of this shift in the application of computing technology is the move from a mainframe or mini-computer-based architecture, with few vendor choices and where custom development is the dominant activity, to a networked environment of heterogeneous mainframes, servers, workstations, and PCs, with many choices of vendors and operating systems. Second, enterprise-wide integration of existing legacy systems and commercial off-the-shelf products dominate the development activity. Component integration is becoming the focus of many system developments. Last is the move from back-office systems that few highly trained staff use to front-office and revenue-generating systems that are operated by many employees with a wide range of skills. This has fundamentally changed the role of computers and software from promoting operational efficiency to creating a competitive edge.

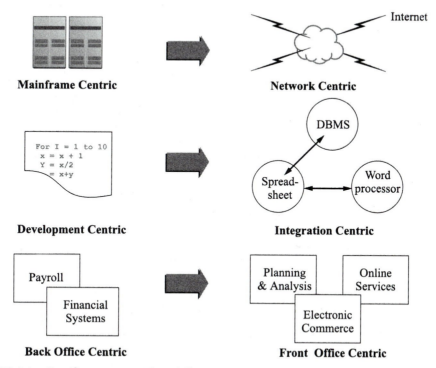

FIGURE 1.1   Significant computing shifts.

Common object request broker architecture (CORBA) is the technology that will help transform organizations so that they can deal with challenges such as those faced by Karen's organization. This book provides an introduction to CORBA from the perspective of system development.

1.3   Challenges in System Development

System development today is about rapid change and responding to the realities of the business environment. The key to successful system development is how well an enterprise can (1) perform system integration, (2) manage the future, and (3) find suitable supporting technology. Software development itself (programming) is no longer the central issue.

1.3.1   System Integration

Information systems development methods have changed from a reliance on unconstrained design and development to an increasing reliance on software integration methods in which new systems or applications are created by connecting existing components, as shown in Figure 1.2. These software components could have been previously developed, could be under development, or could be acquired from a vendor.

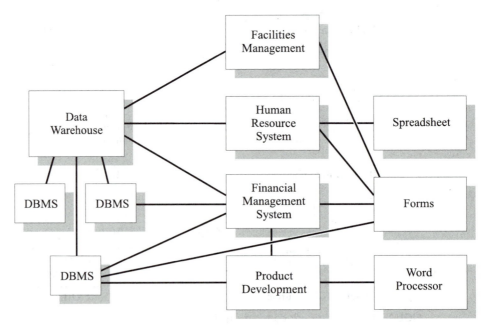

FIGURE 1.2   Sample integration scenario.

Integration is often viewed as a simpler process than new development. Unfortunately, integration has not resulted in deployment of new capability at either a faster or a cheaper rate. This is primarily due to the need to customize interfaces for components that were not originally designed to work together. In addition, a networked environment requires communications across heterogeneous hardware platforms. The time and energy spent to develop the interfaces can easily exceed the effort required to develop the code for the functions themselves.

Other stumbling blocks to good systems integration:

- Development and integration are fundamentally different activities requiring different talents and experiences.

- The potential always exists for locking into proprietary products and custom development, limiting flexibility in the future.

- Off-the-shelf products do not always work together or meet the needs of users.

1.3.2   Managing the Future

The art of managing the future is the key to making organizations more competitive. Rapid changes in the computer hardware and operating system software industries have changed the face of information systems development. The proliferation of networks, workstations, personal computers, and graphical user interfaces have shifted the functional and economic advantage to client-server systems. An expanding software application marketplace has produced an abundance of low cost, easy-to-use end-user applications. This has also produced increasingly sophisticated users, with much higher expectations for system performance, capability, and utility. And information technology has become a key to economic survival in the competitive global environment.

These changes have produced increased system complexity, intensified user demands, and heightened management expectations, which have resulted in higher economic stakes for organizations, information systems, and software developers. These pressures are further exacerbated by the requirement to maintain and grow a large portfolio of legacy software and systems.

1.3.3   Technology Availability

While system software manufacturers have long recognized the need for tools that support system integration, many have fallen short of satisfying the needs of the system implementors. The tools that do exist consist primarily of scripting languages, code libraries, and clipboard functions. Most of these provide only low-level communications-oriented functions, such as sockets and remote procedure calls. Rarely do these tools support integration across heterogeneous operating system platforms. In many instances, the tools are designed by people with limited experience in the development of large systems, which results in ineffective tools. In other cases, the complexities of the tools themselves actually increase the burden on the system implementer.

1.4   CORBA Overview

In recognition of this technology vacuum, the Object Management Group (OMG) was created in 1989. The OMG solicited input from all segments of the industry and eventually defined the CORBA standard. The OMG does not create products; it focuses on creating specifications that can be implemented and used by all. The CORBA specification is supported by more than 700 (and growing) hardware and software manufacturers, government organizations, and user groups. The CORBA specification has been implemented by numerous hardware and system software manufacturers, creating a rich and robust framework that successfully operates across heterogeneous computing platforms.

CORBA is proving to be one of the most important innovations in the recent history of information systems. It addresses the two most prominent problems faced in the software industry today: (1) the difficulty of developing client-server applications (2) by rapidly integrating legacy systems, off-the-shelf applications, and new development.

CORBA is a specification for an emerging technology known as distributed object management (DOM). DOM technology provides a higher-level, object-oriented interface on top of the basic distributed computing services. CORBA has emerged as the leading standard among DOM solutions, with only one significant competitor, Microsoft's distributed component object model (DCOM). DCOM, formally known as network object linking and embedding (OLE), is the natural evolution of the component object model (COM) and OLE. Later in the book, we will look at how DCOM and CORBA compare.

At its most basic level, CORBA defines a standard framework from which an information system implementer or software developer can easily and quickly integrate network-resident software modules and applications to create new, more-powerful applications. It combines object technology with a client-server model to provide a uniform view of an enterprise's computing system—everything on the network is an object.

The highest level specification is referred to as the object management architecture (OMA), which addresses four architectural elements, as shown in Figure 1.3. The term CORBA is often used to refer to the object request broker (ORB) itself, as well as to the entire OMG architecture.

The role of the ORB is to route requests among the other architectural components. CORBAservices, CORBAfacilities, and CORBAdomains are also

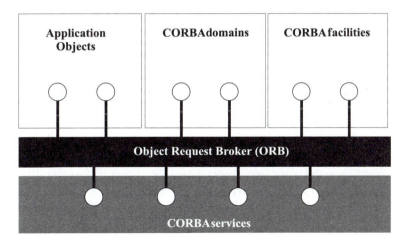

FIGURE 1.3   Object management architecture.

defined as part of the specifications. CORBAservices provide some basic system-level services, such as Naming, Persistence, and Event Notification. CORBAfacilities are a set of higher-level functions that cover a broad range of generically applicable facilities in areas such as user interface and information management. CORBAdomains are specific to particular application domains, such as manufacturing, finance, and telecommunications. Finally, application objects provide the new business capabilities that are created by the system implementors.

The key to integrating application objects is the specification of standard interfaces using the interface definition language (IDL). Once all applications and data have an IDL-compliant interface, communication is independent of physical location, platform type, networking protocol, and programming language. An information system is created by using CORBA to mediate the flow of control and information among these software objects.

1.5   CORBA Concepts

CORBA's theoretical underpinnings are based on three important concepts:

- Object-oriented model
- Open distributed computing environments
- Component integration and reuse

OMG has devoted considerable effort to developing the CORBA object model. The first version of this model was completed in July 1992, in an updated *Object Management Architecture Guide.* An industry standard model of the fundamental CORBA architecture was needed to assure consistency across implementations and because no single, uniformly supported object model had been developed by the computing industry. Arguably, however, there is agreement in the industry about the benefits of using an object model. Chief among these is the ability to contain the complexity of the overall system. Another key benefit is to improve the reusability of system components.

Distributed computing, in a generic sense, is rapidly emerging as the defining architecture for the entire computer industry. All modern business systems employ a network to connect a variety of computers, facilitating improved communication of information among applications. Furthermore, most up-to-date business applications feature an open environment, based on the connection of heterogeneous platforms. In the future, there will be continued evolution toward applications that exist as components across a network, which can be rapidly migrated and combined without significant effort. This is where CORBA shines, by providing unified access to applications, independent of the location of each application on the network.

The concept of component software has been a dream pursued in many forms for a long time. CORBA is arguably the first commercially successful version of a back plane, with which software objects can be plugged into the system. It achieves this distinction by providing:

- Uniform access to services
- Uniform discovery of resources and object names
- Uniform error handling methods
- Uniform security policies

These capabilities facilitate the integration and reuse of systems and system components, independent of network location and the details of underlying implementation technology.

1.5.1   The Object Model

CORBA is solidly grounded in fundamental object-oriented concepts, as shown in Figure 1.4. These concepts, important to understanding the contents of this book, are:

- Objects—Software entities that contain attributes and exhibit behavior through methods. In traditional terminology, attributes can be thought of as data or data structures and behaviors can be thought of as operations.
- Classes—Clusters of objects that share common behavior.

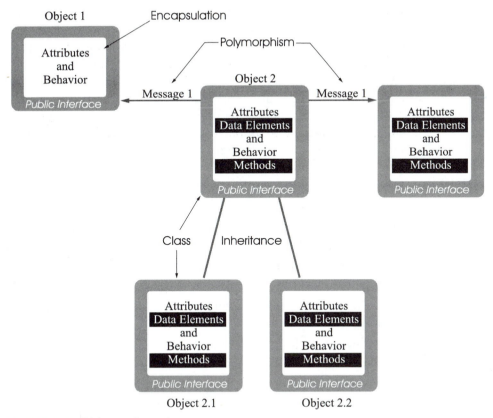

FIGURE 1.4   Object-oriented concepts.

- Encapsulation—The bundling of attributes and behaviors into well-defined software packages, concealing the internal structure of attributes and the details of behaviors through a public interface.

- Inheritance—The ability of a class to pass on attributes and behaviors to its descendants.

- Polymorphism—The ability of two or more classes to respond to the same message, each in its own way.

These same concepts are applied to many other aspects of computing technology. For example, object-oriented analysis and design techniques (the art of understanding the system and how to implement it) focus on discovering objects, attributes, and relationships, as well as the required behavior of objects. Database systems based on these concepts provide for the storage and management of objects. However, detailed nuances of these concepts allow for different implementations and conflicts (as you will quickly discover if you put two object-oriented methodologists in the same room). The CORBA object model defines key boundaries and meanings to enable unambiguous interpretation of these concepts. Without a common object model, the implementation of CORBA-compliant tools by independent software manufacturers might otherwise produce fatal incompatibilities.

CORBA's object model is based on a complete object approach in which a client sends a message to an object. The message identifies an object, and one or more parameters are included. The first parameter defines the operation to be performed, although the specific method used is determined by the receiving object (or in some cases, the ORB).

The CORBA object model consists of:

- Objects—An encapsulated entity that provides services to a client.

- Requests—An action created by a client directed to a target object that includes information on the operation to be performed and zero or more actual parameters.

- Object Creation and Destruction—Based on the state of requests, objects are created or deleted.

- Types—An identifiable entity defined over values. Legal values are shown in Figure 1.5.

- Interfaces—The specification of operations that a client can request from an object.

- Operations—An identifiable entity that defines what a client can request from an object.

Object implementation in CORBA, illustrated in Figure 1.6, is realized through a model consisting of two parts: the construction model and the execution model. The construction model describes how services are defined; the execution model describes how services are performed. With respect to the construction model, the object implementation definition provides the information needed to create objects and allow them to provide services, including definitions of methods and the intended type of an object. The execution model ensures that the requested service is performed by executing code that operates on data.

1.5.2   Open Distributed Computing Environment

CORBA is based on a client-server model of distributed computing. In the client-server model, a request for service is made from one software component to another on a network. CORBA adds an additional dimension to this model by inserting a broker between the client and server components. The broker

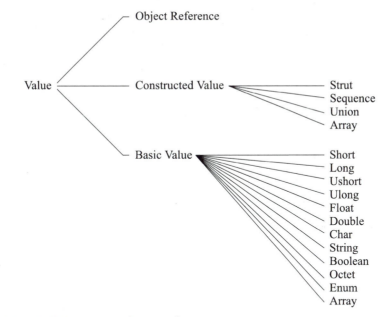

FIGURE 1.5   CORBA supported type values.

reduces the complexity of implementing the interaction between the client and server.

The broker plays two key roles. First, it provides common services, including basic messaging and communication between client and server, directory services, meta-data description, security services, and location transparency. Second, it insulates the application from the specifics of the system configuration, such as hardware platforms and operating systems, network protocols, and implementation languages.

CORBA is based on a peer-to-peer communications model and supports both synchronous and a limited version of asynchronous communications. The underlying interprocess communication in CORBA is handled through

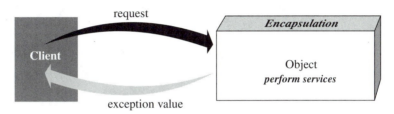

FIGURE 1.6   CORBA object implementation model.

the general inter-ORB protocol (GIOP). The GIOP was specified to allow interoperability among ORB implementations. It assumes an underlying connection-oriented transport layer. The GIOP defines a transfer syntax, known as common data representation (CDR), and seven basic message types.

The mapping of GIOP to TCP/IP is referred to as the internet inter-ORB protocol (IIOP). The interoperable object reference (IOR) is the mechanism through which objects are accessed through the IIOP and between ORB vendors. The IOR includes the ORB's internal object reference, Internet host address, and port numbers. It is managed by the interoperating ORBs and is not visible to application programmers.

In addition to IIOP, the DCE environment-specific inter-ORB protocol (DCE ESIOP) provides support for DCE's RPC mechanism, allowing CORBA to coexist with a DCE-based system.

The ORB itself handles the communications routing of a request, as well as any ancillary services required to perform the request, as shown in Figure 1.7. The object that makes the request is referred to as the client. If an abnormal condition occurs during the execution of a request, an exception value is returned to the client. Requests can be of both a static and dynamic nature.

Static invocations are requests that have been fully defined at compile time and are made through an IDL stub to a skeleton on the server side. Dynamic invocations provide the ability to add new objects and interfaces without requiring changes to the client code. Dynamic invocation requires the use of the dynamic invocation interface (DII). The dynamic skeleton interface (DSI) is the server-side equivalent.

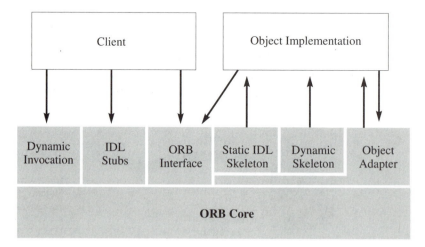

FIGURE 1.7 Object request broker interface.

1.5.3   Component Integration and Reuse

The twin concepts of software reuse and software integration are closely related since integration is the combination of two or more existing components. Without good integration tools and techniques, reuse is difficult and will probably not happen to any significant degree because, without a back plane or broker, custom interfaces must be defined for each interaction between components. With a broker, however, each interface is defined just once and subsequent interactions are handled by the broker. With CORBAidl, these interfaces can be defined in a standardized, platform-independent fashion. The advantage to the software developer is a significant reduction in complexity.

Without the broker, the number of interfaces is an N-squared problem; with the broker, only N interfaces are required, as shown in Figure 1.8.

The advantages of this are clear when one considers the cost of extending a relatively large and complex system. With the custom interface solution, the integration of each additional component requires the development of $N + 1$ new interfaces while the broker-based approach requires only one, as shown in Figure 1.9.

Extending the broker to include carefully selected services can further facilitate the rapid integration and reuse of components. The CORBA Interface and Implementation Repositories are examples of these types of services. The Interface Repository allows clients to discover interface information. Clients can determine which operations are valid and perform invocations at run time. In addition, the Interface Repository is used for storing other type and interface information, including stubs, skeletons, routines to browse interfaces,

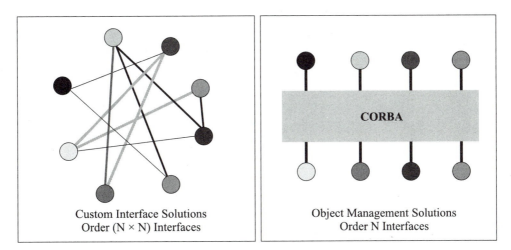

Custom Interface Solutions
Order (N × N) Interfaces

Object Management Solutions
Order N Interfaces

FIGURE 1.8   Custom interfaces versus object management solutions.

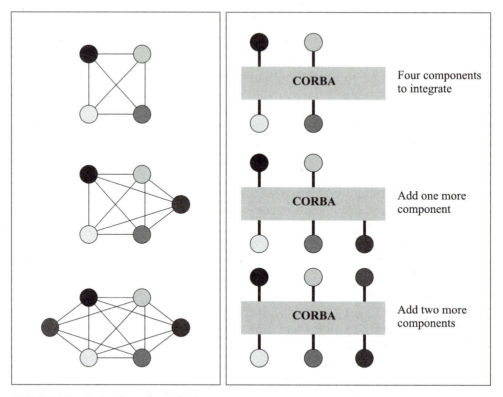

FIGURE 1.9   Extending the solution.

and debugging information. The Implementation Repository allows ORBs to locate and activate implementations of objects. Used in combination, these repositories provide the developer with the ability to browse, select, and locate objects at either development or run time.

Furthermore, CORBAservices contain a rich assortment of additional tools. The completeness of this assortment of services is the reason why CORBA eclipses all other currently available distributed technology solutions. CORBA includes well-developed service specifications in each of the following areas.

Lifecycle	Object transaction	Properties
Naming	Concurrency	Object trader
Event notification	Security	Object startup
Persistent objects	Time	Object collections
Relationship	Licensing	
Externalization	Object query	

In addition, CORBA provides a set of higher-level CORBAfacilities to support the development of applications and to handle object interoperability. The facilities are composed of four basic categories: User Interface, Information Management, Systems Management, and Task Management. They support compound document presentation and interchange, internationalization and time services, data and information exchange, rendering management, printing, change management, system management, scripting, agents, rule management, and other sophisticated capabilities. The CORBAdomains specifications are also currently being developed to describe objects for various vertical industry domains, such as healthcare, financial services, and telecommunications.

1.6   **CORBA's Growth**

CORBA has rapidly achieved two critical distinctions. The first is its robust and complete set of technical capabilities, including:

ADA language mapping	C++ language mapping
COM/CORBA (Part A)	CORBA 2.0
CORBA interoperability	Common secure IIOP
Document component facility	Concurrency service
Event notification service	Externalization service
IDL fixed-point extensions	IDL type extensions
Licensing service	Lifecycle service
Naming service	Object collections service
Object query service	Object security service
Object trader service	Object transaction service
Properties service	Query service
Relationship service	Security service
Smalltalk language mapping	System management facilities
Time service	

In addition, OMG-sponsored technical committees are working in the area of CORBA on financial facilities, repositories, Asian input facility, internationalization and time facilities, data interchange facility, mobile agent facility, meta-object facility, and printing facility. In the area of ORB and object services, committees are working on Internet, real time, COM/CORBA, ORB portability enhancement, COBOL mapping, multiple interfaces and composition, messaging service, objects-by-value, Java language mapping, secure socket layer/security,

IDL type extension, and CORBA core revision. In addition, a variety of other committees are working in the areas of analysis and design, business objects, manufacturing, product data management enablers, electronic payment facility, asset and content management, enabling technologies for electronic commerce, financial currency, financial insurance, and patient identification services.

DOM technology, in general, has been accepted by all major hardware and system software vendors. The second distinction for CORBA is the overwhelming support from more than 700 organizations for its DOM technology. This makes the OMG the world's largest consortium.

Over the next few years, DOMs will become pervasive. In particular, technology with both CORBA and DCOM support the creation of an available, mature, and interoperable set of distributed technology foundations.

1.7   What You Will Learn from This Book

The implementation of a large new information system and the successful integration of several existing information systems involve a significant degree of complexity, as seen in our beginning scenario. CORBA provides a framework to manage that complexity. However, to gain the full benefits of this framework requires knowledge of CORBA and its related services and facilities. This book provides a complete, illustrated introduction to this information. Chapter 2 introduces you to the CORBA interface definition language, the *lingua franca* of CORBA standards. Chapters 3, 4, and 5 discuss the specifications for CORBA, CORBAservices, CORBAfacilities, and the CORBAdomains. After reading these chapters, you will have a complete understanding of CORBA and its related standards. Chapters 6, 7, 8, and 9 focus on the application of CORBA to a business enterprise. The respective roles of the system architect, developer, and manager are explored, and the role played by CORBA in these jobs is explained. We will revisit our scenario in each of these chapters to help illustrate the points. Finally, Chapter 10 takes you through a case study of a CORBA migration project.

However, the book is just a guide and reference. Success with CORBA depends on two additional things. The first is proficiency. Proficiency is gained through hands-on application of the technology. The authors' experiences suggest that it takes six months for an individual to gain sufficient knowledge to be truly proficient. The second requirement is the commitment of the entire team (managers, architects, and developers) to the goal of successfully adopting and applying CORBA. The bottom line is that CORBA is not an individual productivity enhancement; rather, it enhances the productivity of entire teams in developing systems with significant and lasting business impact.

CORBA Standards

CORBA Interface Definition Language

2.1 An Overview of CORBAidl

The Object Management Group's (OMG) interface definition language (IDL) is an important tool for software engineers. In our opinion, IDL is comparable in significance to Backus-Naur Form and other major computer science advances. IDL is the most important part of the CORBA standard; therefore we will cover it first. IDL stands alone as a universal notation for software interfaces. We suggest that a working knowledge of IDL is an essential skill for every practicing software architect and software developer.

2.1.1 The Most Significant Element of CORBA Is the Interface Definition Language

IDL is a universally applicable notation for application program interfaces (API). IDL defines an opaque boundary between client code and object implementations (or services).

2.1.2 OMG IDL Is a Stable Standard

OMG IDL was first standardized by OMG in 1991. Today, in CORBA 2, IDL is virtually unchanged. IDL is the basis for every specification that the OMG adopts (more than a dozen, so far), so the OMG must keep IDL stable or break most of its own standards and commercial products. In addition, the International Standards Organization (ISO) has extracted the IDL section from CORBA to be drafted as an international standard (ISO DIS 14750). ISO adoption is the ultimate recognition of stability and credibility. The ISO standards writers see the many benefits of IDL; these benefits are also applicable to the needs of software architects and developers.

2.1.3   One IDL File Creates Multiple Language Bindings

IDL is language independent; it supports multiple language bindings from a single IDL specification. Standard bindings include C, C++, SmallTalk, Ada95, and others. Software designers need write software interfaces in OMG IDL only once and they have effectively written bindings for multiple languages.

2.1.4   IDL Enables Platform Independence

IDL is also platform independent. Because of the standard language bindings, the interface specified in IDL will be presented consistently on any object request broker and platform. What may differ from platform to platform are vendor-defined interfaces, such as operating systems and windowing interfaces. As long as programmers use interfaces defined by OMG standards and their own IDL, they are unlikely to encounter any platform portability problems due to the use of CORBA.

2.1.5   IDL Is Pure Specification, Not Implementation

IDL defines the interfaces to a CORBA-based object, but it does not otherwise constrain the object's implementation. For example, the implementation may be in any programming language, in the same address space, on the same machine, or on a different machine. The implementation may use a sophisticated algorithm, highly tuned for performance, or use a simple algorithm. Clients may use IDL interfaces without knowledge of these object implementation details. A strict separation of client software from object implementation details is a key advantage of the CORBA approach. This enables software reuse and reduction in the number of software builds.

2.1.6   The Quality of IDL Designs Is Critically Important

IDL is used to define the significant interfaces in an application system, including subsystem interfaces, enterprise model interfaces, library interfaces, and so forth. These interfaces are the design points on which reusability and interoperability will be based in the application system and across the organization. Changes in IDL designs will affect multiple software modules, so getting these designs correct is critically important.

Quality IDL designs will be reusable across many object implementations, systems, and clients; it will greatly enhance the interoperability within and among application systems; and it will promote the adaptability of application systems, which will result in substantial savings in software maintenance.

On the other hand, ad hoc, poorly conceived IDL designs will have the same shortcomings of systems built on previous technologies: lack of reuse, interoperability, and adaptability.

In this first section, we have described the key rationale behind the use of IDL. In the following sections, we will introduce the syntax and semantics of IDL.

2.2   An IDL Tutorial

This chapter is a companion to the OMG IDL specification contained in CORBA [OMG 1995b]. The CORBA standard provides a reference manual for IDL. This chapter contains a less formal user's guide discussion of IDL and many examples of the application of IDL features. An attempt has been made to address the needs of the CORBA novice as well as the more advanced user. If additional explanation is needed, please refer to the IDL reference manual, which is Chapter 3 of the CORBA specification [OMG 1995b].

IDL is a relatively simple notation because it is rigorously defined in the CORBA specification in about 40 pages. This guide walks through the features of IDL. Following this overview, we provide some examples of the application of IDL to OO systems design.

Before we get started, here are some notational conventions. IDL code is printed in a `courier` font. IDL comments have two forms: single line comments that begin with a // symbol; and multi-line comments enclosed by /* and */ symbols, as shown in the following example:

```
// This is a single line comment.


/* This is a multi-line comment. (First Line)
   This is a multi-line comment. (Second Line) */
```

2.2.1   IDL Modules

IDL modules create separate name spaces for IDL definitions. This prevents potential name conflicts among identifiers used in different domains. Modules do not inherit from other modules. Only IDL interfaces are capable of inheriting specifications.

Modules can be nested. This feature is infrequently used in practice, perhaps because nested modules can lead to long, scoped name references. In practice, most modules are used at the base definition level to enclose one or more IDL interfaces and their associated type definitions.

Since modules define scopes, IDL also defines a syntax for referencing in foreign scopes; these are called scoped names. Scoped names use the symbol :: as a separator. For example the following is a scoped name:

```
Part::Assembly::ComponentWidget.
```

In the following example, three modules are defined. The modules Assembly and Part are base-level definitions (that is, at the outer-most scope in the IDL file). Optionally, base-level definitions can be referred to by using a scoped name beginning with the :: symbol. In the example, a type string is redefined as a renamed type in all three modules. Without the use of scoped names, the type names Widget, PartWidget, and ComponentWidget are only known within their respective modules. In addition, IDL definitions are only known after they appear in the IDL file.

```
module Assembly {
  typedef string Widget;
};

module Part {

  typedef::Assembly::Widget PartWidget;

  module ComponentPart {
    typedef PartWidget ComponentWidget;
  };


};
```

CORBA 2 uses an IDL module called CORBA to enclose the scope of its definitions. To refer to definitions in module CORBA, one must use a scoped name, such as CORBA::Container. Without modules, CORBA definitions might conflict with other name spaces and user-defined identifiers.

CORBAservices also make extensive use of modules, each service defining one or more modules. Each CORBAservice module encloses a cohesive set of definitions. For example, there are modules for containment and reference management in the Relationship service and another specialized set of modules based on these definitions in the Lifecycle and Externalization services.

2.2.2   IDL Interfaces

IDL interfaces define the exposed details of distributed objects. Each IDL interface defines a new object type. The operation signatures are the essence of the interface. These are the entry points for service requests.

Another way to think about an IDL interface is that it specifies a software boundary between a service implementation and its clients. The IDL declares what is exposed by this interface, and all other details are hidden. Also unwanted, brittle code relationships, which are not specified in the declared interfaces, are prevented.

IDL interfaces can inherit from other interfaces. The complete set of definitions are inherited, and the inherited identifiers cannot be redefined without causing a conflict.

The following example defines three interfaces: a common interface for account and more specialized interfaces for checking and savings accounts. The IDL indicates that the checking and savings interfaces inherit all the definitions from the account interface.

```
interface Account {
  // Account definitions
};

interface Checking: Account {
  // Inherits all Account definitions
  // Then adds Checking definitions
};

interface Savings: Account {
  // Inherits all Account definitions
  // Then adds Savings definitions
};
```

IDL supports multiple inheritance; an interface may inherit from several other interfaces. The inherited definitions must not conflict and must be unambiguous.

2.2.3   IDL Forward

The IDL forward statement is used to declare an interface name before its complete definition appears in the IDL file. For example:

```
interface Employee; // forward declaration
struct EmployeeContacts {
  Employee supervisor;
  Employee secretary;
  Employee union_shop_leader;
};
```

```
interface Employee {
  attribute EmployeeContacts contacts;
  typedef string JobTitle;
  // other definitions
};
```

Forward declarations can also be used to create recursive (or self-referential) definitions. Forward declarations do not establish their enclosed definitions. In the above example, the type definition JobTitle is not known as a result of the forward declaration; it is only known after it actually appears in the IDL file.

2.2.4   IDL Constants

IDL allows the definition of constant values. There is a restricted set of types, including integer, character, Boolean, floating point, string, and renamed types. The constant definitions can include some arithmetic expressions. For example:

```
const unsigned long kilometers_per_mile = 2.2;
const char separator = '/';
const char carriage_return = '/';
const boolean tautology = TRUE;
const float pi = 3.1415926;
const double avagodro = 6.02e25;
const string state = "Virginia";
typedef string LastName;
const LastName my_lastname = "Mowbray";
const float days_per_month = 364.5 / 12;
```

2.2.5   IDL Type Declaration

The purpose of type declarations in IDL is to enable strong type checking of operation signatures. Type declarations include renaming of the intrinsic types in IDL, as well as the creation of user-defined types that can be either enumeration, structures, arrays, sequences, or unions. The following are examples of each kind of type declaration.

```
typedef unsigned long PhoneNumber; // Renamed type unsigned long
typedef string GuestName, Address; // Renamed types of strings

// Enumeration Types
enum ChargeCard { MasterCard, Visa, AmericanExpress, Diners };
// A Structure Type
struct GuestRecord {
```

```
    GuestName name;
    Address address;
    PhoneNumber number;
    ChargeCard card_kind;
    unsigned long card_number, expiration;
};


// A Sequence Type
typedef sequence<GuestRecord> GuestList;


// Another Structure Type (alternative style definition)
typedef struct EmployeeStruct {
    string name;
    Address address;
    unsigned long social_security_number;
} EmployeeRecord;


// An Array Type
typedef EmployeeRecord Employees[100]; // Array Type


// A Union Type
enum PersonKind { A_GUEST, AN_EMPLOYEE, AN_OTHER };
union Person switch ( PersonKind ) {
  case A_GUEST:
    GuestRecord guest_record;
  case AN_EMPLOYEE:
    EmployeeRecord employee_record;
  default: string description;
};
```

The declaration of enumeration, structures, and unions may take two forms: one beginning the `typedef` token and the other not. The two forms have the same effect, except those that begin with the `typedef` token declare two names for the new type.

The discriminator in the union type must be either a restricted type (integer, char, Boolean) or enumeration. A special case label (called `default`) is defined to allow for other cases.

2.2.6   IDL Sequences

Sequences are a special data type that is unique to IDL. Sequences are essentially variable-length arrays. Since every programming language has a binding to IDL that is natural, sequences are defined as appropriate within the programming language environment. If the programming language already has a variable-length element type (Common Lisp, Smalltalk), that is a suitable representation. In C++, the details are encapsulated behind a C++ class definition.

The C binding to IDL exposes how this might be implemented. Within C, sequences are mapped to a structure type as in the following.

```
/* IDL */
typedef sequence<long> LongSeq; // A Sequence Type
struct Automobile {
  string make, model;
  unsigned short year; };
typedef sequence<Automobile> AutomobileSeq; // Another
Sequence Type

/* C */
typedef struct {                    // A Sequence Type in
C
  CORBA_unsigned_long _maximum;
  CORBA_unsigned_long _length;
  CORBA_long *_buffer;
} LongSeq ;
typedef struct {
  CORBA_char *make, *model;
  CORBA_unsigned_short year;
} Automobile;
typedef struct {                    //Another Sequence
Type in C
  unsigned long _maximum;
  unsigned long _length;
  Automobile *_buffer;
} AutomobileSeq;
```

In C, each sequence maps to a structure type with three members, _maximum, _length, and _buffer. In memory, storage of the sequence values are allocated as a contiguous array of the indicated buffer type. The size of this allocated area is indicated by the member _maximum, where there are _maximum* sizeof(<element_type>) bytes allocated. The amount of valid data in the sequence buffer is indicated by the member _length (again in units of <element_type>.).

2.2.7 The Dynamic IDL Type Any

IDL provides capability for strongly typed interface definitions. In addition, there is a capability for loosely typed data values through an intrinsic type, the CORBA type any. Examples of type any definitions are:

```
typedef any DynamicallyTypedValue;
struct RunTimeValue {
  string description;
  any run_time_value; };
exception UserError {
  string explanation;
  any exception_value; };
```

A value of type `any` is self-identifying. It contains information about the run-time type and the current value of the data. The run-time type information is represented as a CORBA `type code`. IDL compilers generate `type code` values for user-defined types, and the CORBA interface repository interfaces include facilities for generating new type codes at run time. In addition, the `type code` object has on-line information that the application software can use to discover the attributes of the type.

Type `any` is useful for defining reusable interfaces. For example, `type any` is used extensively in CORBAservices because these services are intended for reuse in arbitrary applications.

2.2.8   IDL Attributes

IDL definitions expose public attributes and operations. If an attribute or operation is private, it should not appear in a public IDL definition. By default, all IDL definitions known by the ORB are public because they are publicly retrievable from the Interface Repository.

Attributes may be read-only or read-write. Each attribute has an IDL data type and appears within a specific IDL interface definition. The following are examples of attribute definitions.

```
interface CensusData {
  attribute unsigned short age;
  readonly attribute string birth_date;
  attribute string last_name, first_name;
  struct HouseHold {
  string address;
  unsigned short number_of_occupants;
  };
  attribute HouseHold house_hold;
};
```

After the attribute keyword, there is a type specification. This can be any IDL type, but it cannot be an unnamed type—that is, the type of the attribute must be given a name in a separate declaration. This same restriction applies to parameters in operation signatures.

In the language bindings, attribute declarations map to accessor functions. For read-write attributes, there is a `set` function and a `get` function generated for each attribute. For read-only attributes, a single `get` function is generated.

2.2.9 IDL Exceptions

CORBA makes the important guarantee that the client making an invocation will always receive a successful return or an exception. This is a significant simplification of the complexities of distributed computing and can greatly reduce the amount of client code needed. Exceptions are also an important part of an interface specification. Exceptions define the values passed by the interface in case something goes wrong.

Exception values are declared similar to IDL structure types. Here are some examples.

```
exception CardExpired { string expiration_date; };
exception CreditLimitExceeded
  { unsigned long credit_limit; };
exception CardReportedStolen {
  string reporting_instructions;
  unsigned long hotline_phone_number; };
```

The implementation of an `exception` is defined by the IDL language mapping. In general, an `exception` is an opaque structure. The user-defined part of the structure (as in the above examples) is exposed. There is other information included in the `exception` that is specific to each ORB implementation. Any other information is accessed through various accessor functions. In general, the accessor functions will return an exception code and a string-valued explanation. Both of these values are controlled by the system. All other user-defined values are controlled by the application code in the object implementation.

There are two general kinds of exceptions: user-defined and CORBA-defined. A relatively comprehensive set of exceptions, called the Standard Exceptions, are defined by CORBA. Standard Exceptions may be returned by any CORBA operation. These are worthwhile to learn; here is the IDL from the CORBA specification that defines the Standard Exceptions.

```
#define ex_body {unsigned long minor; completion_status completed;}

enum completion_status {COMPLETED_YES, COMPLETED_NO,
COMPLETED_MAYBE};
```

```
enum exception_type {NO_EXCEPTION, USER_EXCEPTION,
SYSTEM_EXCEPTION};

exception UNKNOWN ex_body;
exception BAD_PARAM ex_body;
exception NO_MEMORY ex_body;
exception IMP_LIMIT ex_body;
exception COMM_FAILURE ex_body;
exception INV_OBJREF ex_body;
exception INTERNAL ex_body;
exception MARSHAL ex_body;
exception INITIALIZE ex_body;
exception NO_IMPLEMENT ex_body;
exception BAD_TYPECODE ex_body;
exception BAD_OPERATION ex_body;
exception NO_RESOURCES ex_body;
exception NO_RESPONSE ex_body;
exception PERSIST_STORE ex_body;
exception BAD_INV_ORDER ex_body;
exception TRANSIENT ex_body;
exception FREE_MEM ex_body;
exception INV_IDENT ex_body;
exception INV_FLAG ex_body;
exception INTF_REPOS ex_body;
exception BAD_CONTEXT ex_body;
exception OBJ_ADAPTER ex_body;
exception DATA_CONVERSION ex_body;
exception OBJECT_NOT_EXIST ex_body;
```

Note that the Standard Exceptions are indicated by the enumeration value
`exception_type` expressed as `SYSTEM_EXCEPTION`. Regardless, the
Standard Exceptions may be returned by the ORB and by application code (the
object implementation).

The semantics of the Standard Exceptions depend on their application.
Some Standard Exceptions used in particular IDL language mappings and their
semantics are defined in language-dependent ways. Most Standard Exceptions
invoked by ORB implementations have semantics defined by the ORB supplier.
Standard Exceptions appear in CORBAservices and other OMG specifications.
Their semantics are defined accordingly when they are used in specifications.
When Standard Exceptions are returned by object implementations, their
semantics are defined by the implementation or corresponding specification.

2.2.10   IDL Operation Signatures

The specification of operation signatures is the underlying purpose of IDL. An operation signature defines the acceptable ways to access an object. No other hidden interfaces are allowed. All operation definitions are declared within specific IDL interfaces (as are attributes definitions). Here are some simple examples of operation signatures.

```
interface Hospital {
  typedef string PatientId;

  // An Operation Signature
  PatientId admit_patient ();
  // Another Signature
  void release_patient (in PatientId patient);
};
```

In IDL, only the user-defined parameters are specified. When compiled into a particular language mapping, each signature has a target object. The IDL type of the target object is the declared name of the interface (which always happens to be a renamed type of CORBA type Object). In addition, each operation can return exception information in case any errors are detected by the ORB or the object implementation.

By default, IDL operations are synchronous. There is an asynchronous option denoted by the oneway keyword, which indicates that the operation will be executed at-most-once, using a best-effort semantics. Operations that are oneway can have only input parameters.

Operation signatures include the following elements: the operation attribute (oneway or none), the operation type specification, the operation identifier, the parameters declarations, an optional raises expression, and an optional context expression. The operation type specification is the return value from the whole operation. This may be any IDL type or the keyword void, indicating that there is no return value. Note that there are no pointer types in IDL. The use of pointer types is a language-specific mapping issue.

The following are some more-sophisticated examples of operation signatures.

```
interface AirlineReservation {
  typedef unsigned long ConfirmationNumber;
  enum SeatKind { Window, Aisle, Middle };
  exception BadFrequentFlyerNumber {};
  exception SeatNotAvailable {};
  exception BadConfirmationNumber {};
```

```
  ConfirmationNumber make_reservation (
    in string passenger_name,
    in unsigned long frequent_flyer_number,
    inout SeatKind seat_kind,
    out string seat_assignment )
    raises( BadFrequentFlyerNumber,
      SeatNotAvailable )
    context( "TicketAgent", "Agency" );

 oneway void cancel_reservation (
    in ConfirmationNumber number )
    raises( BadConfirmationNumber )
    context( "TicketAgent", "Agency" );
};
```

In the above example, the operation make_reservation uses all three parameter modes: in, inout, and out. Both operations have raises expressions and context expressions. The raises expression indicates potential user-defined exception conditions that may occur. The context expression is translated into a set of string-valued properties that are attached to the invocation and conveyed to the object implementation.

Note that if an exception is returned, none of the output values is valid and the client cannot be certain about completion unless it is specifically required by semantic documentation accompanying the IDL. For this type of application, one might choose the enhanced semantics of the OMG Transaction CORBAservice, which would be able to guarantee rollback if an operation could not successfully complete.

2.2.11   Pre-Compiler Directives

IDL has pre-compiler directives, as do C and C++. The most important one is the include statement, which allows IDL files to reference each other's definitions. By convention, IDL files are often named after the module they contain.

The following #include statements enable access to CORBAservices definitions.

```
// Naming Service
#include <CosNaming.idl>
// Event Service
#include <CosEventComm.idl>
#include <CosEventChannelAdmin.idl>
// Persistence Service
#include <CosPersistencePID.idl>
```

```
#include <CosPersistencePOM.idl>
#include <CosPersistencePDS.idl>
// Life Cycle Service
#include <CosLifeCycle.idl>
// Concurrency Service
#include <CosCocurrencyControl.idl>
// Externalization Service
#include <CosExternalization.idl>
// Relationships Service
#include <CosObjectIdentity.idl>
#include <CosRelationships.idl>
#include <CosGraphs.idl>
#include <CosContainment.idl>
#include <CosReference.idl>
// Transactions Service
#include <CosTransactions.idl>
//Query Service
#include <CosQuery.idl>
#include <CosCollection.idl>
```

If the IDL compiler implements the #include semantics directly, the compiler will generate header files, stubs, and skeletons for all the included interface definitions. This is usually not desirable. A future extension to CORBA may include an import statement that allows the definitions to be accessible within user IDL, without generating code for the original definitions. Several ORB products currently support this capability for the #include statement.

In this section, we have described the syntax and semantics of IDL. In the next section, we describe how to extract IDL from OO designs.

2.3   Conversion of OO Designs to IDL

IDL is a useful notation for representing selected information from an OO design. IDL can best be used to capture a key subset of the static OO models, in particular, the public attributes and public operations. The static OO model includes the inheritance hierarchy, or class hierarchy, among other object relationships.

Generally, the IDL captures the inheritance relationships. Other relationships may be represented indirectly as IDL attributes or not at all (if they are private or implemented otherwise). Inheritance relationships in IDL are subtyping relationships. By this, we mean that the IDL defines interface inheritance, but IDL does imply implementation inheritance (the usual notion of inheritance).

IDL expands the details of attributes and operations included in the static OO model. For example, the IDL will have detailed type definitions, strongly typed operation signatures, and exception definitions.

A common misconception is that IDL should capture all the semantics of an OO design. This could not be farther from the truth. IDL only captures the interface information inherent in OO models. IDL is not intended to represent implementation characteristics, such as dynamic models (behavior), object instances, and object relationships.

2.4 From OO Design to IDL Example: Course Registration Object Model

This example is illustrative of the information that IDL captures from an OO design. We use the unified modeling language notation for the OO design diagrams in these examples, as we do throughout the book. Although this example implies a direct mapping from a formal OO design process to an IDL description, we believe that much more design input is needed to generate a robust architecture. Architectural concepts and techniques are discussed in more detail in Chapter 7 and the case study in Chapter 10.

2.4.1 The OO Design

An example OO design is shown in Figure 2.1. This is an object hierarchy (static model) showing object classes for students, courses, and faculty members. Each of the object classes has attributes and operations. The object classes are linked by various relationships (note that relationships are not represented in the IDL).

2.4.2 An Abstract IDL Representation

The following preliminary IDL contains the interface information extracted from the OO design model. This first-cut specification does not attempt to add detail, so it is easy to notice that information is missing. For example, there is no `type` information for the attributes and there are no parameter lists or return values for the operations. For the attributes, we have specified the `type any` to denote data types unspecified by the OO model. Other missing elements of the interface are the exception values.

```
module CourseRegistration {

  interface Student {
    attribute any name;
```

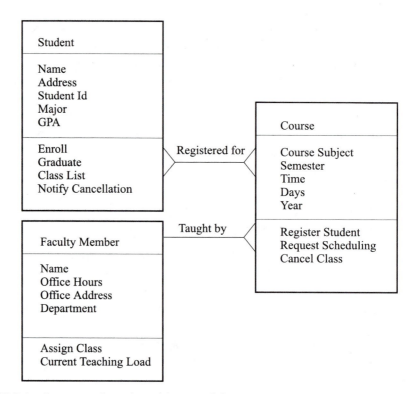

FIGURE 2.1   Course registration object model.

```
        attribute any address;
        attribute any studentId;
        attribute any major;
        attribute any gradePointAverage;
        void enroll();
        void graduate();
        void class_list();
        void notify_cancellation();
    };

    interface Course {
        attribute any courseSubject;
        attribute any maxSize;
        attribute any semester;
        attribute any time;
        attribute any days;
        attribute any year;
```

```
      void register_student();
      void request_scheduling();
      void cancel_class();
    };

    interface FacultyMember {
      attribute any name;
      attribute any officeHours;
      attribute any officeAddress;
      attribute any department;
      void assign_class();
      void current_teaching_load();
    };
  };
```

2.4.3   A Concrete IDL Representation

The following is an example of a more complete IDL specification for the above
OO design. There is significantly more information than is present in the original OO model. Some of the key additions include the typing information (for
attributes, operation return values, and parameters), the exceptions, the addition of parameters, and so forth.

  This first step to formalizing the IDL specification based on an OO design
is only the first step in creating a robust IDL-based architecture. Further
concepts and processes are presented in Chapters 8 and 9.

```
  module CourseRegistration {
    // Forward Declarations
    interface Course;
    interface FacultyMember;

    interface Student {
      attribute string name;
      attribute string address;
      attribute unsigned long studentId;
      attribute string major;
      attribute float gradePointAverage;
      exception ClassFull {};
      void enroll( in Course course )
        raises (ClassFull);
      exception HasNotCompletedReqts {};
      void graduate()
```

```
                  raises (HasNotCompletedReqts);
              typedef sequence<Course> CourseList;
              CourseList class_list();
              void notify_cancellation(
                  in Course course );
          };


          interface Course {
              attribute string courseSubject;
              attribute unsigned short maxSize;
              enum SchoolSemesters
                  { FALL, SPRING, SUMMER };
              attribute SchoolSemesters semester;
              attribute unsigned long time;
              attribute string days;
              attribute unsigned short year;
              void register_student(
                  in Student student );
              exception RoomSpaceUnavailable {};
              void request_scheduling( in Time time,
                  in string days,
                  in SchoolSemesters semester,
                  in unsigned short year )
                  raises (RoomSpaceUnavailable);
              void cancel_class();
          };


          interface FacultyMember {
              attribute string name;
              struct OfficeHours {
                  string time, duration, days; };
              attribute OfficeHours office_hours;
              attribute string office_address;
              attribute string department;
              exception TeachingLoadExceeded {};
              void assign_class( in Course course )
                  raises (TeachingLoadExceeded);
              typedef unsigned short TeachingHours;
              TeachingHours current_teaching_load();
          };
      };
```

Note that forward declarations are used to declare the name of an interface type that is used as an operation parameter before its definition appears in the IDL. This is necessary because IDL is defined to support single-pass compilation, unlike Java.

In this section, we described how to extract IDL from OO designs through an example. In the following section, we provide some general guidelines for writing IDL code and specifications.

2.5   IDL Guidelines

The following are some general guidelines when writing IDL interfaces and specifications.

2.5.1   IDL Identifiers

Although there are few written guidelines for ISO IDL coding style, the style of the IDL in the adopted OMG standards is very consistent. Some of the commonly observed conventions include the following.

- Use initial capitals on all module names, interface names, data type names, and exception names. For example:

```
interface AnExampleInterface {
  typedef sequence<long> AnExampleType;
  exception AnExampleException {};
};
```

- Use lowercase letters and underscores for operations names, formal parameters, and attribute names. For example:

```
void an_example_operation(in long
  a_formal_parameter);
attribute string an_attribute;
readonly attribute long another_attribute_name;
```

Conventions on other types of identifiers are less well established. Suggested styles include:

- Use uppercase with underscores for enumerations and constants.

```
enum AnEnumeration { AN_ENUMERATOR,
ANOTHER_ENUMERATOR };
const unsigned long A_CONSTANT = 0;
```

2.5.2   Parameter and Return Values

Some general guidelines are applicable to parameters and return values when designing IDL operation signatures. These guidelines make the operations easier to use, clearer for documentation, and more consistent.

- Avoid an excessive number of parameters. Use one to four parameters in most operation signatures.

- If there is a single output value, it should be defined as the return value, not an out parameter.

- Avoid the use of output parameters and a return value on the same operation. Both have a return value and no output parameters or several output parameters and no return value.

- Order parameters by the parameter mode. Start by listing all input parameters, then output parameters, then inout parameters.

- Avoid the use of inout parameters. Often, their purpose and usage is difficult to convey to other developers. Inout parameters can also encourage misuse and undocumented usage of interfaces for purposes other than intended by the IDL designer.

2.5.3   The Use of Attributes

IDL attributes are used sparingly in OMG standards such as CORBAservices. There are perhaps two reasons. The first is that attributes are generally associated with domain-specific information. Since OMG standards are widely applicable, the use of attributes is delegated to application-specific specialization of the standards. Designers who attempt to maximize reusability may also want to avoid attributes. The second reason is more subtle. Note that operation signatures can have user-defined exceptions. There is no comparable feature for attributes. Attribute accessor functions (set and get) are limited to the CORBA Standard Exceptions. Some designers consider this an unreasonable constraint. The functionality that attributes provide can be implemented in several ways, such as in ordinary IDL operation signatures and through the Properties CORBAservice.

2.5.4   Use of Type Any

Use the type any with caution. Its use requires extra performance overhead, avoids compiler type checking, and entails added complexity for application software. Type any is often misused by IDL designers as a place-holder for future needs. Use of a specific data type is preferable to type any in most cases. Type any is appropriate for highly reusable specifications (such as CORBAservices) in which the data type is specialized for particular applications.

2.5.5   IDL Modules

It is a good idea to put all IDL definitions within IDL modules to avoid global definitions outside the modules. This is important because potential conflicts may occur among name spaces.

One widely used convention involves the ordering of definitions within modules. If several interfaces appear within a module, it is customary to define all the data types and exceptions at the beginning of the module. Then the interfaces will include only attributes and operations. This convention allows sharing of data types and exceptions without redefinition. The convention also simplifies naming of data types and exceptions for developers by making them consistent since they all appear in the module scope. An alternative is to place these definitions near their use in attributes and operation signatures (as we have done for the example in this chapter). This aids clarity by placing the definition and usage close together. Experience has shown that this approach is usually not very scalable, and IDL code tends to evolve toward the above convention as designs grow.

2.5.6   IDL Documentation

The IDL code itself is a rigorous specification, but more is needed for complete descriptions of software architectures. OMG standards require at least two pieces of addition specification: the semantics of the IDL and the sequencing of the operations in the IDL. Both are typically specified by using prose (informal) descriptions.

We find that one must go even further if a specification is to guarantee application-level interoperability. The semantics and formatting of the data in parameters is an important additional specification to complete the description of semantics. In addition, we find that a healthy dose of meta-data description is needed to build robust, flexible systems.

2.6   Concluding Remarks

In this chapter, we have introduced the interface definition language (IDL). This notation is universally applicable for specifying software interfaces regardless of programming language or platform. The next chapter introduces the common object request broker architecture (CORBA). CORBA provides an object model and distributed communication infrastructure for IDL.

3

The CORBA 2 Standard

3.1 An Overview of CORBA 2

CORBA is the fundamental standard for distributed objects. The CORBA specification is one of the key OMG specifications. There are others, including CORBAservices and CORBAfacilities, which are covered in separate chapters. CORBA's key features include a standard object model, a way to specify interfaces for multiple languages, and the basic interfaces that enable interobject communication.

This chapter is a companion to the CORBA specification, with a focus on the key CORBA concepts that are useful in design and development with CORBA. In addition, it provides some useful insights into what the standards mean and what they are able and unable to achieve.

It is recommended that the reader's knowledge of CORBA specification include a detailed knowledge of IDL, at least one language binding, as well as a working knowledge of the CORBA architecture and the enabling object request broker (ORB) interfaces. IDL language competency is covered in Chapter 2. This chapter provides the balance of the essential knowledge needed to understand CORBA. In addition, hands-on training with any ORB product of choice is highly recommended and will greatly enhance chances of success with CORBA.

CORBA is a standard from the world's largest software consortia, the OMG. The CORBA standard is jointly authored by more than a dozen corporations. It is a joint publication of the OMG and X/Open, representing an overwhelming worldwide industry consensus. Core parts of the specification (in particular OMG IDL) have also been adopted by the European Computer Manufacturers Association (ECMA) and the International Organization for Standardization (ISO) as formal standards for specifying software interfaces.

CORBA is simultaneously three types of standards: formal, de facto, and de jure. OMG IDL is a formal standard through ECMA and ISO. CORBA is a de facto standard because of its widespread adoption and support by middleware vendors, independent software vendors, and developers. It is a de jure standard because its use is recognized and approved in part by the United States and other governments.

More than a dozen ORB products support CORBA. Market and product support are growing rapidly. In addition, a number of freeware packages provide CORBA support.

The role of CORBA is defined in the object management architecture (OMA) reference model (Figure 3.1). In this referenced model, CORBA is the central component through which all other objects communicate. CORBA is an enabling infrastructure for communication among object-oriented systems, as well as legacy systems, in non-object-oriented technologies. Other object-oriented technologies include object-oriented programming languages (OOPL) and object-oriented database management systems (OODBMS). CORBA extends the object-oriented model in other object-oriented technologies with distributed computing capabilities that cross platforms with language boundaries.

The OMA is the root diagram for all OMG standards activities. The OMA defines the role of CORBA and four other categories of objects. The first category is called CORBAservices. CORBAservices are standardized objects that provide primitive and enabling capabilities, such as creation of objects, movement of objects, and other more sophisticated capabilities, such as query services, transactions services, concurrency control, and directory services (naming and trading).

All other standards that might be adopted are either in the CORBAdomains or the CORBAfacilities category. CORBAdomains are the vertical market

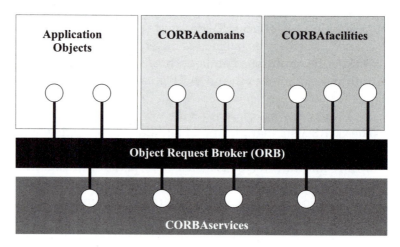

FIGURE 3.1 The object management architecture.

standards within the OMG. Examples of vertical market areas include financial services, which will be standardized by the CORBAfinancials task force, and healthcare, which will be standardized by the CORBAmed task force. Other areas of vertical market standardization include telecommunications (CORBAtel), manufacturing (CORBAman), and business objects. CORBAfacilities standardize all interfaces that are common across all CORBAdomains. Examples of CORBAfacilities include compound documents and system management. Both of these areas may be applied in multiple vertical domains and are independent of a domain's specificity, although the corporate domains may add and extend those standards.

The final category of objects within the OMA are called applications, or user-defined interfaces and proprietary interfaces. The interfaces may be reused from other standard parts of the OMA and they can be extended from the OMA standards. In addition, other kinds of independent specialized interfaces, called application interfaces, can be defined. Note that the overwhelming majority of software interfaces in today's systems would be categorized as application interfaces (interfaces that do not correspond to particular standards).

3.1.1 The ORB

The ORB is the infrastructure mechanism standardized by CORBA. The role of the ORB is to unify access to application services, which it does by providing a common object-oriented, remote procedure call mechanism. Remote procedure call technologies have been around for more than a decade, starting with the introduction of open network computing (ONC) by Sun Microsystems. Sun decided to promote this technology by making implementations freely available on other UNIX platforms.

Note that the remote procedure call technologies provided similar promises to those CORBA makes today. The only widely used remote procedure call interface with the ONC open network commuting technologies is the network file system. The file-sharing capability is important for interoperability but cannot meet all the operability needs. This results in the need for additional effort in system integration.

More recently, the Open Software Foundation (OSF), now part of The Open Group, introduced the distributed commuting environment (DCE), another remote procedure call technology with the same primitive capabilities as ONC. DCE's innovation was to provide various enabling services in a standardized way. These services include time retrieval, security, directory, and threads. DCE was also the technology that originated the widespread use of interface definition languages. The OSF DCE was introduced specifically as a competitor to ONC. As such, it provided similar levels of capabilities and was not easier to use than ONC or other remote procedure call technologies. Both ONC and DCE were developed prior to the support for object orientation. The lack of object orientation is the fundamental difference between OSF DCE and CORBA technologies.

Using CORBA technologies with object orientation is a better way to separate interfaces and implementation. It enables programmers to hide what they need to hide and expose what they need to expose, through interfaces. It also allows the CORBA mechanism to greatly unify access to resources and make them uniform. Figure 3.2 is a representational abstraction of how CORBA provides a consistent and uniform way to access distributed services. CORBA provides uniform handling of capabilities that are built into the IDL and common remote procedure call capabilities within CORBA. It provides a uniform way to achieve security and many other capabilities, including uniform access to legacy systems.

Figure 3.3 shows the fundamental role of the ORB in providing an infrastructure for communication among different modules of application software. At the top of the diagram are the two fundamental roles in application software. A client is any piece of application software that invokes a service. Inside an object implementation is a service-providing piece of software that is encapsulated as an object. The client accesses the object implementation by invoking operations through CORBA or the object request broker. This provides a communication independence, but it also separates the client and object implementation from each other and separates both of them from the underlying communication infrastructure and protocol stack so that the protocol stack is replaceable as migration occurs from one implementation of CORBA to another. This gives flexibility for application architectures and simplifies the distributed computing model.

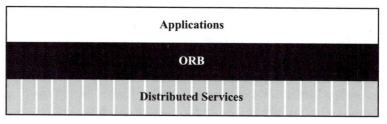

Uniform access to services: Common RPC
Uniform discovery of resources: Common Naming
Uniform error handling
Uniform security policies
Uniform legacy application integration

FIGURE 3.2   Role of the object request broker.

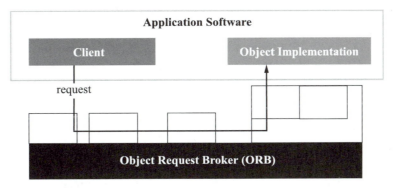

FIGURE 3.3   The object request broker infrastructure.

3.1.2   **CORBA Core**

The CORBA 2 standard includes the core architecture specifications and the specifications for interoperability and language among the products, as well as language mappings for C, C++, SmallTalk, Ada95, COBOL, and Java. The CORBA 2 core architecture includes some other important specifications, such as initialization and the Interface Repository. CORBA 1, first adopted in 1991, has had two minor revisions. The first, which occurred immediately after its adoption, was completed in December 1991 and was called CORBA 1.1. That was followed by another minor revision, called CORBA 1.2, which was adopted in June 1994. Finally, in December 1994, the CORBA 2 specification was recommended for adoption. Each of these specifications represents an upwardly compatible set of technologies.

The core specifications that were included in the original CORBA specification are still valid and have been carried forward into CORBA 2. In particular, the key parts of the specification, which have been in place since its inception, include the CORBA object model, the only common object model for the object-oriented technologies in the computing industry. The architecture specification provides an abstract description of how CORBA works. The reference manual defines the syntax and semantics of the IDL. The other parts of the specification were identified early in the process but were not completely detailed in the original documents. These were later filled in by CORBA 2 and include the Interface Repository, the initialization interfaces, interoperability, and language mappings.

In this section, the object management architecture with its central component, the CORBA infrastructure, is introduced. Even though CORBA comprises a complicated set of specifications, it should be kept in mind that it is performing a simple purpose. CORBA's purpose is to enable communication among application clients and object implementations. This communication is as natural and as convenient as possible for language mapped to a common infrastructure. The infrastructure hides differences among client-object locations, platforms, and programming languages. The next section explains the object model, which is the conceptual basis for this infrastructure, and how it behaves with respect to application software.

3.2   Standard Object Model

A standard CORBA object model is a specialization of the OMG core object model, defined in the object management architecture guide as an abstract model that defines basic concepts such as objects and encapsulations. The CORBA standard object model is a concrete object model in that it defines how the semantics of actual implementations of object request brokers relate to application software. The essence of the standard object model is the definition of an object.

An object is some encapsulated entity that performs services. An object is referred to by a unique object reference. The services that an object performs are accessed by some client software. The client's software can be part of another object or it can be part of a non-object-oriented program that uses objects to achieve its functionality. The client invokes an object's services by generating a request, which is a message sent from a client to an object. The object returns either some results from the performance of the service or exception values.

One of the important benefits of CORBA is that it simplifies the system model for client programs. One of the most important ways that CORBA simplifies client processing is through the exception mechanism. The standard object model guarantees that a request invocation will provide a return. In other words, a client's software will not be left to hang up indefinitely because of some failure in the network or the server software. Either a valid return is supplied or an exception value is supplied. There is a comprehensive set of Standard Exceptions defined in the IDL reference manual that handle most commonly encountered conditions. Figure 3.4 shows how the client accesses services supplied by objects through a request.

Figure 3.5 is the CORBA data type hierarchy. The object model defines a number of different types that are used to describe encapsulations. These types are fundamentally of two kinds: object types and data types. Object types are the result of any interface definition. Each interface defines a set of operations encapsulating an object or legacy software. Each interface definition has a unique object type that is described in the CORBA Interface Repository. The data types form a comprehensive set of strong typing capabilities. The data types include some predefined basic types, such as short and

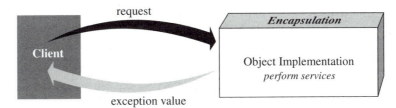

FIGURE 3.4   CORBA object model.

long integers, floating-point numbers, characters, strings, and Boolean. The data types also include an octet type, which is a representation of an arbitrary 8-bit value and can be used for representation and for bit-level representations of data values.

The CORBA extended data types include 64-bit (and longer) numbers, international characters, and fixed-point numbers. The 64-bit integers are designated by the data type long long and unsigned long long. The extended floating-point numbers are designated long double; these are compliant with the Institute of Electrical and Electronics Engineers' (IEEE) specification 754 for double-extended floating-point numbers. IEEE 754 requires at least 15 bits for exponent and 63 bits for the fractional part. International character sets are supported by the data types wchar and wstring, which stand for wide character

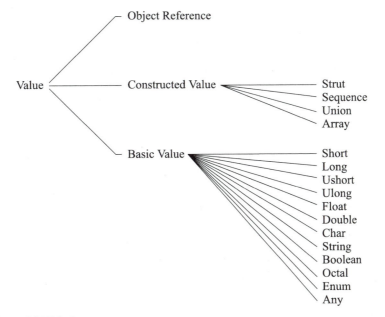

FIGURE 3.5   CORBA data types.

and wide strings. These extended types support arbitrary character sets, and the representation may be of any length, as defined by the implementation. Fixed-point types provide representation of decimal numbers of up to 31 significant digits. The number of digits applied to the fractional part is specified as part of the type. Fixed point types are essential for the representation of money and other quantities that require fixed precision and controlled rounding of calculation results.

One of the interesting types defined within the object model is the CORBA type any. The CORBA type any is a self-describing type that can represent an arbitrary run-time value, both data types, and object references. CORBA also defines constructed types, including enumerations, structures, arrays, unions, and sequences. Most of these are familiar to programmers of C++, Java, and other languages. The sequence type is unique to CORBA and denotes a variable-length array type.

The object model defines the concept of interface that provides encapsulation. An interface comprises a set of operations and attributes that the client may utilize to request services of an object. An attribute denotes some exposed state information. There is no concept of private attributes in the CORBA model. If an attribute is defined in an interface definition, it is a public attribute. All interface definitions are known publicly through the CORBA Interface Repository. In addition to attributes, operations are a component of interfaces.

Each operation denotes a particular service that can be requested by a client. An operation is specified through an operation signature, which defines the input parameters and return values, as well as the user-defined exceptions and context attributes that can be attached to a request. An operation signature can include a one-way specification that has special semantics. A one-way operation is an operation that has no in-out or output parameters and provides an immediate return of control to the invoking client. The semantics of the one-way operation are that the CORBA implementation will make its best effort to deliver the request and the object implementation will perform the request with best effort.

3.2.1 Interface Attributes and Operations

The remaining definitions in the object model include explanations of the meanings of interface attributes and operations. An interface is basically a set of operations that provides the encapsulation for an object and, through this interface, the client requests various services of the object. The interface includes attributes and operations. Attributes are public-state information. In an ideal environment, the object request broker makes all interface information public by providing it on-line in the CORBA Interface Repository. So whenever attribute information exists in an interface definition, it is public information. If there are any private attributes, leave them out of the IDL interface description.

Operations denote the particular services that can be requested. This is similar to the concept of a function prototype in C or a method signature in C++, SmallTalk, and Ada. The operation's signature specifies what is included in a request and what is returned from that request. The core of the signature is the parameter list that includes strongly typed parameters, which can be in three modes: in, in-out, and out. The three modes correspond to parameters that are provided by value, parameters that are provided by reference, and the output parameters that are also provided by reference.

Each operation signature has an operation name and an operation identifier, which is just a particular string value. Each operation can have a particular return value, which is an output value in addition to the output values in the parameter list. The return value is specified by an IDL data type. Each parameter is also specified as a specific IDL data type. As the BNF description of the operation signature shows, there are several other features unique to IDL.

3.2.2   One-Way Keyword

One of these features is the optional one-way keyword that precedes the rest of the signature. When the one-way keyword is specified, the operation gives the client an immediate return to the thread of control. In a one-way operation, only input parameters can be specified; the other two modes are not supported, and the return value is a typed void. The semantics of a one-way operation are that the ORB and the object implementation will make their best effort to complete the particular service request. There is no predefined way the results of the requests are assessed or evaluated. However, a user defining IDL for one-way operations can add some additional operation signatures for retrieving the result of requests.

If the one-way keyword is not used, by default, IDL-based operations are synchronized. In other words, when the client makes the request, the threat of control is blocked until the request is processed by the object implementation and the result of the process or an exception value are returned by the ORB. Ongoing work at the object management group addresses messaging service capabilities that include provision for an asynchronous invocation based on ordinary IDL signatures. The other two features, which are unique to IDL in the operation signature, include the raises clause and the context clause. The raises clause is an optional clause that identifies the user-defined exception values that can be returned by this operation.

3.2.3   Exception Handling

One of the important benefits of CORBA is that it simplifies the client model of the distributed computing environment, primarily through exception handling. Any operation can return a CORBA Standard Exception. About two dozen of these exceptions are defined in the IDL reference manual (Chapter 3 of CORBA 2) and cover most common types of error conditions that can occur in a distributed object system. The IDL for this exception is listed in Appendix B. For example, errors, such as CORBA ::NO_PERMISSION when a particular security or other kind of access cannot be granted to a particular request, and other kinds of error conditions, such as communication failures, memory limits, and object request broker internal failures, are provided by the Standard Exceptions. Standard Exceptions can be returned directly by the ORB or by the object implementation, so the application-defined object implementations have a variety of error conditions that are already defined for all signatures.

Some additional error conditions are introduced by particular CORBAservices. One example is in the transaction service. Because arbitrary operations can be part of transactions, some additional error conditions can be returned if a transaction is failing or must be aborted. In addition to Standard Exceptions, there are user-defined exceptions. User-defined exceptions are an important part of an interface specification and allow the programmer to specify the error handling capability exposed through the interface.

The CORBA object model gives the client certain guarantees. In particular, the client thread is guaranteed not to just hang because of some error conditions in the distributed system. There will be either a successful completion to an operation or an exception value will be returned. User-defined exceptions, then, are recommended to be included with interfaces. They complete the definition of the different kinds of actions that can occur as a result of a request. In particular, when IDL interfaces are defined, they generally include exceptions that relate to each of the input parameters in the operations signature because an erroneous or inappropriate value was provided as an input parameter. This can obviously create problems for the object implementation, and an exception would be the appropriate response. There may be other kinds of exception values that are logically related to the kind of request being processed. Those should be included, as well, in the interface specification.

Often, when users define interfaces by using technologies predating CORBA, their error-handling definitions are left out of the initial interface specifications. Because many interface definitions are not updated to the actual system implementation, it is difficult to discover this error-handling behavior since the information is often buried in the implementation. CORBA gives a clear way to include this information in a structured, strongly typed manner.

3.2.4   Context Clause

The final feature of IDL operations signatures is the context clause, an optional clause that specifies attributes that can be passed with the operation invocation. Context is similar to an additional input parameter. The context is information supplied by the client and attached to a particular request. The use of context is user-defined in virtually every case. There is a use of context in the security service, as well as the transaction service, in order to carry and convey information about security in transactions. This can be done in a way that does not require changes to user-defined IDL. One of the benefits of the context clause is that additional kinds of client environment information can be added without changing the operation signature. The context clause identifies particular context attributes. These context attributes can correspond to any kind of information the client may wish to provide that can help the object implementation provide a better service. An example of the kind of thing that might be included is the client's preferred compression algorithms that it may choose from to provide various kinds of qualities of service. Context information can be used by both the object request broker and the object implementation.

All CORBA ORBs pass the invocation context from the client to the object implementation. We are aware of only one object request broker that actually takes advantage of the invocation context of CORBA: the DEC ObjectBroker, which uses context information in order to influence dynamic binding decisions. The request is made in choosing which particular object and location a request will bind to dynamically. This feature of ObjectBroker allows some interesting run-time behaviors to be specified, such as dynamic load balancing and dynamic matching, or requests to specific processor types and locations in the distributed system. The requirement on the request broker for context objects is that they are passed from the client in an unmodified form to the object implementation as if they were another parameter in the parameter list. The object implementation can use the context information to provide enhanced services that are customized to specific clients. On the other hand, object implementation should be written so that it can provide a basic service without this context information. There may be some cases in which this is not feasible but, in general, context information should be treated as optional hints that provide a more customized value-added service to the object implementation, from the client.

3.2.5   Object Implementation

The final concept in the object model is the object implementation. Everything else we have been talking about in the object model relates to the interfaces of an object and not to its implementation. In CORBA, implementations are handled separately from interface information. In fact, most of what CORBA addresses deals with the handling of interfaces and not with the handling of implementations. This is deliberate. The CORBA specification intends to provide consistent interface handling in a distributive environment and to provide as much flexibility as possible to the handling of implementations. If interfaces are well defined, they hide these implementation details and client software can use interfaces without having explicit knowledge of how implementations are handled. So within the CORBA environment, the object limitations actually provide the software necessary to perform services requested through IDL interfaces.

In conclusion, the CORBA object model is an industry-standard object model for all kinds of distributed object orientation. It also provides a standard object model that is language independent for local object processing, as well as distributed processing. This standard object model applies to all operating systems, languages, and physical distribution schemes. The CORBA object model is an industrial-strength version of object orientation that provides an enhanced definition of object interactions. This object model is robust enough to deal with the complexities of distributed processing and heterogeneous processing across multiple languages and platform environments.

In this section, we explained the conceptual basis for CORBA-based objects and infrastructure, comprising a concrete object model for CORBA products implementation in the infrastructure. In the next section, we will define the architecture underlying CORBA. The CORBA architecture expands the details of the object model and explains how software is configured with, and interacts with, the infrastructure.

3.3   The CORBA Architecture

The CORBA architecture reveals important insights into how CORBA works. It also tells about the parts of the specifications that CORBA constrains and the parts of the implementation that CORBA allows to be unconstrained and implementation-specific.

Figure 3.6 is the key diagram of the CORBA architecture. It shows how application software communicates through the object request broker. CORBA standardizes the object request broker interfaces. On the top of Figure 3.6 are the client and the object implementation. These two pieces of application software are outside the ORB. Everything else in the diagram represents elements found in the object request broker. At the bottom of the diagram is the object request broker core, the details of which are unconstrained by the CORBA specifications. The ORB core can be implemented in any way that a particular prod-

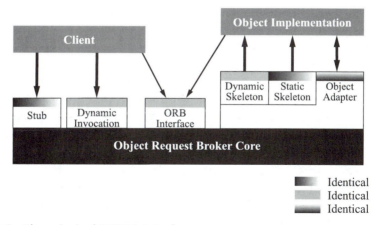

FIGURE 3.6   The principal CORBA interfaces.

uct vendor chooses. It is even possible for a user to replace part of the CORBA infrastructure to substitute unique mechanisms.

Parts of the request broker that are exposed are shown as shaded areas in this diagram. These include the dynamic invocation ORB interfaces, the static and dynamic skeletons, and the object adapter. These components have different guarantees associated with them with respect to the portability of their interfaces and how those interfaces are defined. The first category of interfaces are those that are predefined in the CORBA specification and provided by all object request broker environments, including the dynamic invocation, the ORB interfaces, and the dynamic skeleton. In each case, IDL or pseudo-IDL is included in the CORBA specifications that completely define these interfaces.

In some cases, the CORBA specification includes pseudo-IDL (PIDL), a definition of interfaces to standard ORB objects usually implemented in the client-side address space. One example is the dynamic invocation interface that creates a request pseudo-object. The PIDL includes a void pointer in one of the request signatures that turns out to be the most direct way to specify the implementations passing this type of parameter, which is dynamically typed. This unusual specification is, in general, avoided in all other specifications, such as CORBAservices and CORBAfacilities. It is generally a notational convention that is found in the CORBA specification in special circumstances.

The second category of interfaces corresponds to the object adapter. The object adapter can be a standard interface defined in CORBA. In addition, there can be many other object adapters defined by vendors or future OMG standards. One object adapter is predefined in CORBA today, the basic object adapter. The basic object adapter provides some general capabilities for the integration of object implementation with the ORB environment. Other object adapters may be standardized in the future or provided by specific vendors. An example of such a custom object adapter is in SunSoft NEO's object development framework. This object adapter, currently not standardized, provides convenient ways of developing applications that provide some interfaces that are more abstract than those provided by the basic object adapter.

The third category of interfaces in the CORBA architecture are those that are defined by IDL, including user-defined interfaces. These interfaces can be generated by users of request broker products, and the mapping of these interfaces for use in the CORBA environment is defined for specific languages. Standard CORBA mapping is already defined for C, C++, SmallTalk, and Ada95. Many other language mappings are being standardized, such as COBOL. This category of interfaces provides the most natural and controllable way to use CORBA and will comprise the majority of interfaces used in the CORBA environment.

Figure 3.7 shows the client perspective on the CORBA architecture. The client software can make requests on object implementation in two ways. The choice between these two mechanisms is transparent to the object of implementation. The two mechanisms are static interfaces and dynamic invocations. The static interfaces are defined by IDL definitions that are compiled into stubs, skeletons, and header files as defined by the particular language mapping.

3.3.1   Static Interfaces

The static interfaces are the most natural way for clients to invoke requests in the CORBA environment. Static interfaces provide location transparency in that they are mapped from IDL to a natural set of interfaced signatures. The signatures are natural to the particular language environment. These signatures make CORBA invocations look as much as possible like ordinary language

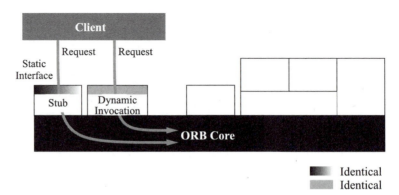

FIGURE 3.7   CORBA client interfaces.

object invocation. For example, if the static interfaces in the C++ environment contain CORBA objects that look like C++ objects, they can be defined with C++ class definitions generated from the IDL. The invocation of CORBA objects uses ordinary method invocation with the same syntax used for ordinary local object invocations. The alternative way that clients can invoke interfaces is through dynamic invocations.

All interfaces in the CORBA environment are defined by using IDL, whether they are static or dynamic invocations. In the case of a dynamic invocation, the client can discover interface information at run time, through access to the CORBA Interface Repository. All IDL definitions that are known within a particular ORB domain are registered and available in the Interface Repository.

The dynamic invocation interface provides a predefined set of signatures that are generic for all operations. For the client to use this interface, all the parameter information is stored in a client-request object, which is then invoked in order to send the request. When processing of the request service is completed, the client needs to retrieve the information from this generic request object. It is fair to say that dynamic invocation is not a natural way for clients to invoke objects. It looks different from an ordinary language invocation.

The advantage of a dynamic invocation is flexibility. Because the dynamic invocation does everything on-the-fly, it enables clients to invoke operations that were not known when the client software was originally constructed. Dynamic invocations are also used in some situations in which the interfaces are known and it is really a client's choice of which type of interface will be utilized.

Figure 3.8 shows the CORBA architecture from the object implementation's perspective. There are both static and dynamic ways that the object implementation can receive requests. It is also true that clients are unaware of which

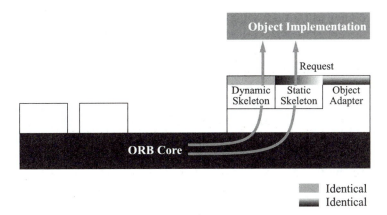

FIGURE 3.8   CORBA object implementation interfaces.

approach is being used by this implementation. In fact, implementations can use a mixture of static and dynamic requested invocations and can perform those transparently to all clients. The object implementation is also unaware of which invocation approach the client is using to generate the request so that there is transparency both ways.

3.3.2 Static and Dynamic Skeletons

The static skeleton corresponds to the static interface requests that are passed through the stub on the client side. In the skeleton, the IDL interfaces that are being implemented are known when the software is written. The IDL is compiled into a set of software with a set of method implementation signatures that correspond to the client-side static interfaces. In each case, when a request arrives, there is an up-call to the object implementation. In the case of a static skeleton, the up-call is in the form of a naturally mapped language signature. The call is similar to any other call made to an object instance.

In the case of a dynamic skeleton, there is a predefined dynamic signature that bundles the request information into dynamic data types that allow the implementation to retrieve the input parameters and to repackage the results. Similar to the case we saw on the client's side, the static skeleton provides a convenient mapping; a dynamic skeleton provides a highly flexible mapping that requires additional software to utilize. Dynamic skeletons have a powerful capability because when used together with dynamic invocation, they allow users to build object implementations that are a gateway to general-purpose applications.

Dynamic skeletons and dynamic invocation can be used together for creating gateways. Gateways have many applications—gateways among ORB environments, gateways among kinds of application implementation, and even implementation of software firewalls. It is also possible to create security domains that are separated by gateway processes that filter requests as they are passed from one security domain to another. This has some exciting implications because in a secure CORBA-based environment, software firewalls may be installed that can actually outnumber the hardware firewalls in the environment. This results in a finer-grained partitioning of secured domains than is the case with hardware firewalls.

The third set of interfaces provided to object implementations is through the object adapter. The object adapter defines additional operations needed by object implementations that are not specifically needed by clients. It is the case in the CORBA environment that objects are peer-to-peer. Object implementations can include client invocations of other objects. Every attempt is made for all objects to interact on a peer-to-peer basis in order to reduce the more constrained sorts of architectures that occur in remote procedure call environments, in which it is customary to have some applications that are pure client software and other applications that are pure service software.

Figure 3.9 contains the complete IDL for the dynamic invocation interface. It is interesting to note how concise a notation that IDL can be. This set of interfaces is the total needed to invoke any requests in the request broker environment if all requests are to be performed dynamically. The first signature is for creating a request object. This signature is provided as part of the predefined set of operations on all CORBA object references. So for any CORBA object reference, a programmer can create a request object that allows dynamic invocation. This signature is an example of an object creation interface.

To create a request, the client provides a number of parameters that can be sent dynamically. For example, the context object attached to the signature containing the client-specified context attributes is the first parameter. The second parameter is the actual operation identifier, which is the method, or signature, name. The third parameter is a list of arguments. These arguments can be specified at the time the call-create request is initiated or there is another interface that enables an add-them-on-the-fly option after the request object is created. The fourth parameter identifies the operation result, which is the additional return value provided by the overall operation as indicated by the operation type specification in the BNF for operation signatures. The final parameters return the actual request object reference and input a number of flags that can control the handling of this request.

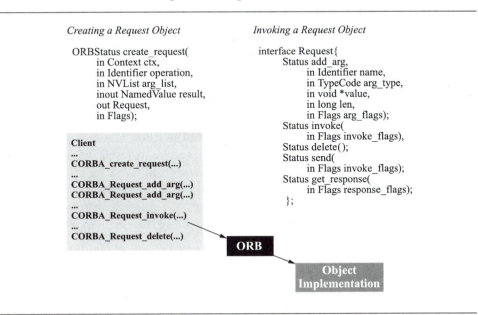

FIGURE 3.9   Dynamic invocation interface.

Once the request object is formed, it has its own IDL-specified interface, which is also shown in Figure 3.9. The request interface includes signatures for filling in the content of the request object and for invoking the request object, both synchronous and asynchronous. The first signature is for adding arguments. It allows identification of the name of the argument from the IDL and the type code of the argument. These dynamically indicate which type this argument has and then supply the value of the argument as a pointer to a void type—in other words, an unconstrained type. This is an example of pseudo-IDL. Normally, IDL would not have any pointer types specified. In this exception to the normal IDL, syntax provides a somewhat more convenient handling of this case than would be the case with ordinary language mapping mechanisms. The final arguments in this signature allow a specific length of the value and any flags that correspond with this argument. The other signatures in this interface include a delete operation for destroying the request object and de-allocating all its resources, as well as the invocation operations.

The first invocation operation is called invoke and simply sends this request through the ORB synchronously. When the invoke operation is used, the client thread blocks until either an exception is returned or the service is successfully performed and a normal completion status is returned. The remaining operations allow requests to be sent asynchronously. This asynchronous handling is unique to the dynamic invocation interface, although when writing custom IDL, the same ideas may be used to specify signatures for asynchronous handling of application-defined interfaces.

The first signature is the send operation, which essentially gives an immediate return value and sends the request through the request broker to be processed asynchronously. The final signature is the get response signature, which allows retrieval results or exceptions from this particular invocation.

Figure 3.10 explains some of the key trade-offs between the choices of static interfaces and dynamic interfaces. We anticipate that static interfaces will be used by most of the code, most of the time. Static interfaces require that the IDL is known at compile time so that the particular object type is known when the client software is written. The actual binding to an object instance is dynamic. There can be several instances of any object type, and the ORB allows concurrent interaction. Applications can bind invocations at run time, so there is still tremendous flexibility in the static interface approach.

3.3.3   Static Versus Dynamic Invocation

Right now, static interfaces are the status-quo approach supported by all CORBA object request broker products. Static interfaces are natural mappings to specific languages and use normal function call or method invocation syntax and semantics. The parameter types, which are used with static interfaces, are

Static Interfaces	Dynamic Invocation Interface
General Purpose: Used by most code, most of the time	Used in special purpose code needing extra flexibility; debuggers, desktops, browsers, etc.
Interfaces must be known at compile time, binding can be dynamic /run-time	Interfaces can be discovered at run time using data in Interface Repository
Supported by all current CORBA compliant products	Appeared before static interfaces in first generation products, 2-3 years ago — similar to current OLE2 Automation

API is natural to the language
  – uses normal function calls
  – uses natural parameter types
  – thorough compile time checking
	DII is pre-defined, single API for all method invocations

Easier to use, less code needed

FIGURE 3.10   Static versus dynamic invocation.

natural high-level parameters because each language and static interface provides complete, thorough, and strong type checking when compiling those interfaces. In general, static interfaces are easy to use and require a minimal amount of software. In contrast, dynamic invocation interfaces can invoke the same signatures as static ones, including signatures that are discovered dynamically on-the-fly. It is anticipated that dynamic invocation will be used by specialized code programs that need additional flexibility and by developers who are willing to write additional software to achieve it.

Some examples of applications that might need dynamic invocation include debuggers in which some operations discovered at run time may need to be invoked for the debugger to debug new programs, and desktop applications that may encounter new software interfaces as software is installed. One of the important advantages of dynamic invocation is its ability to discover interfaces on-the-fly at run time. Any interface that is known can be discovered through the CORBA Interface Repository present in all CORBA-compliant environments.

Note that dynamic invocation interfaces preceded static interfaces in the market, and the first generation of CORBA products was based almost entirely on dynamic invocation interfaces. This was feasible because dynamic invocation gives complete flexibility for invoking an arbitrary interface. The market has matured since 1992 and users realize that static interfaces are the way to go for most software needs. It is also interesting that the signatures between OLE automation and the CORBA dynamic invocation interface are quite similar. However, CORBA dynamic invocation allows user-defined data types and OLE automation does not.

The dynamic invocation interface is the predefined interface that gives a single application programming interface (API) for all signature invocations. Because it does that, it is somewhat unnatural compared with ordinary static types of signature invocations provided in most programming languages. When dynamic invocation is used, extra software must be written, which recasts the parameters from their strongly typed high-level language form into a generic dynamically typed form that uses a specific CORBA type to make these values known dynamically to the object request broker so that it can perform its marshaling activities. In summary, the dynamic invocation interface is more difficult to use and requires more code but gives some additional flexibility for a price.

This section explained how the CORBA architecture model works and what fundamental guarantees are provided by the infrastructure. Note that CORBA defines only interfaces, not implementations. This means that the behavior at the interface is constrained by the CORBA specification but the underlying algorithms and technologies are implementation-specific. The next section will explain in more detail how application software interfaces to the CORBA infrastructure. In particular, the focus will be on CORBA clients and object implementations. CORBA clients comprise any application software that makes CORBA invocations, whether contained within an object or not. Object implementations provide the service-side of the picture. Typically, clients and services are application software, although the next chapter will cover some standard interfaces for objects that can be implemented by both vendors and application developers.

3.4   CORBA Clients and Object Implementations

Figure 3.11 shows the structure of a typical client program in the CORBA environment. The top half of the diagram represents client software written in a particular programming language. In this language, there are various object references that correspond to objects known in the ORB environment. For example, if a client program is written in C++, its object references look like any other C++ object reference and are accessed through C++ class definitions.

There are various pieces of software that are linked together with the client program. At the time of compile and linkage, these are in the form of object libraries, as in machine-code-linkable libraries. These object libraries include any stubs corresponding to static interfaces that are known when the software is written.

If dynamic invocation is used, the dynamic invocation interfaces can be linked and any other ORB interfaces known to the client are linked. The ORB

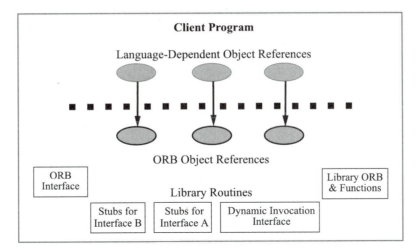

FIGURE 3.11   Structure of a typical client program.

interfaces comprise some generic functions that provide utility capabilities—for example, conversion of object references to strings and vice-versa, as well as operations on object references in basic data types that are known to CORBA.

3.4.1   Local Objects

In addition to these capabilities, there may be some object implementations that are actually linked into the client program. In other words, there can be some CORBA objects in the same address space as the client. CORBA hides the differences in location of objects—this is called location transparency. Objects can be local to the clients address space; they can be on the same machine; or they can be on a remote machine—perhaps even in a different language or on a different platform without the client having to know the difference between these different cases. They are all invoked in the same way, and the ORB deals with any differences in location or platform or language as needed to provide the same semantics, regardless of which case is implemented.

3.4.2   Marshaling

The stub program and the dynamic invocation interface provide marshaling of parameter information from language-dependent interfaces. These stubs translate high-level language parameters to a form that is necessary for transmitting information across the network and reassembling it on the object implementation side. The purpose of marshaling is handling high-level language data types in a transparent manner. When sent in through requests, these data types, if they are sent through a network, have to be converted and flattened into an externalized form (in other words, a byte stream). The externalized form can be sent across a low-level communication network protocol.

The choice of protocols is ORB-implementation-dependent, and the client does not have to have explicit knowledge of which protocol is being used. The ORB is also responsible when it is unmarshaling the parameters to provide any necessary conversions that are appropriate. For example, different platforms have different byte ordering for the representation of integers. These are called little-endian and big-endian hardware architectures. The ORB is responsible for transparently translating between these differences so that when the information is presented to application software, it is in the appropriate form. This transformation is possible because the IDL definition provides typing information with all parameters. In the case of static interfaces, the type information may be completely specified when the software is written at compile time so that when the stubs are generated, the particular ORB product may use this compile-time information to provide highly optimized marshaling transformations.

In some ORB environments, such as IBM SOM, the marshaling information is acquired dynamically at run time and the run-time information is used to perform the parameter marshaling transformations. The dynamic marshaling is also used in the case of dynamic transformation interface, which may not actually have information about the data types until the invocation is made. A similar situation occurs when the CORBA type any is invoked and used in interfaces. The CORBA type any has self-identifying type information that must be used on-the-fly to provide any marshaling that is needed. Because of the potential complexity of the CORBA type any, some ORB products are capable of marshaling only a fairly restricted set of data types representable by using CORBA type any. In particular, at a minimum, all distributed ORB environments can marshal basic data types and structures.

3.4.3   ORB Libraries

Figure 3.12 is the diagram of an object implementation software and the different libraries linked with it. This provides the view from the implementation side as opposed to Figure 3.11, which showed us the client side. We have a similar situation on the implementation side. The top half of the diagram represents the application program in which we have software written in a programming language that implements various objects. If some of these objects are known to the ORB, the ORB can send up-calls to the objects representing CORBA-based requests. These up-calls can come in through a static skeleton linked with the object implementation or through the dynamic skeleton.

Any object implementation may have one or more objects' instances represented in its program. Each object instance has a particular set of state information associated with it. The software supporting an object's instance may be the

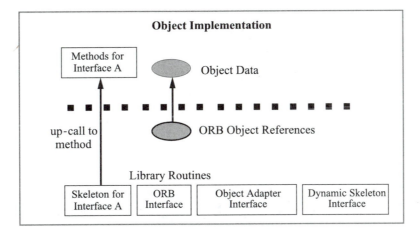

FIGURE 3.12   Structure of a typical object implementation.

same software supporting other instances. This is the capability that the ORB and the language run-time environment need in order to work together and implement properly.

Some other pieces of software that are linked with the object implementation include the direct ORB interfaces, which provide various kinds of utility capabilities used by both clients and implementations. The other item that is linked is the object adapter interface, which provides the additional interfaces needed by object implementations in their communication and interaction with the ORB. The object adapter interfaces can include capabilities such as registering objects and activating an object within the ORB environment. An important capability of the object adapter is the ability to create new object references that are stored persistently by the ORB. This will ensure that when requests are sent, the object request broker can determine which implementation is supporting this object instance and, if necessary, it can activate that implementation transparently to the client.

3.4.4   Client Invocation Process

Figure 3.13 is the client invocation process. This client invocation process is one of many examples of how a client can use CORBA to request a service. The first step in client invocation is to obtain an object reference. Object references in the CORBA environment are robust in that they can be stored persistently in a file in a string-valued form also known as a stringified object reference. When an object reference is stored in a file, it can later be retrieved, and if that object instance is still in existence, this object reference can be used to provide invocations on the reference.

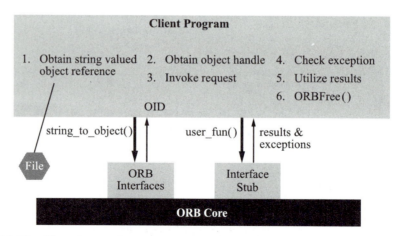

FIGURE 3.13   Client invocation process scenario.

This guarantee is in contrast to other technologies, such as remote procedure calls in the distributed component object model (DCOM), which use transient pointers to interface instances. The transient pointer becomes invalid whenever an object instance loses a connection, perhaps via a network error or if the program crashes or the machine crashes. In the CORBA environment, the object model guarantees that if these failures occur, the object reference will still be valid and the object request broker will do what is necessary to reestablish communication using this object reference. In some cases, it may even restart the object's server. If the ORB is unable to reestablish communication, it can return an exception.

There are ways of obtaining object references other than through files. The most common method of obtaining object references from other objects is through various operations signatures. The CORBA Naming Service is a white-pages directory service that is a common way for objects to obtain signatures for other objects. If a string-valued name is known for the object that is wanted, a naming service is available to return its object reference. Most applications will likely use the Naming Service as a primary way of obtaining references.

Another CORBA service that supplies object references is the Trader Service, a yellow-pages directory service that allows retrieval of object references with respect to some of the characteristics and qualities of service that objects can provide. Object implementations can register and advertise their availability to provide services in the Trader Service, and clients can send queries against the service to discover which object implementations are best able to provide the service they require.

Another way to obtain object references happens when the client first starts executing. It needs to obtain at least one application object reference before it can perform any invocation. There are initialization interfaces defined in CORBA for this purpose to allow discovery of references for the Name Service, Interface Repository and, potentially, other well-known objects. The final way that clients can obtain object references other than through files is through application-defined IDL interfaces with other application objects. User-defined IDL can pass object references as parameters and return values.

In this scenario (see Figure 3.13), the object reference is initially obtained through a file. Once the stringified object reference is obtained, it needs to internalize that reference by using one of the ORB interface methods, called string to object. When string to object is invoked, an internalized object identifier is received, after which invocations on that object can be made. Object identifiers can be used more than once. If this scenario started with the object identifier, the request could have been invoked on the first step. Note that some ORBs differ slightly from the actual CORBA object model and may require an additional step.

The next step is to invoke the request. A static interface is used as an example operation, called userfun(), to represent our static signature. After the invocation occurs, the client thread blocks until either an exception is returned or a normal completion results.

Many things that may happen in the background are transparent to the client during this request invocation. A few of these are described in the object implementation scenario below.

When the return occurs, it is important for client software to check to see if there are any exception conditions. Because it is a distributed-object environment, regardless of where the objects are located, there may be failures that can occur during the processing. Some of these errors may be application-level failures; some may be related to the distributed networking environment. There is always a greater-than-zero probability that something can go wrong. Therefore, we recommend that exception checking always occur after every ORB invocation. If an exception is returned, none of the output values from the invocation are considered to be valid. In other words, they cannot be used. If there is no exception and this is a normal completion, then it is acceptable to use the results of the invocation.

After all the results have been referenced or copied as appropriate, it is important to free the resources. Freeing the memory resources is not required in all language environments. For example, Ada95, SmallTalk, and Java have automatic garbage collection and do not require the use of memory deallocation functions. Other environments, such as C and C++, do require explicit memory management, and there are functions provided by CORBA for management of memory allocated by the request broker.

3.4.5 Invocation Scenario

Figure 3.14 is an example scenario that focuses on the object implementation side of the invocation process. This is a particular example of an invocation process, not the general case. There are certainly many other possible scenarios. In this one, the object request broker core has received an invocation request. When the request gets to the object implementation side of the system, the ORB discovers that the implementation is inactive. In other words, it is possible for an object instance to be in a nonrunning process that is out somewhere in a disk file. In this case, one of the pieces of information that the ORB stores persistently includes the object implementation repository. This repository contains enough information associated with each object reference to activate the object implementation from a completely inactive state, if necessary.

If we had encountered the object implementation in an active state, we would have been able to immediately deliver the request invocation and then return the result. However, in this scenario, a more general case is shown, in which the first action includes the object request broker working with the object adapter to activate the implementation. Depending on the operating systems, this could occur by executing a system call to an address stored in the implementation repository. For example, in a UNIX environment, this information might correspond to a path name and an argument list for a particular executable. The ORB would be responsible for invoking that executable process and creating the process in the appropriate account space with appropriate privileges.

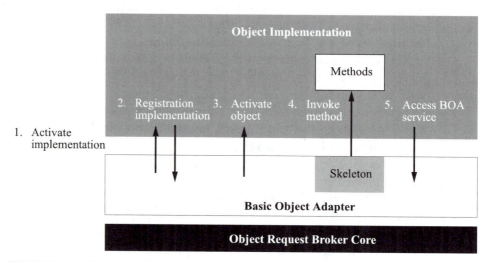

FIGURE 3.14 Object implementation invocation scenario.

Once the server process (which contains the object implementation) is activated, there is then a protocol for registering the implementation. In other words, the server needs to initialize the connection with the ORB and notify the ORB that it is in the active state through a protocol for activating objects. Object activation is required to make sure that the ORB knows that the particular objects are able to receive invocations. Objects can be in active and inactive states even if the object implementation process is running. This useful capability can be controlled through additional object adapter interfaces.

Once the objects are known to be active, the invocation can be made, which is an up-call from the skeleton to the implementation methods. This is the point at which the object reference is used to associate this object instance with some state information in the object implementation. Once the method services are completed, results or exception values are returned through the skeleton and back through the object request broker core to the client.

There are additional interfaces that the object adapter provides that can be invoked as a result of a method invocation or as a result of one of the background threads running in the implementation server. These interfaces include capabilities such as managing the activation state of objects and generating object references when new objects are created.

In this section, we explained how application software is linked to the CORBA infrastructure. Also explained was how application software interacts with the infrastructure through some scenario examples. This establishes a basis for how CORBA works with application software. In the next section, interface and implementation CORBA repositories are discussed. These complete the architecture model by explaining how interface and implementations are registered within the infrastructure.

3.5   Interface and Implementation Repositories

CORBA provides an explicit separation between interfaces and implementations. All interfaces in the CORBA environment are defined in IDL. IDL is used in several different ways. First of all, the IDL definitions are stored in the Interface Repository and therefore made accessible to all application software as public information. The IDL is also compiled into stub and skeleton programs—stubs linked with the client software and the skeletons linked with the object implementations.

Interfaces are handled independently of implementations (Figure 3.15). Implementations are installed in an Implementation Repository that provides a persistent record, known to the ORB, of how to activate and invoke operations on object implementations. CORBA is primarily constraining interfaces. The

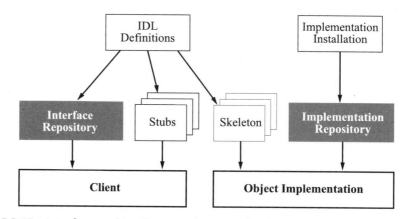

FIGURE 3.15   Interface and implementation repositories.

definition of how the implementations are handled is left to the specific ORB implementers. This allows flexibility in the way ORBs are implemented. If CORBA does a good job of constraining the interface information, it is not necessary to know all the details of how implementations are handled.

3.5.1   Interface Repository and IDL Object Models

The Interface Repository is one of the original facilities defined in CORBA, along with the interface definition language, dynamic invocation, basic object adapter, and so forth. Unfortunately, in the original version of CORBA, this was just a minimal capability. In CORBA 2, the Interface Repository is extended to provide a comprehensive schema for interface information. In essence, the improvement allowed the user to take all the IDL features and provide additional IDL interfaces that allow discovery of and access to the details of each interface. For example, take a definition of an array type with fixed bounds. There is an IDL to enable the discovery of the array element type, the number of bounds, and the sizes of the bounds, as well as the name of the array interface and the object references to each of these parts of the on-line specification. Similarly, the Interface Repository has an IDL schema defined that models all other features of the interface definition language for describing software interfaces.

It is interesting that IDL definitions are actually a fairly small subset of the overall design and analysis information that may be compiled in order to create application software. All that IDL captures is the sum of the information on the object hierarchy or the static object model diagram. In particular, it models the existence of the interface classes, the inheritance between interface classes, and the presence of the public attributes and public methods. Additional detail is required to create a complete IDL specification from this information—for example, the definition of all appropriate data types used by attributes in operation signatures and the definition of the strong typing of the attributes' operation return values. This includes the definition of the parameter modes and their strong typing data types. All of these details are not generally part of a typical object analysis and design documentation but must be added to IDL. There are other things, such as the exception values and context objects, that go beyond the level of detail of object diagrams.

Elements of the analysis and design documentation that are modeled in IDL are a small subset of the overall analysis model. Features such as the dynamic object design models are not captured at all in IDL specifications. In particular, the object design of the dynamic models really describes characteristics of object implementations. IDL is a pure interface description notation that does not model relationships other than inheritance. There are other kinds of relationships that occur among objects in systems that cannot be captured by IDL. Because they cannot be captured in IDL, by implication, they also are not represented in the Interface Repository. Additional standards are being worked on at OMG meetings to extend the capabilities of the standard specifications to include capabilities such as modeling relationships among objects. This is in addition to the enabling mechanism provided by the relationship service. The new facility that will capture these semantics is called the Meta-Object Facility. In addition to capturing relationship information, the Meta-Object Facility will also capture business object semantics, rules, and sequencing constraints.

3.5.2   Applications of the Interface Repository

Because of the complexity of the schema provided by the Interface Repository and the number of IDL interfaces involved, it is believed that the uses of the repository are probably limited to some relatively specialized applications. For example, development tools would access the repository to retrieve interface design information and other pieces of software. In our opinion, it is unlikely that the Interface Repository would be widely used by application client software because of the amount of software that would be required to use the information in the repository to invoke interfaces in the CORBA environment.

There is also another important consideration—the Interface Repository does not store any semantic information about the interfaces it is describing. It is not clear how automated software would take advantage of the interface information contained in the repository. For example, why should a method be invoked by an automated piece of software, or what does it mean to invoke this method? What type of service is being requested unless this service is already known? At a more detailed level, are there questions about what the parameters mean? What kind of data values should be supplied for those parameters? What do any returned results mean? None of this information is directly stored in the repository, although it may be part of the future meta-object facility standard that is directed at extending the overall ability of the CORBA system to model additional characteristics and details of object-oriented analysis and design models.

The final capability in the Interface Repository is a definition of the CORBA type code facilities. In the original CORBA 1.2 environment, there was a set of type code facilities to describe dynamic typing in the CORBA environment. In CORBA 2, these type code facilities have been extended and completed to provide a robust model. It was found that in the earlier CORBA products, due to some of the ambiguities in the CORBA 1.2 specification, the implementation of type codes was not consistent across ORB products. These problems are addressed in the CORBA 2 type code facilities.

This section discussed the interface and implementation repositories. These capabilities provide a way to register interface and implementation information so that it is accessible by the infrastructure and other application software. In the next section, CORBA language mappings is discussed. This will define how languages view IDL, the CORBA object model, and architecture.

3.6   Language Mappings

Figure 3.16 shows how IDL definitions can be compiled to support multiple language mappings. A particular IDL definition is processed by a compiler supplied with the object request broker. There may be one or more compilers supplied, depending on the different language mappings supported by the ORB. One capability supported by all object request broker products is the transformation of the IDL code into the Interface Repository representation available on line. Additional IDL compilers may be provided for various language mappings.

Most CORBA products support one or more of these language mappings. Multiple mappings have been created including C, C++, SmallTalk, Ada95, COBOL, and Java. Multiple products are available for most of the language mappings. Each language mapping is defined in a way that provides the most natural mapping among interfaces defined in IDL and interfaces defined in the language. In the case of the C mapping, header files are generated that describe the function prototypes, as well as stub and skeleton code that provide the mechanism immediately behind those interfaces for accepting the client invocation and delivering the up-call into the object implementation. Similarly, C++ generated header files, stubs, and skeletons for the C++ mapping from the IDL compiler provide a natural mapping from IDL interface objects to C++ class definitions.

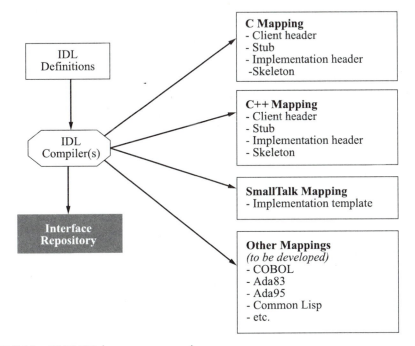

FIGURE 3.16   OMG IDL language mappings.

In the SmallTalk mapping, IDL interfaces are mapped into SmallTalk objects, providing a natural way for SmallTalk applications to interoperate through CORBA. In the Java mapping, IDL modules are mapped to Java packages and IDL interfaces are mapped to Java interfaces and support classes. The intention is that these languages will be able to interoperate in a seamless manner so that client software in one language can access services and object implementation in other languages without having to explicitly accommodate other differences in the language mappings.

3.6.1   C Language Mapping

Resolving the impedance match between these mappings is the responsibility of the ORB products. Figure 3.17 is an example of the IDL mapping to the C programming language as defined in CORBA 2. A simple example IDL interface is defined for an interface with a single operation. This interface has a user-defined parameter and causes for the raises expression and the context expression. When this IDL is processed and compiled through an IDL compiler, part of the header file that is generated is shown here. The first thing done because each IDL interface defines a new object type within the C header file is that the object type is defined as a renamed type CORBA object of the generic object

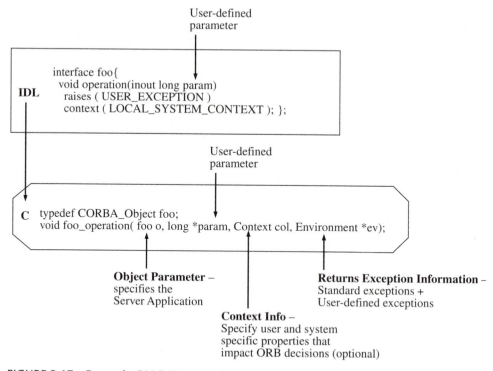

FIGURE 3.17   Example OMG IDL mapping to C.

type defined by the object request broker. In other words, all interfaces are equivalent to a CORBA type object in the C environment. Then the next statement in the header file corresponds to the operation signature generated from the IDL. In this case, the operation signature in the IDL generates a function prototype in the C programming language environment. The name of the function prototype is a combination of the module name(s), the interface type name, and the operation name.

In the C environment, there is a flat name space in which all the object type definitions and their operation signatures coexist. The C programming language does not explicitly support objects and the appropriate scoping mechanisms that objects provide. The IDL mapping provides naming conventions for combining the interface type name with the operation name. This is used to discriminate among operations supported by different object types.

There are a number of parameters in the function prototype, some of which are automatically generated by the IDL compiler. The first parameter is the object parameter that specifies the object implementations to which the message is directed. This parameter enables the dynamic binding of calls on the operation to different object instances. In other language environments that directly support objects, this parameter is implicit in the syntax of the method invocation. The second parameter shown here is generated from the user-defined parameter included in the IDL. If there were additional user-defined parameters, they would appear in the same order as in the IDL here in the C function prototype. In the language mapping, there is a well-defined set of transformations from IDL parameters to C data types. The mapping defines rules for the three argument-passing modes—in, in-out, and out—to the C data types provided in the function prototypes. In this case, we have an in-out parameter that is a long integer. In the C mapping, such a parameter is mapped into a pointer type to provide a reference to the long integer in the C language, which enables the function prototype to pass this parameter as both an input and an output value. The additional parameters in the function prototype generated by the IDL compiler correspond to the context object and the exceptions. The second-to-last parameter is of type context, which is a reference to a CORBA context object and contains all the context attributes included by the client to be conveyed with each invocation. The final parameter is the environment parameter, which is information returned by the ORB or object implementation that indicates any exception conditions that occur as a result of the invocation of this function.

3.6.2   C++ Language Mapping

The CORBA 1.2 C mapping is an OMG standard that preexisted the CORBA 2 C/C++ mapping. The new C/C++ mapping accommodates the use of C and C++ in the same program and does it in a relatively seamless way. The original CORBA 1.2 mapping is actually a simple transformation of this mapping. The most significant change is in the ordering of implicit parameters. The context and environment in the CORBA 1.2 mapping were included at the beginning of the function prototypes instead of at the end of the list. These automatically generated parameters are at the end of the list in the CORBA 2 mapping because that is where they occur in the C++ mapping if they are not defaulted. Since the CORBA 1.2 mapping is still an OMG standard and will be supported by CORBA-compliant products, this mapping will be available in CORBA products, selected by a compiler argument at the command-line level. There are many products supporting the legacy mapping to C, and it is anticipated that this mapping will be available to previous users of CORBA in the foreseeable future.

One of the advantages of OMG standards is that they are defined to avoid becoming obsolete whenever possible, and the CORBA 2 specification is an upwardly compatible specification when considered in contrast to CORBA 1.2 specification. This philosophy is used throughout the CORBA standards, including the CORBAservices and CORBAfacilities. The C++ binding is another standard mapping defined by CORBA. Before this mapping was standardized, there were some product-specific mappings supported in the C++ ORBs in the market. This new C++ mapping is based on significant experience with the alternative ways this mapping could be defined and represents a universal consensus from the vendor community, which unanimously submitted this specification.

The C++ mapping is a direct mapping from IDL because of the similarities in syntax between IDL and the C++ data definitions, although IDL and C++ data definitions are different notations. In particular, the C++ data definitions expose various implementation details through the interfaces, which would not be appropriate through the distributed object environment. Some of the basic features of the C++ mapping include the mapping from IDL modules to C++ name spaces, the mapping from IDL interfaces to C++ class definitions, and other straightforward feature mappings.

3.6.3   Variable Type and Pointer Type

Object references from the CORBA environment are actually mapped into two C++ types: variable type and pointer type. The variable type of object references has the same semantics as the CORBA object model. In other words, these references can be stringified, stored persistently, and also have restrictions in that they are opaque, meaning that they are not intended to be parsed by application software and they may indeed be product-dependent. So it is generally a mistake to refer to the internal contents of object references in application software. The other type of object reference defined in C++ is the pointer reference. This is a more primitive object reference and has semantics similar to C++ pointer types. In fact, CORBA pointer types support most of the C++ pointer capabilities. The primary exceptions are: It does not support casting to void star type and it does not support pointer arithmetic or relational operations in C++, although there are relational operations that are provided as method signatures in the standard mapping.

Some additional operations, such as the relation operations and others, are defined in the mapping and allow the safe handling of CORBA object references in the C++ environment. One of the most important of these operations is the narrow operation. The narrow operation allows casting of object references from more-general types of references to more specialized types. When there is a more specialized inheriting from a more general type, there may be additional kinds of operation signatures and attributes that are added to the definition. These would not be known by the ORB implementation unless this particular object reference was cast to the more specialized type.

The other kinds of data types supported within C++ have fairly straightforward mapping to C++ and are similar to the C mapping. In particular, the basic types, such as integers, floating points, and characters, are mapped from their

IDL types to the corresponding C++ basic types. Compound types, such as structures, arrays, and sequences, are mapped into C++ classes. That gives these types the additional convenience and protection of encapsulation within the C++ environment.

Figure 3.18 is an example of the C++ mapping. Shown in the upper-left corner is a small segment of IDL. In this case, we have an interface with a single operation and a single defined parameter. When this IDL interface is run through the IDL compiler, we get a header file output from the compiler, which is shown here. The example is of a compliant mapping of C++ and is not the only compliant mapping possible. Shown in the C++ code is the class definition for the CORBA type object that is recast into the pointer type, which is the pointer to this class. In the class definition, there are a number of public methods defined for a manipulation of pointer references. The duplicate operation allows the safe copying of pointer references. The narrow operation, as discussed above, allows the safe typecasting from more general types to more specific types of references, and the nil method signature allows for testing nil references.

The next mapping is from the user-defined operation signature that appeared in the IDL. Following the class definition is the definition of the variable type that provides the creation and copying operators. Shown in the public method signature definitions are some of these predefined method signatures. The first one is called the default constructor, and it allows the creation of a nil variable type reference. The second one deals with the conversion

```
//IDL
interface A
{ A op(in A param); };
```

```
//C++
class A;
typedef A *A_ptr;
typedef A_ptr ARef;
class A : public virtual Object
{ public:
    static A_ptr_duplicate(A_ptr obj);
    static A_ptr_narrow(Object_ptr obj);
    static A_ptr_nil();

    virtual A_ptr_op(A_ptr param) = 0;
  protected:
    A();
    virtual ~A();
  private:
    A(const A&);
    void operator=(constA&);
};
```

```
//C++ (continued)
class A_var: public_var
{ public:
    A_var() { ptr_ = A::_nil(); };
    A_var(A_ptr p) {ptr_ = p};
    A_var(const A_var a&)
        {ptr_=A::_duplicate(A_ptr(a)); }
    A_var &operator=(A_ptr p)
        {if (p!=ptr_) reset(p); return *this};
    operator A_ptr() const { return ptr_; }
    operator A_ptr&() {return ptr_;}
    A_ptr operator->() const {return ptr_;}
  protected:
    A_ptr ptr_;
    void free() {release(ptr__); }
    void reset(A_ptr p) {free(); ptr_ = p;}
  private:
    void operator=(const A_var &);
    void operator=(const_var &);
};
```

FIGURE 3.18 C++ mapping example.

of pointer references to object references. Some additional operations deal with copying—for example, copying the variable reference, as well as copying the actual state information in the object. The experience with the C++ mapping indicates that once the basics have been mastered, it turns out to be a convenient way to use CORBA in a C++ environment. The initial exposure to the complexity of this mapping does take some people by surprise, but after more exposure, it becomes evident that these features support highly productive application development in C++.

3.6.4 SmallTalk Language Mapping

The SmallTalk mapping for the SmallTalk programming language is another CORBA 2 standard. It is based on the SmallTalk 80 language defined in the popular textbook by Adele Goldberg. This SmallTalk mapping is a natural mapping. For example, the mapping uses the garbage collection capabilities of SmallTalk to manage CORBA objects, as well. The IDL operations and attributes map directly to SmallTalk messages in this mapping so that they provide the most natural way of handling these capabilities. Each object reference from the CORBA environment maps into a SmallTalk object reference, which allows SmallTalk objects to respond to message signatures defined in the IDL interfaces.

Some other important details of the mapping include the way data types in IDL map into SmallTalk objects. Some IDL data types map into existing standard objects within SmallTalk to provide a natural correspondence. In particular, IDL structure types map to SmallTalk dictionary classes, and IDL exception types map to dictionary classes. It is interesting that exception types and structure types are similar to each other at the IDL level, and it is also interesting to see that they map to a common type in the SmallTalk environment. The IDL sequence type also maps to the SmallTalk ordered collection class, which is useful because it is the natural way SmallTalk manipulates these variable-length sequences of objects. IDL array types map to the SmallTalk array class, which would be the most natural way to handle arrays.

In some cases, new SmallTalk objects are created to support the IDL mapping. One case is for the enumeration type that maps into SmallTalk CORBA enumeration protocol. Another example is the IDL union type that maps to the SmallTalk CORBA union protocol. Figure 3.19 is an example of the SmallTalk mapping. The IDL operation signature returns a type Boolean and has two input parameters. One of these parameters is an input parameter and the other is an output parameter. In the SmallTalk language environment, this maps into a SmallTalk invocation shown at the bottom of the figure. The message would be sent to the self object. It has a return value that is a Boolean object and basically accepts a message for the input parameter and a protection value to support the handling of the output parameter.

OMG IDL
boolean
      has_property_protection(in string key,
          out Protection pval);

Would be invoked in the SmallTalk language as:
aBool:= self
      hasPropertyProtection:aString
      Pval: (protection := nil asCORBAparameter).

FIGURE 3.19   Example of SmallTalk mapping.

3.6.5   JAVA Language Mapping

The IDL/Java language mapping contains several approaches to accommodate Java's unique language features. Every data type and interface type defined in IDL generates an additional class, called a holder class. The holder class is needed to pass parameters for the IDL out and in-out modes. This is necessary because JAVA only supports a call-by-value parameter mode analogous to the IDL input parameter mode.

Basic types from IDL are mapped into their corresponding basic types in Java (with the additional holder classes). Since Java has no construct analogous to IDL typedef, most compound data types are mapped to Java classes (including structs, unions, and `type any`). This is not the case, however, with arrays and sequences, which are mapped directly into Java arrays.

The IDL/JAVA mapping can be used with several infrastructure options, depending on those supported by the ORB product. These include protocols layered over TCP/IP, Java remote method invocation (RMI), environment-specific inter-ORB protocols (generally ORB-specific), and the Internet inter-ORB protocol (IIOP).

In this section, the CORBA language mappings for several programming languages were discussed. CORBA enables the construction of single or multiple language applications by providing natural mappings to a common infrastructure (CORBA) from a common interface definition (IDL). This is possible because the same client-service separation required to support distributed computing is also useful for isolating client-service language differences. In the next section, portability issues and CORBA will be discussed. In this case, we refer to portability of application software between middleware infrastructures, not just hardware platforms and operating systems.

3.7   **Portability**

The purpose of CORBA standards and most standards is to provide risk reduction for consumers, as well as suppliers. One of the capabilities for risk reduction is portability of application software between different vendor-supplied CORBA environments. With portability, the application software is as independent as possible from each CORBA product and would allow the application software to run on a variety of CORBA environments with minimal modification. Today source code portability is not fully guaranteed by the CORBA standards but is guaranteed to the extent that porting among CORBA products is a relatively straightforward process and is less expensive than trying to port among different proprietary middleware technologies.

People have war stories about committing their application software to middleware products and running into problems later when the products changed or were withdrawn from the market. We strongly recommend that this issue be considered in application software design and that everything necessary be done to isolate the majority of the application software from any product-specific extensions that are exposed through software interfaces. Some of the standards discussed in this section helped to resolve portability issues and represent additional attempts by CORBA vendors to eliminate remaining differences that might hinder source code portability.

In the CORBA 2 standard, the most important interfaces supporting portability are called the initialization interfaces. Note that most application software will be using IDL-defined interfaces most of the time. Since the standard language mappings are defined to be consistent across products, these mappings will provide portability under most circumstances. There are some circumstances in which the language bindings do not cover all cases. One case is initializing, which corresponds to the processing needed when a client or object implementation process first begins activation. In other words, the application software needs to initialize its relationship to the ORB and discover any initial object references needed to begin processing. This area was not well addressed by the original CORBA 1.2 standard. The initializing interfaces in CORBA 2 do address this area in a comprehensive way, however.

If you are currently using a CORBA product, we strongly recommend that you use CORBA 2 (and beyond) interfaces and layer them on top of any product dependencies that may be exposed. When the chosen product of object request brokers evolves to CORBA 2, the transition will be relatively straightforward and painless. This technique of complying to the standards rather than to specific products is useful and has proven effective in practice to reduce software risks due to technology advancement and obsolescence. It turns out that the highest-risk features of products, those that may change because of obsolescence, are not standard features but features that are unique and proprietary to individual products.

The initialization interfaces cover the operations needed when application software first begins executing. In particular, the ORB init operation is a general operation for both clients and object implementations and initializes their association with the object request broker. Another interface, called the basic object adapter (BOA) initialization, is a request that allows object implementations to initialize their relationship with the object adapter whenever the object implementation is activated.

An important challenge as an object or client starts running is to obtain its initial object references so that it can start to generate requests. When a process starts running, it may not have access to any object references. Processes can obtain object references from files, as we discussed earlier, but it is more likely that useful object references will be obtained from other objects. The initialization interfaces allow an object or client to retrieve an initial set of object references so that it can obtain additional references from those objects. In particular, there is a signature, called list initial services, which returns a sequence of string values that are identifiers to the initial objects and that can be returned through the initialization interfaces.

Another operation signature, called resolve initial references, takes one of these strings as an input parameter and returns the appropriate object reference for that object. There are a few predefined string-valued identifiers for well-known services, in particular, the Name Service and the Interface Repository. We anticipate that there will be other predefined object identifiers that use this interface for the Trader Service and, potentially, for other services. In addition, there can be application-defined object identifiers that are registered with the object request broker and can be retrieved through these initialization phases.

In this section, the portability support within CORBA was explained. This provides a much-improved model over earlier middleware infrastructures, which were entirely proprietary. In the next section, how middleware infrastructures can operate with similar or different infrastructures is discussed.

3.8   Interoperability and OLE Integration

Figure 3.20 shows various ways CORBA supports the integration of object-oriented systems. CORBA can be used for integration of object-oriented software, as well as non-object-oriented software. In fact, it is useful for the integration of legacy software and commercial software in cases where there is no explicit access to the internals. Within an object-oriented environment, an important role that CORBA plays is integrating different object run-time

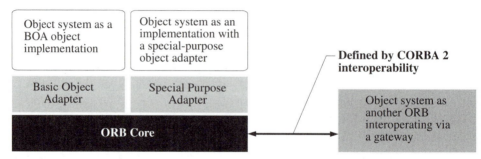

FIGURE 3.20   Different ways to integrate object systems to the ORB.

systems. For example, each programming language environment, such as C++, SmallTalk, Ada95, and others, provides a particular type of object system. These object systems are integrated through the standard language mappings, which are adopted for CORBA. There may also be other types of object systems that programmers might want to integrate through the CORBA environment.

CORBA provides a basic object adapter as a standard way to integrate object systems. This general-purpose capability is useful across the board. Unfortunately, it does not always provide the convenience or performance appropriate for all object environments. In that case, a special-purpose adapter could be provided in a standard or a product-specific form. This provides an additional way to integrate a unique object system. One example of a unique object system might be an object-oriented database with 10,000 or more objects. If we attempted to integrate all 10,000 objects into the CORBA environment using the basic object adapter, we would spend time every time the application was activated registering every object and activating them so that they were known to be accessible through the ORB. These 10,000 objects would probably overload the internal tables of the object request broker and may affect the overall performance of the CORBA system.

An alternative is to have a special-purpose object adapter, which would provide a more dynamic way to register objects when it becomes necessary that they be known in the CORBA environment. For example, it is possible to have an object adapter that registers the existence of an object only when it is referenced by a CORBA object or when it sends a reference to itself to another object through the special-purpose adapter. It would then be possible to have a large number of fine-grained objects that can be seamlessly and conveniently integrated in a CORBA environment. Another way to integrate with foreign object systems is through CORBA 2 interoperability. There can be a direct integration to the object request broker core environment as defined by one of the specific protocol stacks in CORBA 2. This is a direct integration into the CORBA environment and can provide excellent performance, as well as interoperability. A wide range of CORBA products support this approach.

3.8.1 CORBA Interoperability

CORBA interoperability is an important part of the specification but not for application developers. CORBA interoperability deals with the interoperability of multiple ORB products, not vdirectly with the interoperability of application software. The specification of CORBA interoperability is independent of application software interfaces and, in general, would not affect application software in the underlying mechanism used. Only in specialized applications would application programmers use the CORBA interoperability specifications directly. An example would be if some programmers were doing some high performance real-time satellite communication processing integration, but this type of situation is highly specialized.

The CORBA interoperability specification defines an architecture for various solutions for ORB-to-ORB communication. This overall solution is called the combined submission because it contains elements of various submissions tendered to the OMG. Within the combined submission, there is an overall architecture, called universal networked objects, which defines several categories of interoperability solutions. These categories include the general interoperability protocols and the environment-specific interoperability protocols. General interoperability protocols are mandated for use by all CORBA products. If a product calls itself CORBA 2-compliant, it must comply with all general interoperability protocols.

Only one of these protocols is standardized—the Internet interoperability protocol (IIOP). The IIOP is based on the standard Internet technologies, including the transmission control protocol/internet protocol, or TCP/IP, which is universally available on platforms since it is used by the Internet. The IIOP is an efficient protocol for ORB-to-ORB communication and will be supplied with all CORBA 2-compliant products. In order to encourage the use of this protocol in the market, one vendor, SunSoft, has created an IIOP reference implementation that they have made available through the OMG as freeware.

The other predefined protocol is an environment-specific interoperability protocol not mandated for implementation—the distributed computing environment common inter-ORB protocol (DCE CIOP). It is based on the popular Open Software Foundation technology for remote procedures calls—the distributed computing environment (OSF DCE). This protocol was submitted by several vendors who delivered DCE products and were interested in having their customers use that technology as part of their CORBA environment. There are some advantages to DCE because of some of the layered services in the DCE environment, such as the cell directory service and the security service. The OMG, however, is defining a secure extension to the IIOP that would minimize the necessity for using the DCE approach.

One common misconception about the DCE interoperability protocol is that it would imply that the CORBA products would be layered directly on top of existing DCE technology. This is unlikely because most CORBA products are layered on some lower-level networking technology, which is more efficient than remote procedure call. For example, many products are layered directly on top of socket technologies. These come in different forms, depending on the product. If a CORBA product were layered directly on top of DCE, it would perform worse than DCE and would not be competitive, compared with products using more-efficient protocol stacks.

An important way to think about CORBA is that the ORB is an intelligent manager of some lower-level networking layer and once the initial communication is established, the additional ORB software gets out of the way and enables direct communication between the client and the object implementation software through the lower-level networking layer. We have seen in practice that this often results in performance advantages in CORBA products, which are superior to legacy remote procedure call technologies, such as DCE. The products that may claim some comparability with DCE are probably not using DCE in a conventional way. They are used only for interoperability purposes for bridging environments or as special-purpose ORBs dedicated to secure environments or other specialized applications.

3.8.2   CORBA and Microsoft

Another important capability of CORBA is interoperability with the Microsoft technologies. The OMG has completed work on interoperability between the Microsoft common object model and the CORBA 2-based object request brokers. This work is called the Part A COM/CORBA interoperability—COM stands for component object model. COM is the technology basis for the object linking and embedding technology on Microsoft platforms. The COM on Microsoft desktops today is a nondistributed processing technology that supports only single platform software. The COM/CORBA interworking standard allows CORBA to extend the capabilities of the existing COM to distributed processing and integration with other platform environments. As the distributed COM (DCOM) becomes more widely available, OMG will adopt distributed extensions based on COM/CORBA interworking.

Most organizations have a variety of platforms in-house and need to do distributed processing to provide their capabilities. It is possible for application software to operate seamlessly with commercial software supporting technologies like OLE. With the COM/CORBA interworking, it is possible to integrate application server software with client software on OLE COM platforms. The COM/CORBA interworking standard provides a risk reduction for developers in that the technology that leverages the integration of OLE COM and CORBA will be supplied by multiple vendors and supplied in a consistent manner across all products. This technology is widely available in a variety of CORBA products, such as Expersoft Power Broker, SunSoft NEO, Iona Orbix, and DEC ObjectBroker, among others.

Figure 3.21 shows how this technology could be used to integrate mission-critical application software. The suggested approach is not to provide direct integration to the OLE technologies from current mission-critical application software because the complexity of the direct OLE interface integration will require writing a significant amount of software and provide a tight coupling between the application software and that particular technology.

Another important reason is obsolescence. It is the case that the Microsoft technologies are evolving. As seen in the market, the technologies have the habit of evolving every few years to new interfaces or improved interfaces that address some limitations involved in the previous technologies. It is anticipated that this evolution will occur with respect to the OLE technologies, as well, because many limitations are coming to light, which will lead Microsoft to improved capabilities. So by leveraging the COM/CORBA interworking technology as an OLE gateway, integration can be provided with application

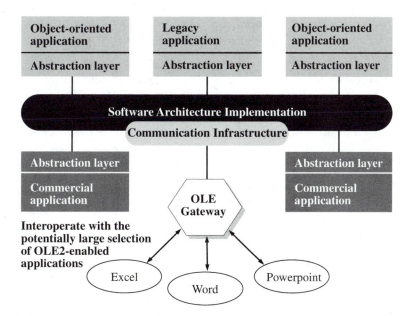

FIGURE 3.21   Integration of complex technologies.

software architecture that provides isolation from the complexity of the de facto standard technology and insulation from any technology changes.

In summary, the common object broker is an object-oriented communication infrastructure that supports the integration of both object and non-object-oriented technologies, as well as legacy software and commercial applications. CORBA simplifies distributed computing. It allows exposure of the interface details that programmers want to expose and hides what they want to hide. It simplifies and standardizes the semantics of object-oriented systems so that client processing and client software can perform distributed processing with a minimum of complexity. In particular, it defines the exception mechanism as a way to consistently specify error conditions likely to occur in any complex system.

The key capability defined within CORBA is the interface definition language and its semantics, which are defined in conjunction with the CORBA object model and the CORBA architecture definitions. Combining these capabilities offers a technology that supports isolation of pieces of software from each other and an independence among pieces of application software. In addition, CORBA provides independence from application software and the underlying communication infrastructure and protocol stacks. CORBA provides independence among programming languages so that languages can operate with each other and integrate in a natural manner. CORBA provides independence from platform and operating systems so that platforms in heterogeneous environments and networking technologies can seamlessly interoperate.

From the application software's perspective, CORBA provides location transparency. Clients do not have to manage the state or location of object implementations. Object implementations can be relocated transparently to optimize performance and functionality of systems without modifying the application software to do so. The other major capability defined within the CORBA architecture is the dynamic invocation interface that provides a flexible extension to the IDL-defined static interfaces enabling special applications to discover interface information on-the-fly and dynamically invoke operations on objects.

In this section, we described interoperability among CORBA-based ORBs and other infrastructures. This completes the description of infrastructure standards. The next section focuses on using these infrastructures for application building. Some interesting issues arise as a result of the characteristics of CORBA.

3.9   CORBA Guidelines

In our experience with teaching and mentoring CORBA developers, we have emphasized several important guidelines for CORBA-based development.

3.9.1   **Location Transparency**

CORBA makes the location of the object implementation transparent. That means hardware-software allocation decisions can be deferred to run time and do not have to be hardwired into the application software. One advantage of location transparency is that it simplifies the client code and makes it more reusable in different configurations. Another advantage is performance tuning. With location transparency, we can move the location of the object implementation and assess performance without changing client code. Three allocation alternatives are remote host, local machine, and same address space.

Use of location transparency is optional. One can easily write code that breaks transparency simply by putting in location information, operation parameters, and return values. For example, we could write the following interface that makes location, file system, and machine type explicit.

```
interface NonTransparentObject {
// Note: Reuse of This Example Not Recommended
  typedef string HostName
  typdef string InternetAddress;
  enum PlatformType { Windows, Macintosh,
    Solaris, OS2, AIX,
    HPUX, VMS, OSF1, SCO, Linix, MVS,
    OS400, IRIX, Other };
  typedef sequence(octet) ByteStream;

  HostName where_are_you();

  InternetAddress what_is_your_address();

  PlatformType which_platform_are_you_on();

  ByteStream get_file_data(

    in string file_path_name);
};
```

One dangerous aspect of breaking location transparency is that it may put brittle assumptions about allocation decisions in the interfaces and implementations, which may cause problems later. In the above interface, if we share file names through IDL interfaces, we make an implicit assumption that we have consistent access paths to a shared file system. In addition, this interface exposes the machine representation of file system data as type sequence ⟨octet⟩. This assumes that mappings among machine representations are handled explicitly by the client software. These assumptions are easily broken when the interfaces are reused or when the system is reconfigured.

To really take advantage of the full power of the CORBA architecture, it is necessary to think about the use of the ORB product and the use of OMG IDL independently. There are several reasons for doing this.

OMG IDL is a tool for rigorously describing software interfaces. It describes these interfaces in a manner that is independent of location, language, platform, and protocol stack.

Brittle systems often use multiple communication infrastructures, and their application code directly depends on these implementation decisions. This complicates the system-level architecture model—for example, in handling security and operations and maintenance (O&M). If we assume that use of the ORB product and OMG IDL are one and the same, then we perpetuate these practices. To have a portable, flexible, and uniform application architecture, it is essential to have a single infrastructure model. By using OMG IDL for all system-level interfaces, this goal can be achieved.

CORBA provides a natural mapping among OMG IDL-defined software interfaces and language-dependent object models (C++, SmallTalk, Ada95, and others). This natural mapping makes it easy and relatively transparent to use OMG IDL-defined interfaces wherever they are needed. This includes fine-grain reusable interfaces, such as class libraries.

Performance management is an important issue, and one can only use CORBA to manage performance properly by exploiting the full flexibility of the standard—for example, by using OMG IDL interfaces layered over user-defined protocol stacks, co-located objects, replicated objects, pseudo objects, and so forth. By taking advantage of CORBA's location transparency, one can co-locate library objects transparently with client software (that is, in the same compilation module). We have exploited this CORBA flexibility in other high performance interfaces, such as multiple-client access to a shared memory system and OMG IDL layered over RPC interfaces. By using CORBA in these ways, the flexibility of the ORB's dynamic binding process will be compromised, but the gain will be the architectural benefit of separating application code from the underlying mechanism, as well as the achievement of desired performance benefits.

Many architects and developers make an a priori assumption that the ORB product is not fast enough or fine-grain enough to support all parts of the architecture. Then they draw the conclusion that they need to expose other mechanisms and protocol stacks to application code in order to meet their performance needs. This is not so. OMG IDL can and should be applied consistently throughout an architecture to describe reusable software interfaces. The appropriate development approach is to first define all interfaces using OMG IDL and use an ORB product for prototyping because the product gives substantial flexibility and support during development. If it is discovered that an ORB product's performance is not sufficient for certain operations, those operations can be selectively layered on other mechanisms.

3.9.2   Rely on the CORBA Standard, Not the ORB Products

Before CORBA, a lot of proprietary middleware had unique software interfaces. These proprietary packages provided significant benefits compared with de facto standards, such as remote procedure calls. To build software systems, one had to risk a substantial portion of the application software investment to exploit this middleware to technical advantage. If the middleware changed or was withdrawn from the market, it involved substantial O&M and porting costs. Experience has shown that middleware migration involves around 18 months to retrain staff and port existing software—18 months in which investments go into porting infrastructure, not new functionality. Losing 18 months of progress can be a catastrophe for many businesses.

CORBA has fundamentally changed the infrastructure options for developers. Now that most distributed computing middleware is either CORBA-compliant or migrating there, there is substantial commonality among middleware environments. CORBA is a stable specification that constrains the most stable and risk-free capabilities of middleware products. In the case of emerging OMG specifications, one can incorporate and anticipate the market direction at a detailed design level.

To take advantage of the inherent risk reduction in using CORBA-based standards and products, one must have a knowledge of the standards, independent of the products. OMG standards suppress the overwhelming majority of product differences exposed to application software, but some differences still exist. Some of these differences provide important implementation advantages. Unfortunately, vendors do not go out of their way to identify noncompliant aspects of their products, nor do they educate consumers sufficiently about the differences. Knowledge of the standards is the responsibility of the consumer— in particular, of the application architects and developers who can provide substantial risk reduction by isolating the majority of application code from noncompliant product features.

3.9.3   Use of Standards

It is not the standard or the product; it is the use that is important. CORBA should be used in more-sophisticated ways than previous technologies. The simplification of distributed computing is one of the keys in making this possible. Before CORBA, developers struggled to survive while creating distributed systems; with CORBA, developers can focus their energies on creating more-sophisticated, adaptable architectures. CORBA enables a focus on the quality of the interfaces in an architecture and allows developers to explore design trade-offs with relative ease, compared with previous technologies.

CORBA and the other OMG specifications are software standards. Some fundamental information about software standards makes their purpose, advantages, and shortcomings clear.

To create a standard, multiple organizations get together to decide a common way to solve a technical problem. Standards reduce technical risk for both suppliers and consumers. Standard compliance is an assurance of important product benefits.

In general, software standards define boundaries. If the boundary is between the supplier and the consumer, then the primary benefit is portability. Portability is the ease with which consumer software can migrate among or support multiple vendors' products. If the boundary is between suppliers, the primary benefit is interoperability. Interoperability is the ability of two pieces of software to exchange information and functionality. The third case is the boundary between consumers and other consumers; the benefit would be interoperability (a case seldom addressed by standards groups).

The majority of standards activities are funded and driven by technology suppliers. Suppliers seek to identify the most common functionality. That is useful across the largest possible customer base. For hardware platform suppliers, that means all computer customers; therefore the standards they propose must be general-purpose. The founders of many important standards groups (OSF, X/Open, COSE, OMG) are hardware suppliers, and their first standards are broadly applicable. Isolation from dependence on the hardware platform (i.e., portability) is the quality that most standards purport to deliver.

The goals of generality and flexibility are at odds with interoperability. To achieve interoperability, there must be constraints and guarantees. Options must be limited and commonality strictly enforced. Flexibility can easily be claimed by providing numerous features.

In a perfect world, standards should exist to provide only technical benefits, including portability and interoperability. However, companies that sponsor standards usually have motivations unrelated to the technical benefits. One of the key motivations that companies have is product marketing. Standards are seen as a key market development tool that generates exposure, credibility, and consumer confidence. The most dramatic example of this is the ISO's standard query language (SQL) standard, which was a key ingredient in the establishment of the industry-dominating relational database market. SQL is certainly an elegant database query language, but it leaves a great deal up to individual vendors, including the APIs and the format of the query results. Virtually every product has a unique dialect of SQL and extensions. SQL provides almost no cross-product portability or interoperability benefits. In fact, a thriving market of proprietary middleware products has arisen to address the interoperability issues created by SQL vendor differences.

At first glance, OMG standards have many of the traditional standards' shortcomings. They are large documents and appear difficult to interpret. The OMG has done a very credible job of streamlining the contents of standards documents, through the introduction of OMG IDL. Because OMG IDL is such a powerful tool for the standards writer, it is catching on like wildfire in the formal standards community. In fact, ISO is extracting the OMG IDL part of CORBA for adoption at the international level (and not the rest of CORBA). This adoption is encouraged by many other standards groups that would like to use OMG IDL but do not yet have a formal standard at which to point.

3.10 Concluding Remarks

In this chapter, the CORBA specification was described. This included elements of the CORBA core, language mappings, and associated specifications. This information adds a standard object model, distribution model, and language mappings to the IDL covered in the previous chapter.

IDL and CORBA are fundamental technologies, on a similar level of abstraction as operating systems and programming languages. These provide enabling infrastructure, but there is substantially more technology required to create sophisticated applications. In the next chapter, the next layer of capabilities, the CORBAservices will be discussed. The CORBAservices provide enabling functionality that builds on this infrastructure.

CORBAservices

4.1 An Overview of CORBAservices

The CORBAservices are a set of enabling interfaces for globally applicable service capabilities. A familiarity with each of the CORBAservices is essential to success with CORBA. A careful reading of this chapter will give all the background needed for basic familiarity. A detailed knowledge of some of the key CORBAservices is also important. The CORBAservices that developers frequently use vary by domain. Most domains make active use of naming and lifecycle services. Other key services might include events, persistence, relationships, externalization, and trading.

This chapter is a companion to the CORBAservices specifications available from the OMG. The CORBAservices specification provides a description similar to a reference manual. These descriptions of services aid in understanding these important standards.

4.1.1 Many Application Developers Have Reinvented the CORBAservices

It is fairly commonplace for developers to attempt to build applications without considering CORBAservices. Many of these developers end up struggling with infrastructure issues, which leads to the construction of new software that replicate the basic functions of CORBAservices. When used appropriately in application system designs, CORBAservices provide design and development leverage.

4.1.2 Considering Vendor Support; Self-Building These Services

Availability of vendor-supplied CORBAservices is an issue for developers and will continue to be an issue for some time. It is unlikely that all vendors will supply the full range of CORBAservices.

One of the key advantages of CORBA is the interchangeability of facilities that are purchased and facilities that are built. The OMG standards enable developers to build specialized implementations of standard interfaces. In addition, if a key facility is missing, it is always a viable option to build implementations of the necessary services. The CORBAservices are reasonably small specifications that can be prototyped quickly and later upgraded to vendor-supplied implementation if that becomes an option.

Figure 4.1 shows the object management architecture with details of the CORBAservices. The majority of CORBAservices have already been adopted. In this architecture, CORBA is the central component through which all other objects communicate. The CORBAservices are fundamental enabling services and are analogous to the services available as system services on operating systems today. The other horizontal category of interface is the CORBAfacilities. CORBAfacilities relate to the CORBAdomains interfaces in that the CORBAfacilities capture any of the domain needs that are in common across multiple domains. Domain interfaces represent different vertical-

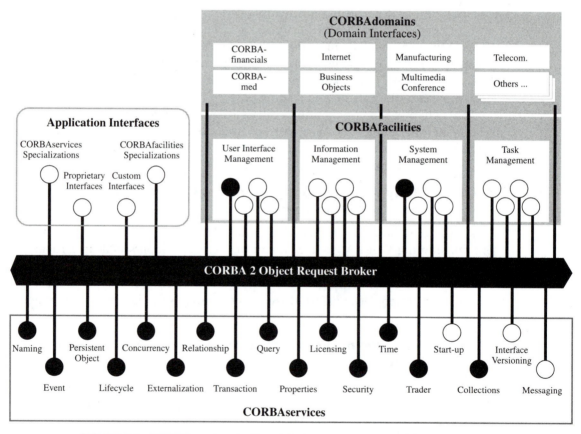

FIGURE 4.1   CORBAservices in the object management architecture.

market areas, such as financial services and healthcare. The final category of objects in the architecture correspond to the applications that are not standardized.

The applications can use standard interfaces from other parts of the architecture, including the CORBAservices, CORBAfacilities, and CORBAdomains. Within the CORBAservices, we have a collection of more than a dozen adopted services, with a few more services in the adoption process. When these final services are completed, the OMG will have completed its work in the services and object request broker areas.

In the preceding discussion, the context for CORBAservices in the object management architecture (OMA) was described. In the following sections, the organization of the CORBAservices and the timeline for adoption—the CORBAservices roadmap—will be described. This partitioning of architecture and roadmap appear in several places within the subdomains of the OMA. The architecture identifies the areas to be standardized; the roadmap is an adoption plan based on technical dependencies, industry needs, and other priorities.

4.1.3   The CORBAservices Architecture

In the top-level OMA, CORBAservices all reside at the same architectural level, without an organizational structure for the services. These services are related logically in the groups in which they were adopted with respect to the OMG's request for proposal activities. This provides a basis for understanding the services in relation to their maturity and the relative availability of products in the market. However, a superior way to categorize the services is to partition them by the architectural and functional roles they play. An architectural structure is necessary to properly abstract and describe the services. The object request broker-object service (ORBOS) architecture provides an organization for the services and infrastructure elements (see Table 4.1).

The ORBOS architecture comprises four categories of service elements: infrastructure, information management, task management, and system management. The infrastructure category includes service elements that are tightly coupled to the ORB mechanism, such as the Security service and inter-ORB interoperability. The information management services include basic services for manipulation and retrieval of data. The task management services include enabling services for managing distributed object events and transactions. The system management includes basic services for enabling the management of meta-data, licensing, and object lifecycle.

CORBAservices are enabling services. They are primitive, fundamental, and globally applicable. CORBAservices are useful for all kinds of applications and are domain-independent in that they are intended to be reused and

Table 4.1   Object Request Broker-Object Service (ORBOS)
Architecture

INFORMATION MANAGEMENT SERVICES	TASK MANAGEMENT SERVICES	SYSTEM MANAGEMENT SERVICES
Properties	Events	Naming
Relationship	Concurrency	Lifecycle
Query	Transactions	Licensing
Externalization		Trader
Persistent Object		Interface Repository*
Collections		
	INFRASTRUCTURE SERVICES & ELEMENTS	
CORBA Core*	Interoperability*	Call By Value
Language	Security & Time	Messaging
Mappings*		
*Addressed in Chapter 4		

specialized by applications. To provide application-level guarantees in the chosen architectures, many implementation choices need to be made—the key implication of their generality. For example, the use of the CORBA type `any` is prevalent in these services. CORBA type `any` is a dynamic data type that allows the programmer to represent any specific data type at run time. To use CORBAservices with the CORBA type, choices need to be made about what that data type will be so that the different applications using the services have a basis for interoperability. Applications that attempt a general unstructured interpretation of the CORBA type `any` will find it very difficult and complicated to execute. This was so complicated to perform that in the early implementations of CORBA, many vendors did not provide a complete implementation of that capability.

Another important feature of CORBAservices is that most service objects are no different than any other kind of objects in the CORBA environment. In other words, there is no private or special relationship between the different CORBAservices and the object request broker. This statement is true with certain well-documented exceptions, such as the Security service. This service also levies some requirements on the object request broker in order to implement its capabilities. An important implication of the fact that CORBAservices are the same as other objects is that CORBAservices may be implemented by anyone. Users might purchase CORBAservices with the object request broker product or may purchase CORBAservices from a third party or they may be implemented by application developers. In fact, it is likely that a developer will build one or more of the CORBAservices in order to give the implementations the unique characteristics required by their application code and application requirements.

The name CORBAservices is a brand name for what is formally called the Common Object Services Specifications (for adopted specifications) and Object Services (in general). In reading OMG marketing literature and technical documentation, the names Object Services and CORBAservices are used interchangeably. The CORBAservices are currently an ongoing activity at OMG meetings. There are many requests for proposals that have been issued relating to these services. Each request for proposals has two to four CORBAservices. The results of the first RFPs—RFP 1 and RFP 2—were fully adopted and published as the first version of the CORBAservices document. RFP 3 and RFP 4 were also completed, and there is still work to complete on additional RFPs.

The document specification for CORBAservices is available for purchase in paper form from the OMG. It is also available on the Internet. CORBAservices documents are large but relatively readable by most developers. One of the key purposes of the balance of this chapter is to give an introduction to these CORBAservices so that users can identify which services are relevant to their application needs.

4.1.4   The CORBAservices Roadmap

The CORBAservices are listed in Figure 4.2. This figure shows the CORBAservices broken down into their request for proposals and the relative dates of adoption. In the first request for proposal, the services include Lifecycle, Event Naming, and Persistence. These are all fundamental services that are useful to most applications.

In RFP 2, services include Externalization, Relationship, Concurrence Control, and Transactions. These services are more specialized to the management of objects in a distributed environment.

In RFP 3, the services include Security and Time. These services are needed and required by many applications, although it is likely they will be available on special versions of ORB products. These products are likely to incur additional overhead and complexity necessary to implement capabilities, as well as the administrative and maintenance costs required for keeping these services operational.

In RFP 4, services include Licensing, Properties, and Queries service. These are all useful services that deal with third-party software applications.

RFP1 Services adopted in 1993
  Object Lifecycle Service
  Object Event Notification Service
  Object Naming Service
  Object Persistent Service

RFP2 Services adopted in 1994
  Object Externalization Service
  Object Relationships Service
  Object Concurrency Service
  Object Transaction Service

RFP3 Services adopted in 1996
  Object Security Service
  Object Time Service

RFP4 Services adopted in 1995
  Object Licensing Service
  Object Properties Service
  Object Query Service

RFP5 Services to be completed in 1996
  Object Trading Service
  Object Collections Service
  Object Start-up Service

Interface Versioning and Asynchronous Invocation to be completed in 1997

FIGURE 4.2   CORBAservices roadmap.

Finally, in RFP 5, services include the Trader and Collection services. These are important for implementing distributed systems.

In this section, the CORBAservices from the top-level viewpoints of the OMA, the ORBOS architecture, and the CORBAservices roadmap have been described. In the following sections, each of the CORBAservices will be described individually. An attempt to provide the necessary abstractions and scenarios needed to understand the purpose and role of each CORBAservice specification is made. The CORBAservices are an interesting set of topics to study because of the breadth and depth of computer science that is incorporated into their definitions.

4.2   The Information Management Services

4.2.1   The Property Service

Properties are a dynamic set of attributes that can be attached to application objects that support the property. In other words, the Property service is an example of a service that requires that application objects inherit the interfaces in the standard and provide additional functionality supported through those interfaces. The implementation of those interfaces can be vendor supplied or provided by the application developer.

The purpose of properties is similar to that of attributes. Attributes are public-state information that is known when the software is written and expressed directly in the IDL. Attributes must be known before compile time and are static in the sense that the set of attributes cannot be extended at run time without changing the IDL and recompiling the software. Properties, on the other hand, are a dynamic capability that allows the addition of properties-on-the-fly.

Properties are implemented by using the CORBA `type any`, which includes type code information to identify the specific type supported. Each property is named with an international character string valued name. This allows self-description of the properties. One important convention an application needs to define is the selection of the names. The coordination of usage of property names is essential for interpretability. It is also important to define the type code associated with each name. In this way, properties can be used without the application providing a complete type code interpreter, which can be very complicated.

Properties are important to many types of specialized applications. Because properties are defined at run time, the application software does not need to know about the full details of the properties concerned. Properties are useful for applications such as desktop managers, debugging tools, browsers, and other kinds of system-management tools.

For example, a desktop manager may need to attach various properties to application objects in order to allow objects to participate in the desktop environment. In another example, the desktop may attach an icon representation that only the desktop needs to interpret. In addition, the desktop may attach various kinds of protection properties, such as whether an object is locked and whether an object is shareable. These properties would be unique to that particular desktop environment.

Another example might be debugging software that needs to attach run-time information to objects during the debugging process. The properties can represent debugging breakpoints that can be used to stop and start the execution at an arbitrary place.

4.2.2   The Relationship Service

The Relationship service is a general-purpose service for establishing linkages and relationships among objects. This service provides a standard way of establishing linkages that would replace ad hoc approaches and unique custom approaches. These might involve the exchange of object references and the storage of this linkage information implicitly in objects. In a sense, the Relationship service moves the potentially implicit relationships of storing object references in the private state of objects and moves it into a common public representation. These relationships are well understood by a variety of other services and application objects that know how to use the Relationship service. For example, the Externalization service and the Lifecycle service have extended capabilities that use the Relationship service to perform their basic functions on graphs of objects.

The Relationship service is a general-purpose service for establishing relationships. It defines object interfaces for relationship objects, as well as full objects. Relationship objects can have any number of roles that are established on-the-fly, and the cardinality of each of the roles can be specified and controlled. For example, there is a minimum cardinality for each role that is set by an attribute value, and a maximum cardinality for each role. Maximum cardinality errors are indicated by the return of an exception value.

Figure 4.3 is an example of the Relationship service. In this case, a document object, a figure object, and an icon object are interrelated. To establish relationships using the service, two relationship objects, relationship B and relationship D, and the corresponding role objects, A, C, and E, need to be created. In order to relate these three objects, at a minimum five additional objects that establish the relationship have to be created.

One of the important implications of this service is that it requires many fine-grain objects to implement relationships. The presence of fine-grain objects implies that there is an efficient object request broker that can support frequent messaging without affecting application performance. It also implies

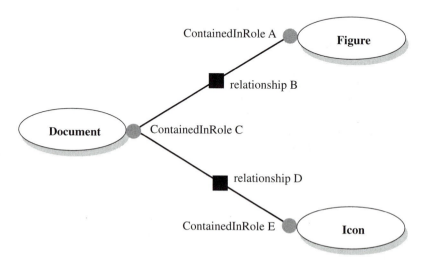

FIGURE 4.3 Relationship service example.

something that is not explicitly stated but is believed a requirement for this service: ORB and operating system support for multithreading.

4.2.3   Multithreaded Environments

An important capability added to operating system technologies is multithreading. It is anticipated that it will be supported across most operating systems within the next few years. Multithreading is important to the implementation of distributed objects. If there are a large number of interoperating objects, they are all sending method invocations and receiving invocations. These objects are implemented in terms of a much smaller number of operating system processes, and the probability of deadlock can be very high. Because each invocation represents a transfer of a thread of control, it is likely to develop situations in which interoperating processes can exchange threads of control in ways that form deadlock situations.

Deadlock occurs when cooperating processes are unable to continue because they require shared resources or each other's resources in order to complete their processing. In a multithreading environment, the probability of deadlock can be greatly reduced because multithreading provides the ability to create new threads of control dynamically. Each operating system process in a multithreading environment can spawn additional threads of control whenever an invocation is received, allowing each invocation to make progress. When a multithreaded process makes an invocation of another process, the thread can block while the invocation occurs. This does not limit the ability of the process to create other threads to make further progress in processing.

The use of multithreading is natural in a fine-grain distributed object environment. Without it, developers are forced to simulate the affects of concurrent processing of multiple threads within a single process and a single thread of control. This simulation can lead to a convoluted program structure, which is hard to understand, and can lead to bugs and other problems. Even though multithreading can help to create a more natural program structure, it is still a significant change in a program's semantics from the more commonplace single-threaded environments. Multithreading involves the creation of many concurrent processes within the same address space. Because these processes share common data values, they can conflict with each other in the update of these values and create inconsistencies and undefined values, which can create subtle errors in programs.

The technology to develop and debug application software using multithreading is still immature. Multithreaded development and debugging environments are still the subject of basic research. Because of the potential for new kinds of program errors and the increased complexity of the run-time environment in a multithreaded operating system, it is believed that there will be substantial development difficulties encountered as end-user organizations migrate to multithreaded technologies. The software tool market also needs to advance greatly until this technology can be adequately supported.

Developers of object request brokers make use of multithreaded technology on a product-by-product basis. Some CORBA request brokers were designed to be used with multithreading from their inception. For example, the SunSoft NEO product and the Hewlett-Packard ORBplus product were designed with the assumption that multithreading would always be available. Multithreading is available on many operating systems; in a few cases, it is inherent to the operating system environment. In some cases, it is necessary to purchase multithreading technology as an extension. For example, one can purchase such capabilities as part of the Open Software Foundation distributed computing environment as an add-on capability to many operating system environments.

The CORBA ORB market is migrating increasingly to multithreaded implementations. It is likely that most ORB products will include multithreading support within a few years. The general availability of multithreading in the commercial market on commercially available operating systems will probably follow in a year or so. Multithreading has some serious affects on application software. Most application software written prior to multithreading would need to be restructured.

The default approach for integrating nonmultithreaded software is to put an exclusive lock around the nonthreaded software, which would exclude any other threads from executing concurrently. Although it is necessary in many cases, this is undesirable because it eliminates multithreading for part of the application processing. This approach is also required with many commercial libraries that are not multithread safe. Because of its use of many fine-grain objects and the need to avoid deadlocks of relationship objects in addition to application objects, the Relationship service needs multithreading support in order to be used effectively in applications.

Because the Relationship service requires many objects to be created in addition to the application objects, it is believed that it will require a great deal of application code to manage and create relationships. It would be useful to have tools that support visualization and debugging of distributed relationships using this service because of the potential complexity of relationships in a distributed object environment.

Figure 4.4 is an example of the Relationship service in an application scenario. In this case, four application software products are represented by a, b, c, and d. These objects are put together in a graph so that they maintain their relationships with each other in an explicit way, which can allow other applications to browse and manipulate this graph. To create the set of relationships

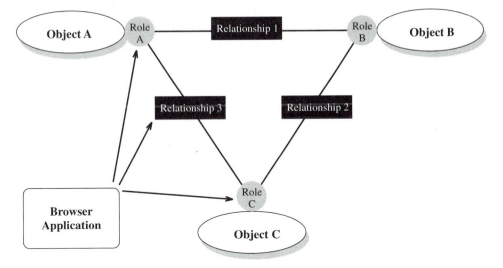

FIGURE 4.4   Relationship service scenario.

among these objects, these objects could work on their own to create the relationships or a third-party object, which has knowledge of these objects, can assist them in establishing the relationships and roles.

Suppose a builder object has this responsibility. The builder object could create the four relationship objects, relationship 1, 2, 3, and 4, which correspond to the one-to-one relationships between A and B, B and C, C and D, and D and A. Then the builder object could create role objects that correspond to each role of the four application objects.

The builder object also needs to create a role object for application B, and then, to fully establish a relationship, the role objects need to have the object references for objects A and B. Similarly, the other role objects and relationship objects can be created by the builder object in order to establish this graph. When another object wishes to browse the graph, it needs to be given an object reference to either one of the role objects or relationship objects in order to start the browsing process.

Given any of these reference objects, the browser can navigate through the graph by using each relationship object to locate the associated role objects. The role object can discover additional relationship objects because role objects store information about the relationship objects, as well as about the application objects. Therefore, by using the information that can be retrieved through the standard interfaces of Relationship service, this graph of objects can be transversed in a standard way that is independent of the specific application objects.

Operations for testing object identity and equivalence are provided in the Relationship service. Using the interface for identifiable objects, it is possible to determine when there are cycles in relationship graphs and when to terminate traversals based on that kind of criteria.

4.2.4   The Query Service

The Query service is a general-purpose set of software interfaces for query objects. For the most part, the service is used with various commercial database products. It supports both relational database models and object database models. The team of submittals to the technology included relational and object-oriented database vendors, including IBM and Sybase on the relational side and a team of database vendors from the Object Database Management Group (ODMG), led by SunSoft.

The Query service identifies and includes current and future database standards, such as SQL92, which is an international standard, the future SQL 3, and the object query language (OQL) from ODMG93. The specification identifies several related programming interface specifications, such as open database computing (ODBC) and remote database access (RDA). ODBC is a de facto API specification from Microsoft that is being phased out. Use of the Query service in application code can provide isolation from obsolescence of proprietary technology, such as ODBC.

All of these technologies are intended to be used with the OMG Query service, and the Query service can be layered on top of implementations of these standards. This service is intended to be a common software interface that crosses all these localized implementation standards.

The Query service supports dynamic querying. Static and dynamic querying are two capabilities commonly supported in database products. Static queries are queries that are represented as an extension to the programming language syntax. These are query statements written directly into application software and, therefore, static queries are known at compile time. The compile time information available in static queries is used by database products to optimize queries in order to provide better performance. The OMG Query service supports only dynamic queries; static queries can be considered a product-specific extension to the Query service.

Dynamic queries are queries that are generated on-the-fly at run time or represented as static strings that are not interpreted at compile time. Dynamic queries are query language statements that are directly represented as strings within the application software. These dynamic query strings are passed through the OMG query service interfaces to the underlying query objects. The query object's responsibility is to parse these dynamic queries and execute the queries, returning query results.

The Query service interface supports synchronous and asynchronous evaluation of dynamic queries. In the synchronous case, the client thread would block when the evaluate message is sent until the query is completed and results returned. There is also an asynchronous set of operations within the Query service so that queries can be submitted and the results retrieved later.

An important gap in previous query standards has been the representation of query results. The OMG Query service only partially resolves this issue. The standard set of query interfaces defined within the service provide for the return of CORBA type any for query results. Because a CORBA type any is returned, the actual representation of the query results is unconstrained by the IDL in the service specification.

There is a separate set of interfaces included in the Query service specification, called query collections. The query collection interfaces represent a recommended way for query objects to return results. However, the use of these query collections is not mandated by the standard. The query collection results are not a complete collections capability but rather a minimal capability that is sufficient for the representation of relational query results and object oriented query results.

Query collection interfaces include an enumeration and a union type that establish a new set of basic types. These extensions add to the basic types in the interface definition language with additional basic types, such as decimal and numeric. The interfaces also include the capability to create, modify, and retrieve from collections of objects. The interface supports direct access interfaces with an array-like index. Alternatively, there is an iterated interface that allows sequential retrieval of query results, which are represented as a sequence of union types. This union type is defined as either a null value that can be present in the result as an actual data value. The allowable values are defined through the set of basic types, which are an extension of the data types in IDL.

4.2.5   The Externalization Service

Externalization is the process of taking program data structures and other object states and converting that information into a form that can be stored or transmitted. This process involves removing pointers and converting binary data into flat representations so that the information can be considered to be a stream of bytes without additional internal structure. The process of externalization is commonplace. It is used explicitly in many cases. For example, externalization is required for the use of the Bento persistence protocol, which is part of the distributed document component facility (an OMG CORBAfacility based on OpenDoc).

Externalization is also one of the processes that are part of the marshaling processing that occurs when static stubs and skeletons convert high-level language parameters to information that can be communicated across the network. Externalization is also used with lower-level networking technologies. For example, TCP/IP sockets and the UNIX System 5 transport location independent interfaces. When externalization is performed, there is a need to do internalization, the reverse of the process. When data exists in an externalized state, any data structures must be reconstituted before it can be used. This process is called internalization.

Externalization is a useful process, with many potential applications. For example, externalization can be used to relocate objects by taking an objects state information, externalizing it, and transmitting through CORBA or through another technology to a remote location, where the data can be internalized and an object can be reconstituted.

There is one caveat. Externalization only concerns object state information. Externalization does not address the conversion or relocation of the machine code software for an object. Therefore, if externalization is used to relocate object state information, it is necessary to have the same software installed at the remote location, where the information is internalized. Another caveat is that the information transmitted to another platform will not be marshaled. In other words, there will be no conversion activities that would normally incur in a CORBA invocation. Operations such as byte swapping for different representations of integers would not be handled automatically. The data would not necessarily be portable among platforms.

The portability issue could be addressed in a revision externalization service, although current implementations are not required to support that capability. Some of the uses of externalization include electronic mail; persistent storage; and, in the future, other kinds of services that can use externalized states such as the CORBAfacilities for data interchange and mobile agents. The Externalization service comprises a large number of operations signatures that have a relatively low-level handling of information.

The externalization process requires application software that traverses all the internal data structures and writes each of the primitive data types encountered in the traversal process. The Externalization service provides operation signatures for writing each of the primitive data types. For example, there are unique operation signatures for writing characters, strings, short integers, long integers, single precision, double precision, floating point, and so forth.

In the internalization capabilities of this service, there is a corresponding set of operations for internalization of the primitive data structures. There are operations for reading short integers, long integers, and characters. The implication of this is that there would be a substantial amount of application software needed to take advantage of this service. This service does not give the developer substantial leverage on performing the operations.

Another interesting implication is that to perform internalization on the remote machine that receives this data, it is necessary to have detailed instructions about how the data structures in the externalized form are traversed and reconstituted into the internalized data structures. There is a need for a lot of information on the receiving end to take advantage of externalized data (including a working implementation of the externalized object). The Externalization service does define an external data format sufficient for transferring information among platforms and not guaranteed to provide full portability of object state among platforms or ORB implementations.

The Externalization service also includes some use of the Relationship service to support compound externalization. Compound externalization is the process of externalizing multiple objects that are configured as graphs of objects using the relationship service. By invoking externalization operations on one object, implementation of an entire graph of objects can be externalized automatically. This assumes that the application software comprising these objects has implemented all appropriate operations for performing this automatic externalization using this extension of the Externalization service.

4.2.6   The Persistent Object Service

The Persistent Object service was jointly created by suppliers of relational database technology and object-oriented database technology. The proposal was a joint submission from IBM, Sybase, and the ODMG, which is a consortium alliance of object-oriented database technology vendors. This service is highly flexible and gives the developer and suppliers of this technology a lot of latitude in how the technology is used. In particular, the Persistent Object service provides for the replacement of the persistence protocols used within the service.

A persistence protocol is a particular set of interfaces used by a persistent object to store its persistent state. The allowable persistence protocols by this service is not constrained. The specification includes an identification of three persistence protocols, although there are many other possible protocols that can be used with this standard. The three protocols identified in the specification include the ODMG 1993 specification, ODMG-93; the direct access protocol; and the dynamic data object protocol.

Other protocols that might be used with this standard include UNIX file IO, Bento, externalization and internalization, and perhaps even the Microsoft structured storage specification for compound objects. The ODMG-93 specification is only identified by reference and indicates that this is one of the recommended ways of using the Persistent Object service. ODMG-93 is defined in a separate document published by the ODMG consortium and is available in book form.

The two other persistence protocols identified in the specification are also fully defined in the Persistent Object service specification. These are the direct access protocol and the dynamic data object protocol. The direct access protocol defines the persistent state through the data definition language (DDL).

The data definition language is a proper subset of CORBA IDL. This subset includes interfaces, data types, and attributes. This subset excludes operation signatures so that the remaining DDL allows the definition of state information without additional operation signatures for manipulating that state. DDL descriptions are intended to represent private state information. This is in contrast to IDL definitions of attributes, which always indicate public state information because IDL definitions are registered in the Interface Repository, a public on-line directory of all interfaces.

DDL descriptions are not public information. They represent the private state information known by the implementation of an object and its persistent store. By implication, the Persistent Object service involves management of the private state information, which is only known by the object and its storage mechanism. Because the direct access protocol uses high-level language data types to define persistent states, persistent objects use those attributes without having to externalize the data types. Additional processing is not required on persistent attribute data to convert them into a form appropriate for persistent storage.

With many other protocols used with the Persistent service, such as traditional file IO, it is necessary to flatten the data structures and do significant processing on the data before it is sent to the persistent store. The reverse of this processing is required when the data is retrieved from the persistent store. This issue will be discussed again later in this chapter.

Another persistence protocol that is comprehensively covered in the object service definition is the dynamic data object protocol, in which the persistent state is stored similar to the property service in that each persistent value is given a string-valued name and the value itself is stored in a CORBA type any value so that the entire persistent state is defined dynamically at run time. This dynamic data object protocol gives some additional flexibility to the run-time definition of the persistent state, compared with the direct access protocol. It is necessary to know the persistent state at compile time when the software is written.

Figure 4.5 is a diagram of the major components of the Persistent Object service. This service focuses on the persistent object, an application object defined by developers. This application object inherits interfaces from the persistent service in order to participate in this framework. The client object is an object external to the service, which interacts with the persistent application

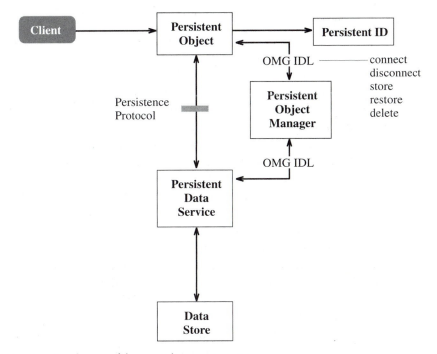

FIGURE 4.5   Persistent object service components.

object to manage the persistent state. This is analogous perhaps to a desktop editor which is able to save or retrieve persistent state from a disk file through explicit menu commands.

The other objects in the diagram are supplied by the Persistent Object service or by third-party vendors. A persistent identification is defined to enable persistent objects to have a reference to their persistent state information. The persistent object manager associates persistent identifications with particular persistent data services. There can be many persistent data services. It is the manager's job to select the appropriate service for a persistent object in its persistent state. The persistent object manager then interacts directly with the persistent data service to manage the persistent state.

Several IDL interfaces shown in Figure 4.5 are similar in that they support five basic operations: connect, disconnect, store, restore, and delete. This applies the client interface to the persistent object, the persistent object's interface to its persistent object manager, and the persistent manager's interface to the persistent data service. The connect and disconnect operations are used to establish the relationship of communication among the objects. The store operation is used to indicate that the persistent state should be written out onto the persistent data store. The restore operation indicates that the persistent state should be read from the persistent data store and replace the current content of the transient state, which is the running persistent object process. Finally, the delete operation corresponds to the removal of the persistent information from the persistent data store.

The interface between the persistent data service and the data store is a private interface that is not defined or standardized by this service and gives the implementors of the Persistent Object service flexibility. This allows substituting different data store mechanisms or having multiple data store mechanisms on the back end. The persistence protocol, which is a direct communication protocol between the persistent object and the persistent data service, is the replaceable element in this specification. This can be the ODMG-93 protocol, the direct access protocol, the dynamic data object protocol, or any other protocol selected by developers.

Figure 4.6 is a scenario using the Persistent Object service. In this scenario, there is a persistent object that is an application object that inherits the interfaces of the Persistent Object service. The application object defines its persistent state using the DDL, attributes of which define the complete persistent state for a persistent object.

This DDL description can be compiled. DDL definitions are known to the persistent data service and to the persistent object, which collaborate using this

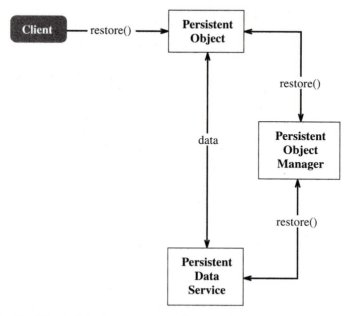

FIGURE 4.6   Persistent object service scenario.

protocol to store the persistent state. In this scenario, there is a client object that has influence over the persistent state. The client object can send the restore operation, which would cause the persistent object to relay that restore operation to the persistent system object manager. The persistent object manager would then relay the restore operation to the appropriate direct access protocol implementation. This persistent data service would retrieve the persistent state from the data store and then retrieve this state and make it available to the persistent object as the set of attributes indicated in DDL.

The persistent object would have a number of accessor functions for getting and setting the attributes in its persistent state, and it would retrieve the transient version of the persistent state by getting these attributes. When the client object wants to store the persistent state, it sends the store operation to the persistent object, which is then responsible for setting the persistent attributes with any transient information intended to be part of the persistent state that is known by the persistent object. After any set operations occur to update the persistent attributes, the persistent object sends the store operation as a request to the persistent object manager. The persistent object manager then selects a data service to which it sends the store message to the persistent attributes, which are recorded into the data store so that the persistent state is committed to the data store and the operations. Following this, the thread of control returns to the object manager of the persistent object and the client object to complete the persistence transaction.

4.2.6   **The Collection Service**

The Collection service provides interface definitions for common groupings of objects. The object collections are structured in various ways. For example, collections can be structured as sequential lists of objects, stacks of objects, queues of objects, bags of objects, and so forth.

The Collection service capabilities have previously been provided through language-specific object libraries. There are a number of commercial object library products with these capabilities, as well as shareware libraries, such as the National Institutes of Health (NIH ++) library. A recent standard extension to C++, called the standard template library, or STL, has collections interfaces suitable for nondistributed objects. The Collections service interfaces standardized by the OMG are inspired by the C++ STL. Because of the requirements for distributed objects, these libraries cannot be completely source-code-compatible with the STL.

The STL is an extensive specification. It is more necessary for OMG standards to be concise and easy to understand and use. For OMG standards, it is important to have clear definitions implemented consistently in distributed object environments because distributed objects may be implemented by independent development teams. For example, geographically distributed development teams may communicate only infrequently; it is necessary for software devised by these teams to be readily interoperable without a lot of direct coordination.

The Collection service interfaces can be implemented for distributed collections and can also be implemented as a set of library objects. For example, the X-Windows6 implementation includes the Fresco object request broker, which is a library ORB. Fresco provides fine-grain objects within the same address space as the client applications. This ORB capability can be used for collections to provide collection objects that are accessed through IDL interfaces and provide the same performance benefits of an object library implementation.

In this section, the enabling services for managing information, including Properties, Relationship, Query, Externalization, Persistence, and Collections, were described. In the next section, another major category of services, addressing control and tasking issues in distributed object systems, will be described.

4.3   Task Management CORBAservices

The following CORBAservices provide primitive task management capabilities for CORBA system developers.

4.3.1   The Events Service

The second object service is the Events service. The Events service defines generic interfaces for passing event information among multiple sources and multiple event consumers. The sources and consumers do not need to have direct knowledge of each other, which is the primary advantage of this particular service. It allows for decoupling of the generators and receivers of events and for a large number of receivers that are managed by the service and not by the event sources. Event notification is one way of using this service.

This service can also be used as a multicast capability. The service provides a general set of mechanisms for allowing multiple recipients of event information to register their interest in events. This also allows the source of a multicast message to post it once and have the message conveyed to multiple recipients without direct knowledge between the events source and the recipients or direct connections between the two pairs of objects.

The Events service supports multiple interaction styles. This means that there are many ways application code can supply or consume events. Applications may choose from many alternative styles to interact with the Events service.

The two principal styles are the push and the pull style. In the push style, the source of the event makes an out-call to the event consumer, so the event consumer receives an event as an up-call to that application object. In the pull style, the event supplier waits for the consumer to make a call back in order to receive the next event notification. In other words, the consumer initiates the transaction.

In the pull style, there are polled and blocking modes. For the polled mode, there is a try-pull operation, which returns a Boolean value that indicates whether an event is ready to be conveyed. This allows the event consumers to be nonblocking. Consumers can first call the try-pull operation, assess the readiness of an event to be posted, and then continue processing if there is no event available. There is also the pull operation, which is a blocking operation. When the pull operation is called, the consumer's event recipient thread will block until that event is available. If the pull operation is called immediately after a successful true return value from the try-pull operation, the pull operation will give a more or less return with the event that has been posted. With these interaction modes, the Events service provides a general impedance match among multiple suppliers and consumers of events and the Events service.

The Events service supports these different interaction styles simultaneously, so there can be some push and some pull consumers, as well as pull and push suppliers, all interoperating at the same time through the same event channel.

Figure 4.7 is an example of the Events service interfaces. An implementation of the Events service provides two object implementations: an event factory

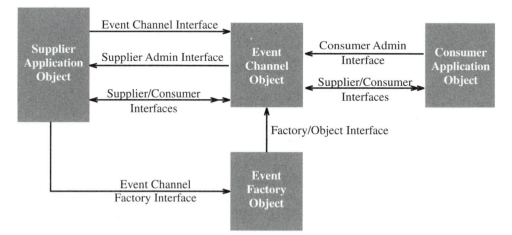

FIGURE 4.7   Events service objects.

object and an event channel object. The other software in this example, the supplier application objects and the consumer application objects, are application software provided by developers using the Events service. Most of the interfaces shown in this example concern the set up and administration of the Events service and the event channels. The only operational interfaces shown here are indicated by the supplier consumer interfaces, which connect the supplier to the event channel and the event channel to the consumer.

The Events service is used initially to call the event factory object. The event factory object implements the Lifecycle service operations specific to the Events service. Event factory objects are responsible for creating event channel objects. When an event channel object is created, it supports a number of interfaces that allow it to be configured for event notifications and the operational interfaces for that purpose.

The first interface on the event channel object to be invoked is the event channel interface that allows suppliers and consumers of events to obtain the supplier and consumer administration interfaces. These administration interfaces are necessary for exchanging object references with the event channel, which indicates that particular suppliers and consumers are registered to supply and consume events or deregistered to no longer supply or consume the events.

The supplier administration interface enables the registration of suppliers with the event channel and the exchange of object references that are necessary to facilitate the communication between supplier application objects and the event channel. The consumer administration interface supports the registration of consumer objects with the event channel that supports the exchange of object references necessary for the event channel and the consumer objects to interoperate.

Finally, the supplier-consumer interfaces allow suppliers to post events on the event channel and allow consumers to receive notification of events in either the push or pull style. The event channel has some internal queuing of event information. Event channels are not required to have persistent records of events, although there may be some implementations of event channels that have this capability. Alternatively, the user could create a special event channel object that has unique capabilities, such as persistence, fault tolerance, and enhanced performance.

Events are posted in two service interfaces. The first service interface is for untyped events. With the untyped Events service interfaces, events are posted as a dynamic data type—CORBA type any. When a supplier posts an event, the event itself is represented as a type any value. When consumers consume the event, they also consume a type any value.

For an event to be meaningful, there needs to be some agreement about conventions among the suppliers and consumers. In particular, it is necessary to determine what will be contained in the type any event value. This is important because consumers need to understand the information conveyed in the event and make use of it for application purposes. With the untyped event interfaces, there is no compile-time checking of event information.

The other Events service interfaces are called type events. Type event interfaces allow user-defined types to be conveyed as the event information. These user-defined types are known at compile time. The compile-time information can be used for type checking. In a strongly typed application design, the use of typed event interfaces is preferable. This is an important advantage to developers of applications. Some conventions for what is contained in event information is actually present in the interface specification (for typed events) and is enforced by the strong type checking by the programming language compilers.

Figure 4.8 is an example scenario of the Events service. The Events service works in two phases. The first phase of initialization involves most interfaces that are defined by the service. The second phase is the operational phase, shown in this example. In this case, a single event supplier application software is using a push mode for posting events. There are two consumers of events. One consumer is using the push mode of receiving events; the other consumer is using the pull mode for receiving events. In this case, the supplier posts an event by invoking a push operation on the event channel object.

The event channel stores the event information in its internal queues. As soon as an event is posted, the event channel makes a push call on the first consumer to deliver the event to that consumer. The event channel tracks each

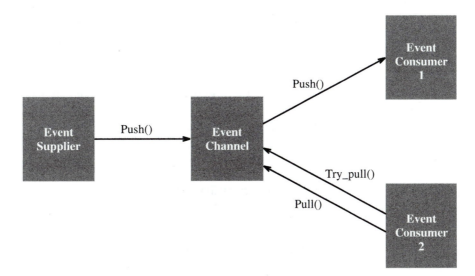

FIGURE 4.8   Events service scenario.

consumer as it receives its events. The channel maintains the event information in its queues until all the pull mode consumers have received the event. The channel must wait for these event consumers to make pull calls to the event channel. For example, a pull-mode event consumer would perform a try-pull operation, and because there is an event present, it would get a true return value from that try-pull operation. Then the event consumer could call the pull operation to receive the event information. After all the push and pull operations are complete, the event channel would then be able to eliminate its knowledge of the event because all consumers of the event had received notifications. Then by using pull mode to see if other events are posted, the event channel would wait for event suppliers or consumers to supply additional events.

There are many potential applications of the Events service. Since it is a primitive service, in many applications, events would probably be used with other services to provide useful functions. The Events service working together with the relationship service could be used to implement capabilities such as publish and subscribe. Events can implement dynamic linking of objects with hot-link updates of information as state information changes. Other applications might use events and delivery of events in a windowing environment. Various input devices, such as keyboards and mice, and rendering engines could work asynchronously to notify the application software of asynchronous events.

Another application of events is real-time systems. Events can be used to convey real-time notifications in a system. One of the key advantages of using events is decoupling of event suppliers from event consumers. A version of these interfaces could tie a particular supplier directly to a consumer. In that case, there would be a fairly brittle relationship between the two objects. This relationship would be monogamous in that there would only be one supplier and one consumer.

By decoupling suppliers and consumers from each other using the Events service, there is a looser coupling among objects. This is advantageous for making a system more flexible. By using the Events service, one eliminates any hardwired assumptions about how many suppliers and consumers are linked together through a common event channel.

4.3.2   The Concurrency Service

The Concurrency service is a general-purpose service for ensuring atomic access to distributed objects. This service extends the capabilities of nondistributed services that apply to individual operating systems. The Concurrency service provides synchronization across distributed environments and allows the locking of individual objects or several objects to provide atomic access when changing state information. This allows applications an enabling capability for assuring coherent state information in distributed systems. Previous capabilities for concurrency control, which are operating system- and language-dependent, do not extend easily to distributed systems. The Concurrency service provides the advantage of portability and the effective use of concurrency across multiple operating systems and languages in a distributed environment.

The key interfaces for the Concurrency service include the lock-set, transactional lock-set, lock-set factory, and lock coordinator interfaces. The core interface in this service is the lock-set interface. The lock-set interface may represent objects supplied by a vendor that are separate from applications or, alternatively, this interface could be inherited by applications to provide locking directly on application interfaces. The interface can be used in both manners. The lock-set interface includes operations for locking and unlocking objects. There are several different kinds of locks that can be applied to objects.

The Concurrency service provides a sophisticated theory of concurrency, which makes for interesting reading and will probably exceed most application requirements for concurrency capabilities. This is an unusual service because it probably already has all the necessary interfaces for application development. In other words, specializations probably are not necessary; however, it is important for applications to determine the conventions for locking. This is a profiling requirement to assure interoperability. The profile should also contain a scheme for avoiding livelocks and deadlocks.

The different kinds of locking modes that are supported include read locks, write locks, upgrade locks, intention read, and intention write locks. The two basic locking modes of read and write support the simultaneous reading of object state information by multiple application clients. The write lock conflicts with read locks. Applications that apply write locks can change object state without having other writers or readers access the state information while it is being modified.

The Concurrency service also provides the capability for applying upgrade locks. This is a special form of read lock that conflicts with other kinds of locks and indicates an intention to modify information. An upgrade lock will conflict with other upgrade locks. Upgrade locks are applied by readers that intend to change their locking mode to a write lock. Through the use of upgrade locks, one can avoid deadlocks. Upgrade locks support concurrent access by multiple clients who may intend to upgrade their locks to write locks after they have applied read locks.

The additional modes of intention read and intention write support locking at multiple granularities. By applying the intentional locks at course granularity, a set of related object applications can apply basic locks to finer-grain objects contained within the course objects. This balances the need for highly concurrent access to objects of different granularities. It also supports deadlock avoidance for access to nested objects of different granularities.

The Concurrency service works with the Transaction service in a closely coordinated manner. Regardless, it is likely that the Concurrency service would be one of the key services used during transaction processing. When the Concurrency service completes a transaction, either by committing the transaction or aborting the transaction, the combined services are responsible for releasing any concurrency locks that were put in place during the transaction. The locks are reset to their unlocked state. This is an important part of clean-up on termination of transactions.

Figure 4.9 is an example of the Concurrency service. In this example, which is well known to computer scientists, there are five application objects, called dining philosophers. These philosophers are competing for access to a shared object representing some food. There are five fork objects needed by the philosophers to eat the food. Each philosopher must have two forks in order to access the food. The philosophers compete with each other to obtain access to a pair of forks. Each fork is placed between two philosophers. In this situation,

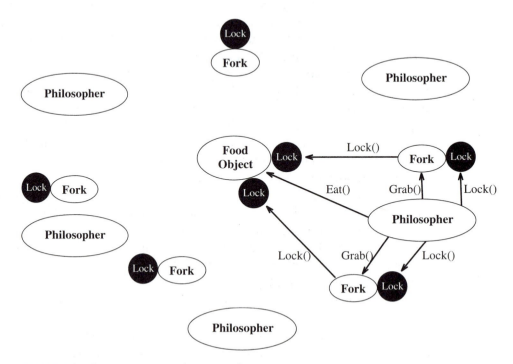

FIGURE 4.9　Concurrency service scenario.

the Concurrency service is used to apply locks to each of the fork objects so that the allocation of forks is controlled. When a philosopher is able to obtain locks on two of the forks adjacent to his or her position, he or she is able to access the food.

This is an interesting example for computer scientists because of the potential consequences of deadlock and livelock. When philosophers grab the lock on the fork resources one at a time, it is possible for each philosopher to have one fork. If the philosophers do not have any protocol for releasing a fork and cannot get another one, the situation would be in deadlock. If some philosophers are much faster than others, it is possible that some may obtain access to forks and be able to eat all the time, whereas other philosophers may never be able to get access to the forks. This would be an example of a livelock situation.

Deadlock and livelock situations are not directly resolved by the Concurrency service. Concurrency control provides the enabling capability for implementing these types of systems. It is an applications responsibility to use the Concurrency service in a safe manner so that deadlocks and livelocks are avoided.

There are many ways that deadlocks and livelocks can be avoided, and they depend on the way the application objects behave. For example, if the application objects are able to access all the resources they require in order to complete a transaction, this is called full allocation. With a full allocation policy, it is possible for the system to completely avoid deadlocks. Other policies for deadlock avoidance would be the avoidance of any circular dependencies in the locking and allocation of resources. In addition, preemption of resource allocation (the removal of partial resource locks) is an after-the-fact approach to resolving deadlocks. All of these strategies for deadlock avoidance are part of the profiling conventions that are necessary to define when using the Concurrency service.

4.3.3   The Transaction Service

The Transaction service is one of the most sophisticated of the CORBAservices. The Transaction service is perhaps the first service that is of high enough value and sophistication to be a profitable service to sell unbundled. This has led to widespread availability of commercial products. Most other services are low-level services comparable with existing operating system services. It is not clear why anyone would pay extra to purchase these other services individually since most organizations would expect them to be bundled with the ORB product.

The Transaction service is a general-purpose set of interfaces that can be used to encapsulate a variety of existing technologies and provide standard interfaces across all implementations of transaction monitors. For example, the

Transaction service is designed to be layered over monitors that are compliant with the X/Open distributed transaction protocol: monitors that use the Tuxedo protocols, the IBM/Transarc Encina product line, and object-oriented databases conformant with the ODMG-93 standards. The transaction service is also interoperable with the IBM system network architecture, including LU6.2 communications.

The Transaction service is a general capability that allows the manipulation of the state of multiple objects in a distributed environment. It builds on the capability of the Concurrency service for controlling access to individual objects. Transaction allows modification of the state of multiple objects to be viewed in a reliable and highly consistent way. The Transaction service supports the ACID properties of transactions (atomicity, consistency, isolation, and durability).

For distributed transactions, atomicity refers to the idea that the transaction appears to be a single operation from the viewpoint of another process accessing the data. Atomic transactions will also appear to be atomic with respect to failures. If a failure does occur during a transaction, the transaction will roll back to the original state of the distributed objects.

The Transaction service supports the consistency property. The result of a transaction leaves the system in a consistent state. Either the transaction operations are committed so that the system state is updated to another consistent state or the transaction is rolled back so that the original consistent state is maintained.

A transaction is isolated in the sense that the operations of one transaction are kept independent of the operations of other transactions. Each transaction appears to be equivalent to a serially ordered execution of the operations that comprise the transaction, even though some of these operations may be executed concurrently. The transaction processing can be concurrent, as well as concurrent with respect to other transactions. To maintain isolation, each transaction needs to appear as if its operations were executed serially in isolation from all other transactions.

The final ACID property is durability. Durability indicates that the effect of a transaction, once it is committed, is permanent. Durable transactions are recorded in the persistent state of the objects and can survive catastrophic system failures.

The Transaction service applies to all kinds of object-based applications that modify the state of multiple objects in a distributed system. The Transaction service can be used specifically with database applications. Database-oriented applications were the primary use of transactions prior to distributed objects. The Transaction service is not solely designed for database purposes and has a wider range of applicability.

The service uses a two-phase commit protocol. Objects participating in transactions become registered resources and support the resource interface. The resource interface includes the prepare, commit, and rollback operations. The commit protocol begins after the transaction has begun and the operational methods of the transaction have been invoked on resources. The two-phase commit protocol begins with the invocation of the prepare operation. Each resource responds with a vote for commitment or rollback. If any resources votes for rollback, the entire transaction must be rolled back. In case of rollback, the earlier operations are ignored. Otherwise, if all resources vote for commitment, the transaction is then committed. At this point, the commit operation is invoked on all resources and indicates that the persistent state of the resources should be modified permanently.

The Transaction service supports both nested and flat transactions. Some transaction-processing products support only flat transactions. In a flat transaction, each transaction would begin, prepare, and commit (or rollback) before any related transactions are initiated.

A Transaction-service implementation can optionally support nested transactions. Nested transactions include subtransactions within large-grain transactions. If a subtransaction fails during the processing of a transaction, it may be reattempted. The overall transaction does not have to roll back.

The Transaction service works in several different modes, which include direct and indirect context management modes, as well as explicit propagation and implicit propagation modes.

Direct context management involves the client initiator of the transaction communicating directly with the other objects in the transaction service. These include the factory and the control object, the terminator object, and the coordinator object. In the indirect context management mode, the client object interoperates with a single object called the current object.

The current object is an object that transparently manages and maintains direct communication with the other objects in the transaction service. Indirect context management is more convenient for application developers who use the Transaction service because fewer objects are managed directly. In addition, fewer messages need to be generated in order to manage transactions.

Another set of modes include implicit and explicit propagation of transaction context. Each transaction has associated context that is used by the ORB, the Transaction service, and certain resources. The implicit and explicit modes concern the passing of specific context information. This context indicates whether the current object context is used or whether direct access to the internal objects in the transaction service is used.

Other kinds of transaction requirement are addressed by the transaction service. More specialized requirements can be addressed in future services or remain as niche markets that are only addressed by some vendor implementations. The start-up service is one example (see description below).

Needs that are not directly addressed in the Transaction service include fault tolerance. The Transaction service provides only a basic capability for consistency, not a complete capability for full tolerance. There are ORB products and research ORBs that address fault tolerant capabilities. These include the Orbix + Isis product, which combines the CORBA technology from Iona with fault-tolerant middleware technology from the Isis company.

Another capability, not directly supported by the Transaction service, is the capability for long transactions. In some applications, it is appropriate to check out objects for extended periods so that they can be manipulated at length. The objects are then checked back into a repository environment. An example of this kind of application is computer-aided design (CAD). In a CAD environment, users check out pieces of a design to perform design work and then return them at the end of the task or work period.

Figure 4.10 is an example scenario using the Transaction service and the Concurrency service. In this scenario, a client process is attempting to write and to change the state of several objects in the distributed environment. A number of reader processes are accessing these shared objects in the distributed environment. These transactions use implicit context management and implicit propagation modes. The writer object registers the beginning of the transaction with the begin operation to the current object. The current object communicates with the coordinator object and other objects in the Transaction service in order to initiate the transaction state. The writer object then acquires any locks on objects it intends to modify. In this case, it would obtain a write lock on the objects called entity A and entity B.

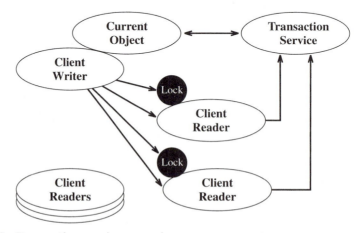

FIGURE 4.10   Transaction service scenario.

These two locks would comprise all the resources necessary for this client to complete the transaction. Since all the necessary resources have been allocated, any possibility of deadlock is avoided. Because write locks on these resources were obtained, any readers present are no longer holding locks on these resources. In other words, readers are not accessing these resources concurrently. After the locks have been obtained, the writer process can set attributes for the application objects by sending appropriate operations. After the writer has successfully completed the modification of the state information, it can commit the transaction by sending the commit operation to the current object. At this point, the current object would again communicate with the other elements of the Transaction service to complete the two-phase commitment protocol. If there were other transactions involving these resources, the Transaction service would be able to return exception values. This may be appropriate to indicate unresolved conflicts over the resources or the consistent state of the objects in the system.

There are several products available and coming to market that support the Transaction service. Products from Honeywell Bull, ICL, IONA, Hitachi, IBM, and others support these interfaces. In addition, because these interfaces are interoperable with other transaction models, it is believed that other organizations supplying transaction monitor technologies will migrate to these interfaces as CORBA enters the mainstream of the market.

In the previous sections on task management services, enabling services for controlling distributed activities are described, including event notification, concurrency, and transactions. In the following section, another major category of CORBAservices, which addresses enabling services for administration of distributed objects, is described.

4.4   System Management CORBAservices

The following CORBAservices provide proactive capabilities for managing resources in distributed object environments.

4.4.1   The Naming Service

The Naming service is a generic directory service that is analogous to a telephone book white pages. In other words, if you have the name of an object, you can retrieve its object reference through this service. This is a useful service for obtaining object references, and it is anticipated that the Naming service would be used by most objects to find other objects. A related yellow-pages service, the Trader service, is described in a separate section in this chapter.

The Naming service is available for most ORB product environments. A knowledge of this service is important to application development. An advantage of using the Naming service is that it allows application software to delegate the management of object references to a separate service so that applications do not need to maintain object references in their own persistent storage. The object references would always be available from this common service.

The key operations in the Naming service include bind and resolve. The bind operation is used to add a name to the service directory. The bind operation takes arguments, including a name and an object reference, and stores this entry in a particular naming context. With the resolve operation, the client supplies a particular object name and receives an object reference as a return value (or an exception). These two operations comprise most of the operations that applications would normally use to interact with the Naming service. The other operations defined in the service deal primarily with how to set up and manage the service so that the names are stored within particular contexts that define particular naming scopes.

The primary objects in the Naming service are naming context objects. Figure 4.11 is an example of some context objects and the names they manage. The interior nodes on this tree diagram denote the naming context objects. Each

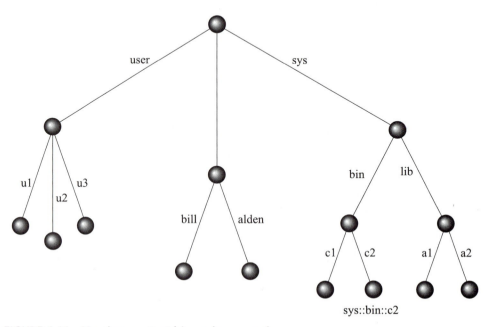

FIGURE 4.11   Naming context hierarchy example.

naming context object exists in a tree of naming contexts that define different scopes and subscopes of the name space. The naming contexts can be singly rooted or multiply rooted—that is, there can be unique root node for all contexts in the directory or multiple, independent directories in an ORB domain. The schema that defines the directory trees and the naming conventions used in these trees is an application design choice. The conventions for how these trees are set up is one of the important conventions that must be defined by application developers in order to use the Naming service.

The leaf nodes on Figure 4.11 correspond to the actual named object instances. The names are indicated by the edges or arrows of the diagram. For example, the object indicated by the sys::bin::c2 is within the root naming context, the sys context, the bin context, and the particular c2 as the leaf-node name within that context. The names are represented in a form that does not include separator characters. One of the key design concepts is that this service could be used as an interface wrapper over existing naming directory services. Each particular implementation of a naming directory service uses different separator characters. For example, many services use forward slash characters, such as the DCE cell directory service, and Internet naming conventions, where some implementations use back slashes and some languages environments use double colons.

Names within the Naming service are represented as a sequence of structures. Within each structure, there are two strings—a string representing the name information and a string representing the kind of that name. The kind field allows for different types of name symbols. The intention is that these sequences of structures (for instance, names) will be converted into pathnames. Each pathname would use environment-specific conventions for separators. For example, the pathname could use language- or protocol-specific separators so that they can be used to interoperate in specific environments (a file system, a directory system, the Internet, and so forth).

Figure 4.12 is an example scenario for the Naming service. In this example, an application object initializes itself with the object request broker and then creates a naming context. The naming context is in an environment that provides a scope within the root naming context. This root context existed before the application started. Within the new naming context, the application binds some names. These bind operations enter some names into the names directory.

When an application uses the Naming service, it needs to know the names of some of the objects registered in the directory. First, an application attempts to resolve a name corresponding to an object. Once an application has an object reference, it can invoke an operation on an object. This is how objects exchange references, using the Naming service that enables application objects to invoke other objects.

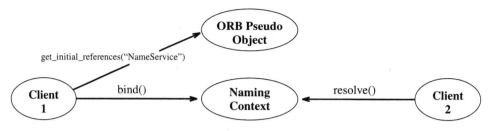

FIGURE 4.12   Naming service scenario.

Continuing in this scenario, if the application object attempts to resolve a different name, not in the directory, it can receive an exception condition. If it wishes to pursue this issue further, the application object can obtain a complete listing of the names that are registered in the directory by using other interfaces provided by the Naming service for iterating through the contents of the directory.

The Naming service requires that the application developers (and perhaps the system administrators) define some usage conventions (profiles) in order to make use of the service.

In particular, the Naming service usually requires the following types of conventions to be defined:

- Definition of the local naming schema
  — Structure of naming contexts
  — Rules of extending the context
- Definition of the local naming conventions
  — Well-known names
  — Conventions for new names
  — Semantics and values for the kind field

The local naming schema includes locally instantiated naming contexts, how they are interrelated, and the naming conventions for objects used within these contexts. A typical installation would include a root naming context for the network domain and a local naming context for each host. These contexts would normally be managed by the system administrator. Users could also create their own naming contexts and application-specific contexts. The unmanaged contexts could be hierarchically related to the host and domain contexts.

The conventions should identify the names of well-known objects, which may be system-wide or defined within each context. Typical well-known objects may include the Naming service, Security service, Printing service, Format conversion service, and the Trader service.

The local naming conventions may include rules for well-defined names, naming new contexts, and naming style conventions. The naming conventions should also include an enumeration and semantics of the kind field within the names. These conventions are analogous to the naming suffix conventions for disk files.

4.4.2   The Lifecycle Service

This service, compared with all other OMG specifications, is more like a guideline than a set of standard programming interfaces (although it contains both). One of the key principles of this service is that the creation of objects is an application issue. It is not possible for the definers of a generic service to predetermine all the attributes and characteristics that must be passed to the object creation function in order to determine the characteristics of new objects. In other words, the application designers need to define the parameters that are conveyed for the purpose of object creation. Usually, this results in the definition of new software interfaces beyond those standardized by a service.

Another important guideline in this service is that all other services, facilities, CORBAdomains, and applications should define lifecycle operations. Lifecycle is pervasive in all services and applications. The Lifecycle service specification provides the conceptual basis for how all other lifecycle capabilities should be configured.

One of the key concepts in the Lifecycle service is the object factory, the purpose of which is to create other objects. Generally, object factories are limited to creating a small set of object types. Factories themselves are generally not created by other factories. They are, in some sense, primal objects that are installed and have a long lifecycle so that they can manage the lifecycles of other objects. Factories are generally created before the objects that they manage and are well-known objects.

There are general ways defined within the Lifecycle service for locating factories. Factories should be readily known in other services, such as the Naming service and the Trader service. Object factories are needed to support lifecycle in a distributed environment. Within OO programming languages, such as C++, Java, and SmallTalk, there are language-dependent approaches for creating objects. Generally, language-dependent object creation makes assumptions about the objects they are creating, as well as the location of those objects. Language-dependent object creation occurs within a single address space. This assumption is not sufficient for distributed processing. In a distributed environment, assumptions cannot be made about the language that is used by the objects about the location of those objects.

Created objects might be in the same address space or they might be on the same machine. In addition, they could be remote objects somewhere else in the enterprise or somewhere in the global computing environment. The CORBA architecture and its location transparency help to hide the complexity associated with these differences in location.

The Lifecycle service introduces the notion that all distributed objects have an abstract location. The meaning of the term abstract location is defined by the implementation and installation. Usually, an abstract location means a particular host processor or set of processors. At abstract locations, the Lifecycle service defines factory finder objects. These maintain a directory of several factories at that same location. Generally, factory finders would be at every abstract location so that factories can be located anywhere on the network. By doing object creation, with respect to the abstract location of a factory, the Lifecycle service is an enabling mechanism for managing object location.

Location transparency is a capability that is not required in application system design. In other words, one can design a system that has location transparency, but one can easily add and expose information in the interface that allows knowledge of location—for example, parameters that pass filenames, URLs, hostnames, and IP addresses. The implementation of CORBA will not constrain the use of interfaces in this manner. However, it is recommended that you avoid such information in interfaces wherever possible. Whenever such information is exposed, it adds to the complexity and brittleness of the application. Frequently, dependence on this information becomes hardwired into application software. Later system extensions and reuses cannot take advantage of location transparency without significant software changes.

The lifecycle interfaces are shown in Figure 4.13. These interfaces are contained within a module called CosLifeCycle. This module contains three interfaces: the interface for the factory finder; the interface called lifecycle object; and an example interface, called generic factory. The IDL starts out with a set of typed definitions that define the basic data types used in the operation signatures of these interfaces. There is a definition of exception values that are used throughout the interfaces in this service. It is also possible, with any of these services, to include these definitions in application IDL files. Given that they are contained in a module, which is a convention used by all services, they limit the scope of the names and can be easily imported between scopes by using IDL's scoped name syntax. Scoped name syntax identifies enclosing module and interface names separated from the symbol name by double colon marks (see the CORBA 2 specification).

The first interface defined in the Lifecycle service is the factory finder interface, which corresponds to objects that have knowledge of factories in a particular location. This interface has only one operation signature—finding factories. The factories are categorized with respect to a key value parameter that is application-defined. In other words, when the application environment

```
         module CosLifecycle{                   interface LifecycleObject {
                                                     LifecycleObject copy(
    typedef Naming::Name Key;                            in FactoryFinder there,
    typedef Object  Factory;                             in Criteria the_criteria)
    typedef sequence<Factory> Factories;              raises(NoFactory, NotCopyable,
    typedef struct NVP {                                 InvalidCriteria,
        Naming::Istring name;                            CannotMeetCriteria);
        any value;                                   void move(in FactoryFinder there,
    } NameValuePair;                                     in Criteria the_criteria)
    typedef sequence <NameValuePair> Criteria;        raises(NoFactory, NotMovable,
                                                         InvalidCriteria,
                                                             CannotMeetCriteria);
    exception NoFactory { Key search_key; };         void remove()
    exception NotCopyable { string reason; };            raises(NotRemovable);
    exception NotMovable { string reason; };     };
        exception InvalidCriteria {
        Criteria invalid_criteria; };
        exception CannotMeetCriteria {           interface GenericFactory {
        Criteria  unmet_criteria; };                 boolean supports(in Key k);
                                                     Object create_object(
                                                         in Key k,
        interface FactoryFinder {                        in Criteria the_criteria);
        Factories find_factories(                    raises(NoFactory, InvalidCriteria,
            in Key factory_key)                          CannotMeetCriteria);
            raises(NoFactory);
                };                                   };
                                             };
```

FIGURE 4.13   Lifecycle service interfaces.

is set up, the applications need to define how the key values are used to indicate categories of object types. The factories need to be installed at these locations to support the creation of objects of the indicated types. The factory finder supports the operation called find factories. It takes as input value a key value corresponding to some specific object type. The operation returns a sequence of factory object references. This list includes all the factories corresponding to that particular object type.

The second interface in the Lifecycle service is for the lifecycle object. This particular interface is intended to be inherited by application software. This enables application objects to take on the characteristics of lifecycle objects. The lifecycle object interface is a set of standard programming interfaces that allow other objects to copy, move, and remove objects. It is useful for applications to support these interfaces instead of supporting unique vertical interfaces for the same purpose. Vertically defined interfaces limit the reusability and interoperability of software. Lifecycle interfaces are applicable across all domains and reuses of software.

The first signature in the lifecycle interface is the copy operation, which performs an application-defined copy. Typically, a shallow copy is implemented by this operation. This means that only the object and its internal state are duplicated. Any references to other objects are copied, but the objects themselves are not copied. Copies are made to the abstract location identified by a specified factory finder object. This operation takes an input parameter, called criteria, which is a list of values represented as a sequence of named value pairs. The meaning and usage of these values is application-defined. This gives the applications a general capability for passing additional information through this interface, which may be appropriate for particular application needs.

The next signature in the lifecycle object interface is the move operation. Typically, this operation also performs a shallow copying of the object and its state information. In effect, the object is then moved to a new factory finder location. The object maintains the same object reference; the ORB transparently forwards future messages to the new location. A criteria parameter is also provided for any application parameters that are passed into the move operation.

The third signature in the lifecycle object is the remove operation. The affect of remove is to terminate the lifecycle of this particular object. The remove operation deallocates any resources managed by the object, which includes persistent storage and running processes. After the remove operation occurs, any other object that references this object will receive an exception condition when it tries to use the object reference.

The third interface in the Lifecycle service is the generic factory interface, which is provided as a guideline and is not intended to be the only factory interface defined. Applications can define their own factory interfaces. Within a generic factory interface, there are two operation signatures.

The first signature is the support operation that determines if a factory supports a particular key value. The key value denotes an application-defined category of objects.

The second signature is the create object operation. This is provided as a prototype signature for factory operations. This operation takes as input a key value. The key value denotes the object type to be created. The create object operation includes a criteria parameter—a user-defined list of named value pairs. The criteria parameter may include information about how to initialize the new object.

In general, factories would not use a key parameter or a criteria parameter. Typical factory methods would have a user-defined parameter list that would be customized for the creation of a particular object type. The parameters should be strongly typed in the operation signature. These parameters would refine the characteristics and initialization of the created object.

Figure 4.14 is an example of the Lifecycle service in operation. There is an object in the same abstract location as the first factory. The client invokes a

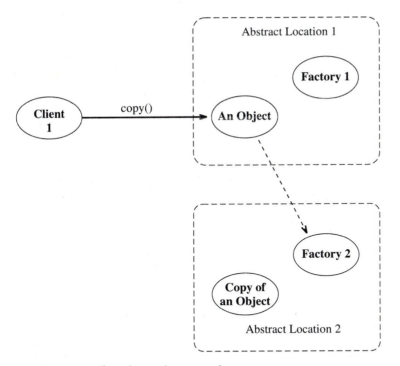

FIGURE 4.14 Lifecycle service scenario.

copy operation. This has the effect of creating a copy of the object in a remote factory location and returns a new object reference so that the client has two object references, one to the original object and one to the object located with the remote factory.

4.4.3   The Licensing Service

The Licensing service supports some general-purpose interfaces for the flexible protection of intellectual property. This service is essential because it is an important key to electronic commerce. In current applications, licensing is used for control of the allocation of software licenses. In a given environment, there can be a pool of software licenses that are allocated to a site. Users in that site may be more numerous than the number of purchased-license holders. A license manager can dynamically allocate licenses from the pool, allowing customers to maintain and purchase a smaller set of licenses than would be necessary if each license were installed on each desktop. In the future, the Licensing service can be used on a finer-grain than current applications of license management.

Licensing can be used to control all types of intellectual property, including computer artwork, commercial publications, and software license pools.

Because objects encapsulate both data and process, licensable objects can represent data-intensive intellectual property, such as artwork, as well as process-intensive intellectual property, such as software licenses.

Licensing is similar in some respects to security but in other ways is very different. Licensing can be more technically challenging than security because security typically concerns the control of computing resources within an enterprise environment. The Licensing service concerns the control of intellectual property and software in external environments. The key difference is presence of the policymaker in the computing environment. Licensing is an attempt to enforce access policies in other people's enterprises, without a direct presence. This provides an increased challenge to protect property even under favorable circumstances.

Another important aspect of licensing is that it controls intellectual property, which has direct monetary value, in contrast to what is normally protected by computer security. Secure information typically involves privacy issues or other areas with no direct monetary valuation. Licensing almost always concerns the external control of resources that have direct monetary consequences.

There are important issues in licensing concerning policy. When an organization releases intellectual property, it needs to have many types of policies implemented for its customers. When the customer relationship is considered valuable and the customer is considered to be trustworthy, licensing policies can be liberal. A licensing organization does not want to deny access to its trusted, friendly customers. By providing a liberal policy, an organization can help that customer to achieve its business objectives. Bending hard and fast rules of licensing is often essential to the business relationship. For example, in a liberal policy, an organization might allow the license pool to be allocated beyond the actual purchased limit. This policy might be implemented on a temporary basis or on a regular basis, depending on the kind of policy the organization wishes to use.

It is estimated that software piracy may be as high as 70 percent of installed software worldwide. Software piracy approaches 50 percent even in ethical organizations. In certain areas of the world, piracy accounts for virtually all installed software. In fact, a popular term for these places is "one-disk countries." For vulnerable software distribution channels, it is necessary to have rigorous licensing policies. In some cases, the licensing organization may wish to prohibit any copying of software and provide hard limits on the number of licenses that can be allocated.

The OMG Licensing service was a joint submission by Gradient, IBM, and Digital Equipment Corp. This service has a close relationship to a de facto industry standard, called the Licensing Service API (LS-API). LS-API is a specification from an alliance of two dozen industry vendors, including Microsoft. The software interfaces in the OMG Licensing service resemble the LS-API interfaces. The OMG Licensing service interfaces can be directly layered on top of LS-API interfaces. Products that are compliant with LS-API can be wrapped to support the OMG Licensing service.

4.4.4   The Trader Service

The Trader service is an important fundamental service. It is a directory that is similar in role to a telephone yellow pages. Offerers of services can register advertisements of service availability in the Trader service. The trader provides a registry of all the publicly known services and may be queried through special software interfaces to allow clients to identify candidate implementations. Each advertisement identifies various service characteristics and qualities of service.

The OMG Trader service is based on the conceptual standards defined for the International Standards Organization's open distributed processing (ISO ODP). In particular, the OMG Trader service is the commercial realization of the ODP Trader. ODP defines the foundational concepts for the provision of trading capabilities. This relationship between ISO ODP and OMG may be utilized repeatedly. Influential organizations, such as Architecture Projects Manage-ment (APM Ltd.), have restructured their standards to enable OMG to conduct the adoption of interfaces for ISO ODP's conceptual standards. The OMG Trader service includes these ideas and additional design details that were discovered in practice in actual software products and end-user environments. It is the opinion of the authors that the Trading service is as fundamental as the Naming service in providing access to object references for clients in the distributed object environment.

In this section, a category of the CORBAservices concerning system management was covered. The key enabling services for exchanging meta-data (Naming and Trader) and managing resources (Lifecycle and Licensing) were described. In the next section, services tightly bound to the underlying CORBA infrastructure are described.

4.5   Infrastructure CORBAservices

4.5.1   Security and Time Services

Security and Time services where adopted together in a joint RFP. In order to have an effective object security service, it was essential to have a Time service, which must also be secure. If the Time service can be subverted, it is possible to create certain types of security system failures. The object security service is different from most other object services because it directly involves and changes the underlying object request broker requirements. Security cannot be thought of as a completely independent service that is on the same level as any other application objects. Security needs to have direct ORB interactions in order to be effective. Therefore, it is categorized with the other infrastructure CORBAservices. It is also important for the ORB to directly support security because a close interaction can be used to minimize the impact on application software. Seamless provision for security was an important goal of the specification, including the minimization of cost required for security implementation.

The OMG Security service includes features that address many important security issues, such as confidentiality, integrity, accountability, availability, and nonrepudiation. Functions in the Security service include access control, auditing, authentication, and policy implementation. The service is implemented at several levels of client awareness. Clients can use the service without any changes to application software to accommodate security.

The Security service uses an implicit context object, which is validated on entry of request to the ORB environment and on exit of those requests on the object implementation side. The implicit context supports integration of unmodified applications in a secure ORB environment, without additional software on the application side.

There are two levels of security-aware application software. Level 1 is an initial awareness that supports some minimal control of the secure environment. Level 2 supports a comprehensive exposure of security features that are appropriate for client access. The majority of the security specification is directed at the ORB developers and implementors of security infrastructure, which includes the administrators of security. The specification has minimal information targeted at client application developers.

The Security service identifies different kinds of security-aware ORB products. The lowest level comprises CORBA 2-compliant ORBs, which have no security capabilities other than those inherent in the operating systems environment. Ordinary ORBs conform to operating system security constraints, such as the ability to read, write, and execute within other users file spaces. The next level comprises security-enabled ORB products. These products support the security access control calls on the client and the implementation sides of ORB invocations. These product extensions enable specialty security vendors to install security functionality into off-the-shelf ORB products. ORB vendors could simply provide the value-added call interfaces or provide complete security mechanisms using the interfaces. All security-enabled ORBs have these interfaces embedded in their software. Some ORBs could support security services implemented at some later time by the ORB vendor, the end-user, or by a third party. The third type of ORB has full security support, which includes a comprehensive implementation of the features specified in the Security and Time services.

The Time service supports the retrieval and synchronization of clocks in a distributed system. Distributed clock synchronization is an interesting theoretical problem. Given that the relative progress of clocks depends on different machines, timing anomalies can result. For example, if the clock's synchronization gets out of step more than the latency of message transmission time, it is possible to receive a message with a time stamp preceding the local time. In fact, theoretical work has shown how to use these anomalies to synchronize clocks.

More-recent technology for clock synchronization includes the use of radio frequency signals generated locally or from government sources. This allows accurate synchronization of time clocks and generally requires the purchase of additional hardware and software. The Time synchronization service supports these and other synchronization capabilities.

4.5.2   Messaging Service

An RFP for messaging and asynchronous invocation has been released by the ORBOS task force. Messaging is intended to address many important areas related to asynchronous processing, using the object request broker. The range of potential services to be adopted includes fine-grain asynchronous processing support all the way up to large scale asynchronous messaging.

By default, IDL interfaces have a synchronous semantics. For fine-grain asynchronous support, it is appropriate for the technology to provide extensions to programming language bindings so that ordinary IDL interfaces can be extended to support asynchronous processing. Current IDL interfaces require that the client thread (which makes the request invocation) block until the message goes through the ORB and the service is performed. Result values or exceptions are returned through the ORB before the client thread can continue processing. This assumption is not sufficient for many types of applications.

The synchronous capability was adopted for CORBA first because it is the more general-purpose capability. It is always possible for application software to provide synchronous interfaces that emulate asynchronous behaviors. An example is the use of the one-way keyword which defines a partial form of asynchronous messaging in IDL definitions. The asynchronous invocation capability of the Messaging service is intended to provide asynchronous semantics to ordinary IDL operations without requiring the modification of IDL to indicate asynchronous delivery.

Asynchronous invocation also has implications on an enterprise level. For example, the Messaging service can extend CORBA technology to cover the functionality addressed by message-oriented middleware (MOM). There are a number of MOM products on the market. An example is the IBM MQ series, which is a three-tiered technology.

MOM technologies provide capabilities similar to object request brokers. However, MOMs define a more primitive technology level for non-object-oriented programming environments, such as legacy COBOL. In these environments, MOM technology provides software interfaces similar to socket-level interfaces (for instance, TCP/IP). In other words, MOM interfaces for legacy software are basic message-sending APIs that which require the externalization of parameters before invocation and additional software complexity for managing a lower-level asynchronous environment. In many MOM products, sets of interfaces are provided for request brokering on different tiers of the architecture. For example, there can be a unique set of proprietary interfaces for the presentation logic layer and another set for the business logic layer. In both cases, these messaging layers provide capabilities that are similar in most respects to those provided by object request brokers.

The key difference between MOMs and ORBs may be the support for reliable delivery and the potential for message confirmation. These are capabilities to be supported by future OMG standards, such as an upcoming telecommunications domain standard—the Notification service. When asynchronous messaging is in place, it would be appropriate for companies in the messaging middleware market to migrate their products toward CORBA compliance. This is the intention of many vendors in the MOM market.

A mail-enabled interoperability protocol is a related future ORBOS service related to the Messaging service. The Messaging service and these future standards may extend CORBA to support capabilities similar to value added networks (VAN). VANs are important outsourcing services provided to support electronic data interchange (EDI). They are commercial companies that allow organizations to transmit EDI messages and store these messages for reliable delivery to the recipients. Messages are retrieved when recipients log into the VAN service. This is an important capability that makes EDI feasible. It is not necessary for senders of messages to have simultaneous connections to recipients of messages. For example, facsimile transmissions can often be delayed because of the unavailability of the recipient machine. The implication of CORBA messaging and future extensions involves the migration of VANS to support distributed objects. The Messaging service adoption will enable interfaces to allow confirmation of delivery and status checking of message delivery.

4.6   The Future of CORBAservices

A small set of additional services have been completed by the Object Management Group to complete the object services architecture. These services complete the OMG's CORBAservices defined in the ORBOS architecture. It is possible that additional services may be identified and solicited for adoption, although, for practical purposes, this completes the CORBAservices activity. Because CORBAservices and the object request broker activities are near completion, they have merged the two task forces into the single ORBOS task force.

4.6.1   Additional Services

A number of services were planned by the task force but were not actually adopted, for various reasons. Some services, such as a replication service, were part of the original architecture but did not have high enough market priority to result in the release of an RFP. Some of the most interesting cases are services for which adoption processes were started but never completed, including the Start-up service and the interface version.

Start-up Service   An additional service within RFP 5 was the object Start-up service. These interfaces augment the Transaction service by providing notification to objects of system events. For example, the service can indicate events as a result of system failure or as the result of a normal restart process. The Start-up service can notify objects whenever the system is going down. It can also notify objects when the system comes back up so that any initialization or recovery actions that are needed can be taken. The Transaction service and the Start-up service can work together so that some transactions can survive system failures and restarts.

The Start-up service originated when it was discovered that additional capabilities were needed to standardize the behavior of transactions in the presence of system failures and system reboot. Initially, the object Start-up service was to comprise a set of standard interfaces. These interfaces are intended to be implemented by application software supporting transactions and are called by operating system software on each platform. The operating system uses these interfaces to notify objects when the system is going down. On notification, objects can save persistent state information that is critical to transaction processing and other forms of reliable processing. The object start-up interfaces also include API's for notifying the objects when the system is starting or booting. These interfaces allow persistent objects to initialize their state on system recovery and perform any other actions necessary to recover from system failures or other consequences of system restart.

The Start-up service adoption process was not completed due to a lack of interest and consensus by the vendor community. For the time being, the start-up capability will remain product-specific.

Interface Versioning Service   The interface versioning RFP addressed change management of IDL interfaces. This RFP has a direct relationship to the Interface Repository because the interface versioning is addressed versioning of interfaces within the repository environment. This service supported the identification of objects and the consistent evolution of these objects. Interface versioning includes version management and configuration management capabilities. Configuration management capabilities are limited to interface information and do not concern implementation versioning. Other kinds of semantics or constraints may be represented by other facilities, such as the meta-object facility.

Prior to the submission deadline, an electronic-mail broadcast by Sun Microsystems suggested that an additional standard for this service was unnecessary. Sun suggested that the same functionality could be achieved by appending version numbers to IDL interface names. Since there were no actual submissions for this service RFP, this reasoning was accepted by default.

There is a related RFP in the CORBAfacilities task force for meta-object facilities, which addresses advanced capabilities for versioning. This is an RFP from the CORBAfacilities task force covered in Chapter 5.

4.7 Concluding Remarks

CORBAservices were originally intended to be ubiquitously available on all ORB environments. The original intention has changed as the CORBAservices have become defined. All ORB vendors intend to provide some subset of CORBAservices, and there are several third-party vendors who will also provide CORBAservices. Not all CORBAservices are readily available today, and it is unlikely that all CORBAservices will be available on all platforms for quite some time, if ever. Various levels of CORBA service support are planned by ORB vendors.

Experience with implementing systems using CORBA indicate that if the CORBAservices are not readily available, application developers spend a significant amount of time reinventing these capabilities in their application architectures. CORBAservices provide some design reuse, which is valuable to application developers. Because all the CORBAservices are not available in every CORBA environment, it is usually feasible for application developers to provide their own implementations. The specifications are publicly available, and the OMG has recently made a decision to make all its specifications available on the Internet. CORBAservices, in general, have fairly simple interfaces, which are described in relatively few pages of specifications.

It is possible for application developers to implement most CORBAservices with relatively modest effort. There are some exceptions to this statement: in particular, the Transaction service and the Security service. For the most part, CORBAservices are relatively straightforward and could be implemented by application developers. A useful implementation technique involves object wrapping an existing service implementation. Application developers might do with the anticipation that commercial products will evolve to support the adopted specifications. Even so, it is always possible for the OMG to modify or replace an adopted specification. Several specifications are targeted by OMG for extension or replacement, including the Persistent Object service and the Relationship service.

In this chapter, basic object services, called the CORBAservices, were discussed. These services are organized into four categories: information management, task management, system management, and infrastructure. The CORBAservices provide the first layer of abstraction above CORBA, which is used by most application domains and systems. In the next chapter, the second layer of abstraction above CORBA—the CORBAfacilities is discussed. CORBAservices are oriented toward enabling infrastructure capabilities; CORBAfacilities provide enabling capabilities for application interoperability.

CORBAfacilities and CORBAdomains

5.1   Overview of CORBAfacilities

The object management architecture (OMA) categorizes the areas of standards adoption within the overall scope of the OMG. The ORB is the communication infrastructure through which all objects communicate. CORBAservices are the fundamental enabling interfaces and are analogous to operating system service calls. The applications represent specialized technology areas that are not standardized.

Everything else that can be standardized within the architecture is either within the CORBAfacilities or the CORBAdomains (Figure 5.1). The CORBA-domains are vertical-market areas. Examples include financial services, healthcare, manufacturing, telecommunications, and business objects. CORBAdomains standardize a level of interoperability needs that are close to the needs of applications. The CORBAdomains will undoubtedly be of high value to developers and to end users for the delivery of component software.

Each of the CORBAdomains takes a vertical perspective. Each CORBA-domain considers only its own interoperability needs and not common needs across the domains, which is the role of the CORBAfacilities. Many capabilities in each domain are useful in other domains. For example, Compound Documents and System Management Facilities are not unique to any particular domain but are useful across many domains (that is, horizontally applicable). CORBAfacilities capture these horizontal interoperability needs and allow another tier of software vendors to provide higher-level capabilities, which are leveraged across multiple vertical markets.

Boundaries in the OMA are not firm. They are defined by the architectural descriptions just discussed and by coordination of the subgroups responsible for these standards areas. The subgroups within the OMG know what each other is doing through the meeting and reporting process built into OMG activities. The architecture board of the OMG is also responsible for coordination across the areas.

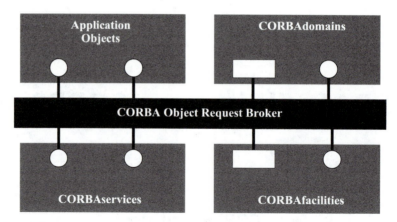

FIGURE 5.1   Object management architecture reference model.

Figure 5.2 is a more detailed model showing the role of application frameworks within the OMA. The technical reference model of the OMA shows, in some additional detail, how the specifications are used together and layered within the object categories. The technical reference model distinguishes between objects and their interfaces. Within each category of objects in the architecture there is a set of interfaces presented to the rest of the environment. In the case of the CORBAservices object, these are primitive services that do not depend on any other service interfaces. Therefore, the CORBAservices objects are encapsulated by their own specifications and by no others.

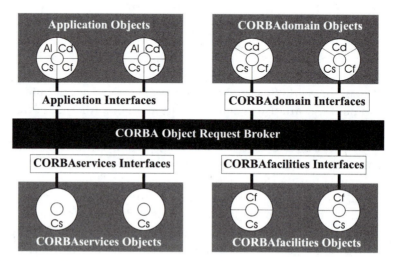

FIGURE 5.2   Object management technical reference model.

In the case of CORBAfacilities in Figure 5.2, there is another layer of technology that augments the CORBAservices interfaces with some extended capabilities, called CORBAfacilities. The CORBAfacilities can reuse CORBAservices, and they can inherit and extend CORBAservices. The CORBAfacilities can also introduce some brand new interfaces that build on the overall capabilities at a higher level of interoperability. One important distinction between the CORBAservices and the CORBAfacilities is that CORBAservices are focused on enabling capabilities. When readily available, the CORBAservices may provide another level of portability to applications; otherwise, this is the role of the application frameworks. Portability has been the primary goal of most vendor-driven standards activities, including CORBA and its predecessor networking technologies, as well as CORBAservices.

The CORBAfacilities and higher-level standards, such as CORBAdomains, are focused on interoperability issues. CORBAfacilities provide leverage because they specify sophisticated frameworks and technologies. Product support is required for most of these facilities because many of them will not be easily implementable by application developers. This was possible in the case of the simple interfaces defined by most of the CORBAservices. The CORBAdomain objects include interfaces from CORBAservices and CORBAfacilities, as well as new interfaces from the CORBAdomains. These represent the highest level of vertical-market standardization within the OMG's scope.

The final category of objects is application objects, which are objects that are not standardized by the OMG. The application objects can reuse standard interfaces from other parts of the architecture, including CORBAservices, CORBAfacilities, and CORBAdomains. Application objects can also add their own interfaces.

Figure 5.3 shows a detailed picture of the OMA with the different services, facilities domains, and application interface categories. In terms of the CORBAservices, virtually all of the standards have already been adopted and approved. This is also the case with the standards directly related to CORBA which have been through more than five years of maturity and are enjoying significant product support in the market.

CORBAfacilities and CORBAdomains are newer areas. There are several initial CORBAfacilities that have been adopted in the area of user interface management, information management, and system management. CORBAdomains are the most immature area of OMG's standards. The different task forces and special interest groups are organized to address each of these areas. The task force areas are empowered to begin the standards adoption processes (see Figure 5.3), including financial services, healthcare, business objects manufacturing, and telecommunications. Active groups in electronic commerce and Internet technologies, as well as in other areas, are forming all the

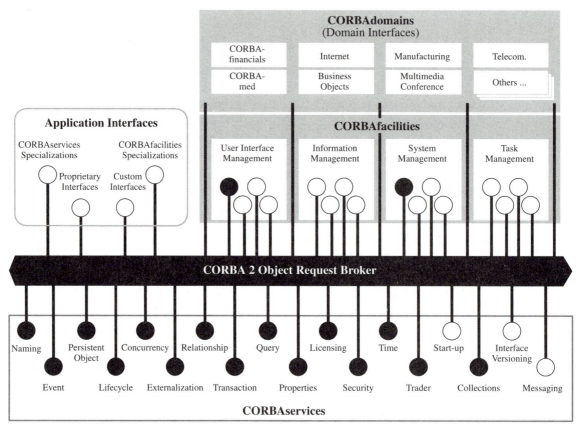

FIGURE 5.3   Object management areas and adopted specifications.

time. In the application interfaces, various categories represent different ways applications can utilize the OMA. Three of these areas are straightforward specialization of the other three categories, including CORBAservices and CORBAfacilities.

Proprietary interfaces are a principal kind of application interface. They are interfaces offered by a particular vendor, either a software product vendor or a system integrator, that represent a lock-in to a product line or set of vendor services. In general, these are the kinds of interfaces the OMG has been trying to eliminate or replace with standard interfaces that represent common ways of interoperating across multiple vendor product lines.

Application interfaces include custom interfaces, which are specified by corporate developers and are needed for application-system-specific interoperability and other needs. There will probably always be a need for such interfaces because standards will progress toward the needs of specific applications but, in general, standards address needs that are horizontal (that is, across multiple systems or domains).

An important way to look at the OMA is that the starting point (CORBA) addresses the most common functionality across all domains and across virtually all software interfaces. CORBAservices address the next level of common functionality. These are capabilities that are often reinvented when individual systems are built. CORBAservices interfaces are generally applicable across all domains. The next level of generality is the CORBAfacility, a higher-level interface that is focused on application interoperability rather than vendor-to-vendor interoperability and will remain domain-independent. The newest level of adoption within OMG is industry-specific but not specific to any organization, enterprise, or system. Certainly, there will be extensions and sub-sets of these that need to be defined for organizational enterprises and system definitions. It is important to know that these interfaces are there for design reuse. It can provide tremendous leverage in providing a well-thought-out starting point for the construction of new systems.

In current software engineering practice, most interfaces are custom interfaces. In other words, there are few interfaces in widespread practice in most systems today that are derived from other sources. Most interfaces are developed for a particular system and, therefore, are customized for that system. An important impact of the OMA is to change this model so that when systems are built, an increasing percentage of the interfaces come from common interface sources. Common sources could be the OMG, but there should also be commonality across enterprises and across multiple systems because the local commonalities may provide the most significant benefits in interoperability and potential for software reuse.

CORBAfacilities are higher-level services. Examples include the Compound Presentation and Interchange Facility from RFP 1 and the System Management Facility from request for comment (RFC) number 1. The focus of CORBAfacilities is on application-level interoperability rather than ORB-to-ORB interoperability. CORBAfacilities is the first area in which the OMG has focused on the application level of interoperability. These are in areas that tie applications together rather than interfaces between applications and vendor-provided services. Examples of facilities focused on interoperability include the Data Interchange Facility from RFP 3 and the Compound Interchange Facility from RFP 1.

CORBAfacilities represent interfaces that are common to multiple domains. For example, the Business Object Framework Facility from CORBAfacilities RFP 4 will be useful in financial services, manufacturing, healthcare, and other areas. The group responsible for adoption of these specifications, the CORBAfacilities task force, works in conjunction with many other groups inside and outside the OMG because of the potentially large scope of specifications that are common across multiple domain areas. In particular, with respect to the Business Object Framework Facility, the Common Facilities task force is working with the Business Object Domain task force to adopt those facilities through the OMG.

5.1.1 CORBAfacilities Versus CORBAservices

A frequently asked question concerns how the CORBAfacilities are different from the CORBAservices. Both are defined in the OMA. However, hard and fast boundaries between these categories are not defined. The groups responsible for each category have knowledge of each other's activities, and the OMG architecture board monitors and approves conformance to the architecture. The architecture board convenes whenever a new request for proposal is issued. They also have approval authority with respect to any technologies proposed for adoption and recommended by the task forces.

The CORBAservices were defined bottom-up, based on the perceived need for enabling interfaces and capabilities. The key benefit of the CORBAservices is their leverage of development activities. CORBAservices were defined and proposed, for the most part, by platform and ORB vendors and represent an infrastructure focus for their capabilities. On the other hand, the CORBAfacilities are typically derived from top-down needs. The benefits of the CORBAfacilities are focused on application interoperability and not on infrastructure and portability issues. The CORBAfacilities also represent a new community of vendors and suppliers within the OMG. This includes, primarily, independent software vendors and vertically-oriented technology groups within the traditional platform and ORB vendor community.

Figure 5.4 represents the reuse of specifications among the categories of OMG standards. The object services are globally applicable, and fundamental capabilities are reused and inherited throughout the architecture by the other categories. In particular, the CORBAfacilities are directly dependent on the CORBAservices interfaces and no other enabling capabilities than the ORB itself. The CORBAfacilities represent high-level capabilities, and in some cases, denote specialization of the object services. CORBAfacilities specialization is globally applicable across vertical domains. The CORBAservices and CORBAfacilities are reused by the domain interfaces, which provide the next level of specialization, in this case targeted at vertical-market needs. The domain interfaces will make substantial use of the more generic services and facilities, although a trend toward the creation of application frameworks such as the Business Object Framework Facility is unforeseen. These frameworks provide a unification and abstraction of the basic services and facilities that are useful for development within more specialized areas.

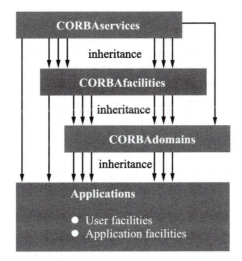

FIGURE 5.4   Reuse of OMG specifications.

The final category of objects is applications, which reuse specifications from all areas, including CORBAservices, CORBAfacilities, and the CORBA-domains. An important goal of reuse for the OMG specifications is that application architectures should be substantially based on standards specifications. Perhaps 70 percent or more of the architecture design for applications could be based on direct use of OMG standards.

In this section, an overview of the role CORBAfacilities and CORBAdomains in the OMA was discussed. This provides a basis for understanding how these facilities relate to and use other standards in the architecture. In the following sections, the existing and future CORBAfacilities and CORBAdomain interfaces will be described.

5.2   Horizontal CORBAfacilities

5.2.1   Distributed Document Component Facility

CORBAfacilities RFP 1 includes the Compound Presentation Facility and the Compound Interchange Facility. For marketing purposes, the OMG has renamed these facilities the Distributed Document Component Facility (DDCF). The Compound Presentation Facility concerns the management of desktop presentation of compound document parts.

A compound document is a collection of information from a variety of application sources. In a compound document, the end user can manipulate these forms of information transparently. For example, if there is textual and spreadsheet information in a compound document, the end user can manipulate the text using text commands and manipulate the embedded spreadsheet using spreadsheet commands. On the desktop, menus and tool-bar capabilities are substituted transparently in accordance with the interfaces presented by the Compound Presentation Facility.

The other facility within RFP 1 is the Compound Interchange Facility, a set of interfaces that provides for interoperability among compound document parts. Each compound document part is an instance of an object that contains state information. The embedded data can be manipulated by a compound document application. Each of these applications can exchange information with other kinds of applications. The approach is similar to the way clipboards are used in personal computing environments to exchange data among a variety of applications.

The interfaces of the DDCF are organized around an application-defined software component, called a part. The DDCF includes all the necessary support objects for part implementation. Starting with a canned part implementation, developers fill in the appropriate sections with software to implement the application-specific capabilities of a part. This approach to application implementation is the evolution of earlier environments such as MacApp. Compound documents are one of the most tightly coupled and sophisticated application integration environments. Much of the complexity of application integration within the compound document environment is handled by DDCF objects supporting the part object.

The Compound Interchange Facility (within DDCF) includes interoperability definitions that support the storage of information in a multiple format, which is part of the proposal. The Compound Interchange Facility also supports clipboard data interchange in a form that is compatible with legacy clipboard interfaces. Compound interchange also supports drag and drop, another form of interchange in which the end user selects data by using the mouse on the screen and then interactively drags that information by depressing the mouse button between different compound document parts displayed on the screen. When the end user releases the mouse button, the compound data is deposited in the destination part. Then the Compound Interchange Facility defines software interfaces that make the seamless and transparent handling of drag and drop possible.

In the adopted specification, based on OpenDoc, the Bento file format representation is used. This file format is similar in principle to the exchange representations used for clipboards. In other words, information stored in Bento is stored in several exchangeable forms, including a form unique to the application in which it was created. By convention, Bento files also include forms that are more generic. For example, text information could be represented in WordPerfect format and, in the same storage, also be represented in an annotated text format and in plain text format. When the information is interchanged with other parts, the other parts use the highest-fidelity format that can be interpreted. In general, a generic format is included so that interchange is possible across the widest range of application parts.

5.2.2   Compound Linking

The third type of compound interchange involves compound linking. Compound documents can store application data embedded in their file representation. Embedding occurs when information is stored with the compound document file. Linking occurs when the application data is stored externally to the compound document file. Active linking allows a single version of information to be updated and modified dynamically in several compound documents. The connection between the data and the compound document application is stored in the file, but it can also be defined on-the-fly when the part is first referenced.

The final form of compound interchange involves linking of parts. In linking, the interchange occurs indirectly by tying compound documents or parts of a compound document together. This creates an active linkage among parts so that when one part is updated, the linked part in the other document can be automatically updated, as well. Linking does not involve embedding of the application data, so there is always the possibility that links can become invalid when documents are changed or moved. This issue is significant in compound document technologies that use file names to represent linkages. In the adopted technology for compound documents, linkages are represented in terms of object references, which are more robust than file references.

The OpenDoc submission adopted by the OMG was a joint submission by members of the Compound Presentation Facility, including the Component Integration Lab and Novell, IBM, and Apple Computer. The adopted OMG technology comprises the two volumes of the OpenDoc specification: an architecture document and a class reference document. The Component Integration Labs also make reference technology available. In particular, they have a freeware code release for OpenDoc in which the complete source listings for the implementation of the OpenDoc-supplied objects can be received. The OpenDoc technology release includes a run-time license to the system object model (SOM), which is the ORB used by Apple, IBM, and other companies for their implementations of OpenDoc. The basis of OpenDoc is CORBA ORB, which enables OpenDoc to be ported to other ORBs. SOM runs on multiple platforms.

5.2.3 OpenDoc Parts Framework

Additional technology is being developed and made into products by Apple and IBM, called the OpenDoc parts framework (OPF). The OPF provides an additional layer of C++ software layered over the IDL APIs for OpenDoc. OPF is not currently an OMG standard because it is language-dependent. The base technology of OpenDoc is a comprehensive solution for compound documents and provides a complete set of interfaces for that purpose. Many other interfaces are needed by compound document parts, including operating system services, windowing, and graphics capabilities, for example. The OPF addresses these areas in a platform-independent manner. When OpenDoc and OPF are used together, developers of OpenDoc parts can be assured of complete platform portability across multiple hardware and operating system platforms. At a minimum, this will include the Apple Macintosh operating system; IBM platforms, such as OS/2 and AIX UNIX; as well as the Microsoft Windows platforms, which include Windows 95 in its current release.

The reference technology for OpenDoc includes an integration solution between OpenDoc and Microsoft OLE. The OpenDoc/OLE interoperability solution is a seamless interface that allows OpenDoc parts to be embedded in OLE documents. The solution also includes the converse capability, which allows OLE parts to be embedded in OpenDoc documents. This provides full bi-directional interoperability between these two technologies. In fact, one of the slogans used to describe OpenDoc is that it provides "an easier way to integrate with OLE than OLE itself."

5.2.4 OpenDoc User Interface

Figure 5.5 is a visual representation of an OpenDoc compound document. An OpenDoc document can contain information from several applications. The overall container for the document (which is also called the root part) manages the file representation for all the embedded compound document parts. The container manages the desktop environment, including resources such as menus and tool bars. The container also arbitrates the allocation of screen space and resources in the compound document. When a compound document is the current part on the desktop, the part receives events generated by the menus for the current window. These menus comprise some general-purpose capabilities from the root part, such as the document and edit windows, as well as some part-specific menus, which vary based on the currently active part.

A compound document part is activated based on the location of the mouse pointer (or sprite). In OpenDoc, the selection of the current part is an efficient and lightweight capability. No expensive context switching occurs between large application software packages as is the case in other compound document

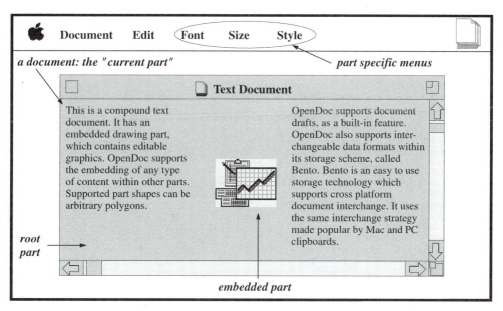

FIGURE 5.5   OpenDoc user interface.

technologies. OpenDoc has created a capability for a lightweight compound document application that makes this efficiency possible.

OpenDoc allows flexible negotiation and allocation of screen real estate in the compound document shown in Figure 5.5. The boundaries of an embedded part do not have to be rectangular. Parts can be of arbitrary shape, and a compound document part does not need to be limited to a single page; it can cross one or more page boundaries. These features are significant restrictions in other technologies.

5.2.5   OpenDoc Framework Objects

Figure 5.6 shows the object relationships within OpenDoc. OpenDoc is a framework technology focused on the needs of a single object class—the OpenDoc part. The OpenDoc part is the application a developer would supply to reuse the other software in the OpenDoc framework implementation. All other objects within the framework, except other OpenDoc parts, are supplied by the OpenDoc implementation. When developers create OpenDoc parts, they are given initial code templates for the parts. The templates have method entry points for all the incoming message signatures. Initially, the methods are filled in with no-operation stub code. If the developer does not modify a stub, it will provide a normal return when invoked by other classes in the framework. This does not define any capabilities.

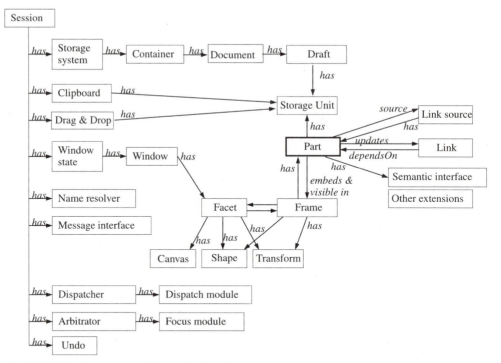

FIGURE 5.6   OpenDoc object relationships.

To develop an OpenDoc part, the developer replaces the default code with his or her own application code. The developer controls which OpenDoc capabilities are supported by replacing the stubs of the template, which allows the developer to add capabilities incrementally and increase the sophistication of the part over time. This capability is also useful to corporate developers who want to rapidly prototype parts or develop end-user parts that require only limited capabilities within the compound document environment. Commercial developers of OpenDoc parts probably will use most of the OpenDoc capabilities for their parts. For commercial parts, competitive implementations should maximize the capabilities of the compound document environment. Because source code is available for the remainder of the framework implementations, it is possible for part developers to understand the inner workings of the compound document framework. This understanding can be valuable for development and debugging purposes.

In this section, the Distributed Document Component Facility (DDCF) was described. This is the basis for standard desktop and document component objects. The DDCF is a good example of how CORBAfacilities differ from services: higher level, more sophisticated, and close-to-actual application programming needs. In the following section, CORBAfacilities for common management will be described. Whereas the DDCF was intended to be a complete set of interfaces for its area, the Common Management Facilities are just the foundational interfaces for system management capabilities.

5.2.6   The Common Management Facilities

The OMG has adopted a foundational interface for system management capabilities, called the Common Management Facilities. This technology was a submission by the X/Open consortium in a technology process called SYSMAN, which was initiated by a submission from the Tivoli Corporation of their Tivoli management environment specification. The Tivoli management environment is a CORBA-based system management development suite that provides extensibility of system management capabilities across many hardware and software platforms. The technology adopted by OMG comprises an enabling infrastructure that System Management Facilities can be built on. The co-submitters of the technology include the X/Open consortium, which is merging with the Open Software Foundation to form the Open Group. Other submitters include AT&T, Honeywell, Digital Equipment Corp., IBM, SunSoft, Tandem Computers, and Tivoli. Note that IBM has acquired Tivoli, Taligent, and Transarc, so their technologies are now IBM products.

System management is an important technology because of the growth of desktop computing and networking in enterprises. System management automates the handling of computer support services across a distributed enterprise. With system management technologies, it is possible to remotely update and install applications. In addition, system management can be used to monitor and maintain security policies and other important operations. These operations previously involved large support staffs that had to physically visit each machine in person to perform the management operation.

As organizations migrated from mainframe technology to personal computing technology, problems of managing computer resources moved from a centralized mainframe machine room (often called the fishbowl because windows around its perimeter allow people to look in) to numerous desktops. When technology moved to the desktop, the management problems handled in the fishbowl were distributed across the enterprise. In many organizations, there were many struggles to cope with these changes. Most organizations are now moving to a decentralized support structure so that support personnel report to local departments and reside in those communities to provide support.

Information Week estimates that support costs, including the lost time of operational personnel, is on the order of $40,000 per year per personal computer. System management technology is positioned to help mitigate those costs and effects through a centrally controlled distributed infrastructure.

Figure 5.7 is the overall architecture of the System Management Facilities in the X/Open submission. Components from the OMA including the ORB, the CORBAservices, and the CORBAfacilities are shown in the diagram.

The Management Facilities are an extension to the OMA infrastructure. They are part of the Common Facilities that are available to application software to provide a common foundation for system management. The application software represented in this architecture diagram includes management applications and managed objects (Figure 5.7). The management applications include user interfaces that exploit the Common Management Facilities and communicate to the managed objects. These management applications include control and monitoring software that configure and operate the system management environment. The managed objects comprise all the objects in the enterprise that are controlled within the system management domain. Examples of managed object applications include desktop applications, databases, file systems, and printing facilities.

To provide consistent system management interface across all these resources, the Common Management Facilities provide interfaces and mechanisms for adding object extensions. Hooks are provided into these managed object applications that the Management Facilities and the management applications can use to conduct system management. Figure 5.8 is a comparison between managed sets, as incorporated in the System Management Facilities, and UNIX file systems, which are the default capability on UNIX platforms.

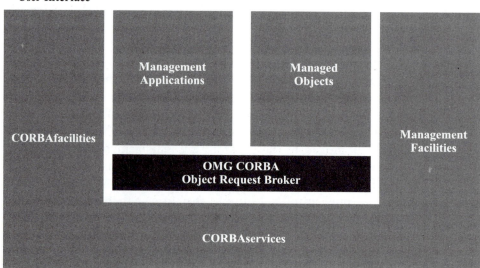

FIGURE 5.7   Common system management facility.

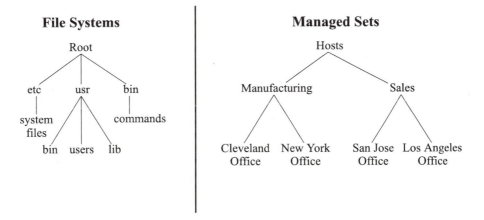

FIGURE 5.8   UNIX files and managed sets.

Managed sets in the System Management Facilities correspond to a logical model of the organization, which partitions the resources to be managed into logical entities and subsets. The overall topology is similar to a UNIX file system, but the UNIX system relates to a physical directory structure corresponding to the way information is laid out in a disk system environment. Using the managed set interfaces, the System Management Facilities can create logical models of an environment or an enterprise that are independent of any hardware or storage schemes. Because the Management Facilities are distributed through CORBA, the distributed object environment can support physical distribution of the enterprise and the managed resources, as well.

Figure 5.9 shows the inheritance relationship in the Common Management Facilities that define the base interfaces for system management. Many other interfaces need to be added to this hierarchy in order to create an actual system management installation. The key interface classes defined in this hierarchy include the policy objects, managed sets, and policy regions. A policy object corresponds to a system management capability that is applied consistently across a managed set. The managed sets correspond to groups of objects and do not need to be mutually exclusive. In other words, managed sets can correspond to groupings of objects along several dimensions that may overlap. The managed instances are a predecessor class of policy region objects. The purpose of policy regions is to define groupings of objects and applicable policies in alternative system management domains. The Common Management Facilities make use of the Lifecycle CORBAservices interfaces, which are used to locate system management objects, as well as copying, moving, and removing system management objects.

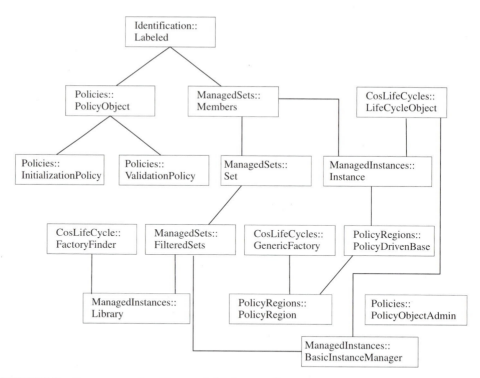

FIGURE 5.9 Common management inheritance diagram.

In this section, the Common Management Facilities were described. These facilities provide necessary vendor commonality across the emerging system management industry. The Internationalization and Time Operations Facilities address some important enabling capabilities for commercial product developers and multinational enterprises.

5.2.7 Internationalization and Time Operations Facilities

The Internationalization and Time Operations Facilities were recommended for adoption through the CORBAfacilities RFP 2 process. The Internationalization Facility supports the localization of object-oriented applications. The facility supports multinational data types (encapsulated as objects) including output formats and conversions among formats. The Time Operations Facility defines similar capabilities with respect to time values. This includes definition of time objects and time data types operations on time objects, as well as time conversions. The Internationalization and Time Operations Facilities were submitted by IBM in conjunction with all their wholly-owned subsidiaries, including Taligent and Tivoli Systems.

The technology basis for the RFP2 facilities are derived from an IBM/Taligent product, OpenClass. The RFP 2 facilities use the same definition of locale that is provided by the IEEE POSIX standard. POSIX defines locale as the subset of the end user's environment that depends on the local language and local cultural conventions. Within the POSIX model, there are six categories of localized information: character classification and case conversion, collation order, date and time formats, numeric formatting, monetary formatting, and text message formatting. The POSIX standard defines a format that can store this localization information in files. The OMG specification is independent of this format. The implementation of the RFP 2 facilities can use the POSIX format or another format because the use of this persistent format is independent of the software interfaces provided by the facility.

The interfaces for the Internationalization and Time Operations Facilities are organized by the number of types of formatters. There are formatters for localizing number information, for localizing date information, for localizing time information, as well as for localizing calendars and messages. The message formatting includes localization and translation of character strings, including parameterized substitutions into formatted strings. The different formatters can be used together so that messages, dates, times, and their component numbers can be formatted. These are all performed by separate formatters working in concert.

Internationalization and Time Operations Facilities take advantage of the adopted IDL extensions for internationalized data types. In particular, these extensions add wide character types and wide string types, which support characters of arbitrary bit length with a minimum of 16 bits required by the specification. An important issue in internationalization is the support for text sorting, which involves the definition of a collating sequence for the different localized character types. This issue is not as simple as a comparison of individual characters. There are certain locales that treat groups of characters differently. For example, some locales consider certain character sequences as a single character for the purposes of collation; some locales consider characters with various kinds of diacritical marks to represent different positions in the collating sequence; others expand diacritical characters to represent multiple characters during collation. In addition, there are characters to be ignored, such as pluralization, which should not be considered when sorting is performed.

The Internationalization Facility allows for evaluation of the collation orders through abstract operation signatures for testing whether a text sequence is greater than, less than, or equal to another text sequence. The underlying conversions involving compression, expansion, and collating sequences are evaluated transparently in the text formatter implementations. The facility supports a capability for performing language insensitive collations by the generation of a new neutral collation order.

Another important capability for localization involves pattern matching. In order to write pattern-matching software, which is language independent, the facility provides a number of pattern-matching functions for comparing text strings. The most basic is a literal match of character strings. Inclusive matches consider any of the contents of the pattern as potentially matching any characters in the strings. Exclusive matches look for characters that are not in the pattern. Boundary matches look for characters at the end or beginning of words.

A number of formatter interfaces are defined in the specification, including the date-time formatter, which provides the capability for converting floating-point numbers into culturally appropriate text. A number formatter converts arbitrary numbers into text. A simple text formatter is used for formatting text values. A parameter formatter can take lists of parameters for formatting. The choice formatter allows developers to build conditional formatters that can be quite sophisticated, depending on its use.

This section described the Internationalization and Time Operations Facilities, which enable the construction of customizable applications based on locale. The Data Interchange Facility is an enabling horizontal facility for application interoperability.

5.2.8   Data Interchange Facility

The Data Interchange Facility for CORBAfacilities RFP 3 was recommended for adoption through the CORBAfacilities RFP 3 process; it is an ongoing adoption process. The proposed facility is the result of a joint submission by MITRE Corp., I-Kinetics Corp., and Objectivity. The I-Kinetics participation is associated with the Component-Ware Consortium (CWC) initiative, a government-funded research consortium to bring component software technology to government systems and the commercial market. The Data Interchange Facility submission is based on the DISCUS technology presented in detail in *The Essential CORBA*, by Mowbray and Zahavi, 1995.

Data interchange represents a fundamental capability for application-level interoperability. This capability is different from the RFP 1 Component Interchange Facility because it is simplified and more widely applicable. Component interchange requires tight coupling with a sophisticated compound document framework software, whereas data interchange may require only loose coupling with conversion services. Also, data interchange does not require externalization of data as is the case in the Component Interchange Facility. The Data Interchange Facility can support the exchange of internalized data, externalized data, and object references, which allows applications to exchange virtually any kind of information through this facility. Data interchange represents a missing key in interface-supporting interoperability. Many other related services and facilities can take advantage of this set of interfaces.

For example, the Externalization service provides a way to flatten out data structures and can be used in conjunction with data interchange.

Data interchange also includes Conversion service, another critical capability. A Conversion service is a general-purpose interface for translating among data formats. This is an important capability because virtually every developed application has a unique data format. For interoperability to be possible, there must be a mechanism for translating from formats that are unique to each application to formats that are exchangeable.

In the above sections, the key CORBAfacilities for compound documents, system management, internationalization, and interoperability were covered. In the following section, vertical facilities and domain area standards activities will be described.

5.3   Vertical CORBAfacilities and Related Activities

5.3.1   Business Object Framework and Common Business Objects

CORBAfacilities RFP 4 comprises the Business Object Framework Facility and Generic Business Object Facilities. This is considered to be the first CORBA-domain specification to be considered by OMG. The Business Object Framework Facility is a unifying set of interfaces for access to the capabilities of all lower-level facilities and services and includes comprehensive support necessary for business applications that need the capabilities of the lower-level services. On top of this framework, a number of generic business objects and vertical-market business objects are built. The common business objects comprise the first set of fundamental business objects applicable across many domains.

Figure 5.10 is the business object application architecture. This figure shows the enabling services and interfaces, including CORBA, CORBAservices, and CORBAfacilities, as the bottom-level layer. Underlying the business object framework are approximately two dozen services and facilities interfaces. The business object framework abstracts and unifies access to these lower-level interfaces. In early adopters' experiences with the CORBAservices and CORBAfacilities, it was found that management of the complexity of these interfaces was key to development success. The business object framework provides a uniform abstraction for business software that manages the complexity of the lower-level services.

The common business objects provide the next level of abstraction. Common business objects use the Business Object Framework Facilities to perform their functions. A number of vertical-market areas use business objects, including financial business objects, healthcare business objects, and other areas. Any additional objects that are enterprise-specific use the interfaces that

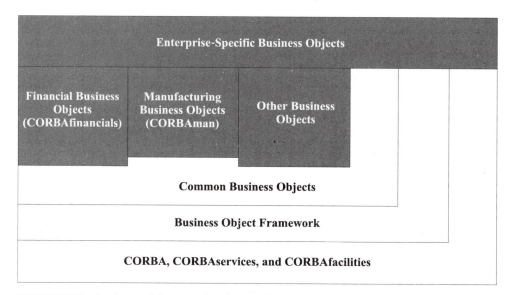

FIGURE 5.10   Business object application architecture.

are defined in these other areas. Application software can still access lower-level services where appropriate.

Business objects are an important addition to the OMG technologies. They represent the first area of domain specialization to the OMG standards. There was much discussion at the OMG prior to the initiation of adoption processes in this area for several reasons. One reason was that business objects make up the first domain area and, therefore, are groundbreaking. Another concern was that the business object framework layer over existing facilities and services, including the basic CORBA interfaces. This layer provides a separation between the platform vendors (including the ORB vendors) and the potentially large segment of the market that uses business objects. Another group of vendor organizations, independent of the platform and ORB vendors, will define this business object operating system for future business object applications.

Another key concern relating to this area is that business objects are open-ended and have a potentially broad scope that might affect virtually any area of standardization that the OMG has or may consider. There is concern that some participants in the OMG process may not fully understand the potential scope of this area and may miss an opportunity to participate.

5.3.2   Meta-Object Facility

CORBAfacilities RFP 5 covers the Meta-Object Facility. An example of the use of the Meta-Object Facility is shown in Figure 5.11. The Meta-Object Facility extends the meta-data definitions supported by OMG standards into the areas of

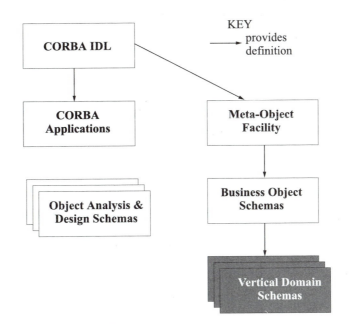

FIGURE 5.11   Meta-object facility.

interface semantics, constraints, and related areas. Prior to meta-objects, the definition of OMG interfaces was limited to the syntax of CORBA's IDL. Note that IDL captures only a subset of the information in object-oriented analysis and design models. In fact, IDL only captures information about the object class hierarchy and the identification of the public attributes in operations. IDL does not capture information about other relationships among object classes other than inheritance. Relationship information is perhaps one of the most needed areas.

The Relationship service can be used to capture physical linkages but does not describe semantics. The IDL interface definitions in a CORBA environment are captured and available on-line in the CORBA Interface Repository, which is part of the CORBA 2 standard. The Interface Repository contains essentially the same information as in IDL code. CORBA 2 defines an elaborate set of interface schema definitions that allow on-line applications to retrieve the IDL information. Unfortunately, the existing Interface Repository by itself is not useful to application software for automatic exploitation, largely because IDL operations are not self-documenting. The meaning of the operation can only be surmised by a human reviewer and is unlikely to be adequately interpreted by automatic software attempting to exploit interface information. IDL contains strong typing information about parameters and return values and the parameter modes, in, in-out, and out. Parameter specifications in operation signatures do not contain sufficient semantic information for software to automatically use the parameters. For example, it is unclear what values to supply or why one would use those parameters. There needs to be additional semantic information to help software interpret the meaning, purpose, and functionality supported by the implementations of the IDL.

These types of definitions are supported in the OMG standard documents by prose descriptions. A typical OMG style specification includes the IDL code that defines the operation signatures and prose descriptions for the sequencing and schematics of the operations in their parameters. The Meta-Object Facility will capture some of this informal information in its descriptions and provide important extensions that can be used for automatic exploitation of interface information.

5.3.3   Printing and Input Method Facilities

Two other facilities that are in process in the CORBAfacilities task force are Printing and Input Method. The Printing Facility, RFP 6, is the first of several planned facilities that address document processing. Document processing is a significant vertical-market area unto itself. Certain aspects of document processing are generally useful in other domains. The Printing Facility is an example, and will be adopted by the CORBAfacilities task force for this purpose. The Printing Facility can include related input facilities within its scope. In this case, the printing and related facilities will define standard software interfaces for integration of software drivers and their component hardware devices, which will make Printing Facilities generally interchangeable among document processing applications.

The RFP 7 is for the Input Method Facility, which defines software interfaces for integration of special purpose input devices and keyboard interfaces that accept Asian character input. In addition to Asian character sets, there are character sets in other parts of the world, such as the Middle East and Africa, that require these specialized capabilities. In particular, when a character set exceeds the number of characters on a typical Westernized keyboard, the need arises to define ways of typing more than one character of Roman-Arabic text to represent Asian characters. Overlapping and redundant solutions to this problem are available from various vendors.

End users of these technologies find that vendors are unable to address the diversity of character sets adequately and that the market could benefit from vendors' cooperation. The Input Method Facility enables vendors to specialize in individual character-set markets. They can provide more-effective, customized support for particular communities. The Input Method Facility will define the common software interfaces that will allow Asian character input software to be interchangeable among software applications, which will allow a market to be created that will provide better market support than is currently available. Participating vendors will be able to take advantage of character sets by relicensing technology from other vendors and licensing their own unique technology to other vendors. The Input Method Facility is an important example of how standard software interfaces can provide for an expanded market and better serve end users.

5.3.4   Vertical-Market Areas

Several additional areas of vertical-market interests are being considered by the OMG. One of the most advanced areas is in financial services. The financial domain task force has created the CORBAfinancial architecture to identify the facilities to be adopted in this arena. Figure 5.12 is a block diagram representation of the CORBAfinancial's architecture. This architecture identifies categories of interfaces that will be the subject of future OMG adoptions processes. These facilities are based on the fundamental facilities defined by CORBA, CORBAservices, CORBAfacilities, and the Business Object Framework Facility.

CORBAfinancials define horizontal and vertical specializations within the financial services market. Some base facilities are used throughout the vertical areas, such as the Accounting Facility, and they define the fundamental capabilities for business. In today's commercial software market, there are more than 6,000 commercial accounting packages, all of which have unique software interfaces. This does not include the proprietary and custom accounting systems that exist in all forms of businesses. In fact, it is commonplace for financial services enterprises to have overlapping systems. Also, it is seldom

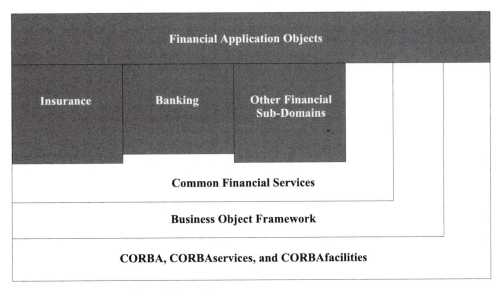

FIGURE 5.12   CORBAfinancial architecture.

feasible to reuse software from existing systems to leverage the development of new systems. The adoption of the CORBAfinancial interfaces will help mature and evolve this market so that there are widely accepted reusable interfaces that are supported commercially. A set of proven standard interfaces can be used to leverage the design and implementation of mission-critical software. These interfaces will support leveraging of commercial software, as well as provide adaptability, reuse, and interoperability across enterprises.

In the above sections, the Vertical facilities and domain-oriented activities of the OMG standards process were described. The following section will describe how to leverage this process for software development and for standards generation.

5.4 Leveraging the OMG Process

Consortia such as the OMG exist to facilitate the growth of software markets. The products of these consortia are technology agreements that lower risks to consumers and suppliers of technology. Consortium organizations create standards to confer credibility on interface solutions that are shared among vendors. A fundamental principle of the OMG is the inherent assumption that vendors in the OMG agree to cooperate on their software interfaces and compete on implementations. This assumption contrasts to the ordinary market principle in which vendors compete on software interfaces and implementation.

When vendors compete on the software interfaces, they create proprietary integration solutions that greatly increase the risk of obsolescence to technology users. Competition on interfaces artificially constrains the size of the software market because of this risk. Whether supplier, end user, or system integrator, it is possible for producers to leverage the OMG process to their advantage.

5.4.1 Exploiting a Predictable Process

The OMG process is predictable. It typically takes from 12 to 18 months from initiating an RFP to the completion of the technology adoption process. Typically, another 12 to 18 months transpires before the technology is generally available in the market. The OMG has delivered significant technologies using this process. The technologies that OMG promised to deliver when it was first formed have, for the most part, been standardized and delivered to the commercial market. The organization is expanding beyond the bounds of its initial charter into vertical-market areas in which even more significant benefits will be realized. Vertical-market areas are the most valuable areas for technology definition because they directly relate to business needs.

Because the OMG process is predictable, it is feasible to align future technology plans to their current and future adoption activities. The OMG publishes its plans in the form of architecture documents and roadmap schedules. OMG architecture documents are top-level descriptions of the facilities that comprise an area of the OMA. The OMA guide is the umbrella over all the architectures within the scope of OMG, including the CORBAfacilities architecture and the CORBAfinancials architecture. These are living plans for ongoing standards activities. The architectures themselves do not define a timeline.

The architecture documents identify the services and facilities for adoption. Each facility is defined by a template, which can range from two to ten pages and includes a section that defines the scope of the facility and the basic requirements. This key description is a place-holder in the architecture. Another section of the template is a bullet list of the relevant standards and references outside of the OMG process that are potentially useful in this standards area. Typically, the standards reference section includes a list of formal standards, such as ISO, ANSI, and IEEE standards, as well as well-known books and other publications. These references help to explain and define the terminology and scope of the facility. The third section is a definition of how the future standard will relate to other parts of the OMA. In particular, the standard template should list which parts of the CORBAservices are relevant and may be reused in the definition of this new facility. This comment also applies to any relevant CORBAservices and CORBAdomains areas. The final section of the architecture template is a listing of unresolved architecture issues that need to be considered prior to the release and initiation of the OMG process for adoption. Together, these sections form a basic definition of the scope of a facility that is sufficient to define the architecture areas the OMG will pursue.

A companion planning document goes with each architecture, called a roadmap. Since the architecture itself does not define a timeline, the roadmap considers the priorities for these services, as well as any technology dependencies among the services and factors, such as industry need and the ability of the task force to pursue adoption processes in parallel. The roadmaps provide timing information that allows one to predict the approximate availability of planned OMG specifications. These roadmaps are synchronized and coordinated among the OMG task forces and also identify external groups working on related standards. Many groups target the OMG process as the final destination for their activities.

In creating organizational plans for exploiting the OMG process, it is important to know the areas that OMG is covering, to avoid replication of effort. In other words, the areas on which OMG is working will be populated by high-quality specifications, which usually involve significant investment by the companies putting these definitions forward. The work of OMG in an area also anticipates the commercial availability of technology supporting these needs. When OMG provides coverage of an area, it is usually possible to obtain early release of specifications and technologies that can help to leverage any application use of these technology areas.

When the OMG specification is adopted, initial use of the adopted interfaces in application architecture is recommended, then migration to the commercial technologies can occur when they become available. This strategy has been used successfully in several areas to minimize development costs and risks. The market will probably reduce software maintenance commitments by replacing end-user software with commercially supplied software. If there is an area in which the OMG is not covering according to its plan, it is often possible to inherit and specialize the specifications. Most OMG specifications are defined explicitly for reuse.

It is not difficult to implement the functionality of IDL specifications for most CORBAservices, with certain exclusions, such as Transactions and Security. If it is not possible to find specifications that match users' needs or come close, then it is appropriate to define individualized interface definitions. If any organization makes a substantial investment in creating a quality architecture with its own specifications, it is potentially feasible and beneficial for it to consider coming back to the OMG to exploit the process and become market leaders.

5.4.2 Application Profiles

When application developers build on the more primitive interfaces, they need to write substantial software to derive benefits from the technology. Developers need to define profiles that detail conventions for how the technology is used, to assure that the technology delivers the appropriate interoperability and portability benefits. It is also important to define these profiles to make sure that complexity is managed appropriately. The motivations of vendors, who author most standards specifications, are different from the motivation of integrators and end users. Vendors want to put technologies with the broadest possible applicability into the market. Sometimes these technologies include significant complexity in order to provide all the features vendors would like to deliver. This need for flexibility and generality contrasts to what users and integrators need. They usually apply the technology to a particular system need that has only one use of a more general technology.

In the profiles, these users and integrators define the appropriate subset of the technology and the conventions for how the technology is used. This approach is not unique to OMG standards but is essential for understanding how to leverage the standards to the needs of applications.

5.4.3   Inside the OMG Organization

The OMG is a nonprofit consortium that operates by using a well-defined process for decision making. It is organized into two technical committees, one for platform technologies and one for domains. Under each of these technical committees there are a number of task forces empowered to pursue adoption processes. These task forces make recommendations to the architecture board and the technical committees concerning adoption. Once the task force completes an adoption process, it is a matter for architectural and business assessments to make a yes or a no decision about whether the technology adoption is appropriate. This process has worked successfully in dozens of instances.

Figure 5.13 is the CORBAfacilities task force mission statement, which is a good example of the charter under which these task forces operate. An important element of the mission is to leverage existing standards wherever they are relevant, including formal standards and de facto standards. The CORBAfacilities task force is an ongoing process, whereas the two previous task forces, CORBAservices and the ORB task force, have merged to form the object request broker-object service task force. This group is near completion of their architecture. CORBAfacilities is still in its early phases but is rapidly making progress since it defined and updated its architecture, and published the CORBAfacilities document. CORBAfacilities has completed its roadmap planning through the end of the process.

Figure 5.14 is an overview of the CORBAfacilities process. This task force followed the same process used earlier for CORBAservices and is being reused by the new domain task force areas. The OMG process starts with request for information (RFI).

Mission:

To populate the Object Management Architecture "Common Facilities" components:

1. To endorse ORB-conformant IDL code and definitions of semantics and sequencing to facilitate application interoperability.

2. To enable application interoperability in vertical market specialty areas: e.g., compound documents, electronic mail, database access.

3. To layer above and conform with the CORBA specification as well as adopted Object Services.

4. To maximize leverage of existing international and national standards as well as existing de facto interfaces in specific vertical market areas.

FIGURE 5.13   CORBAfacilities mission statement.

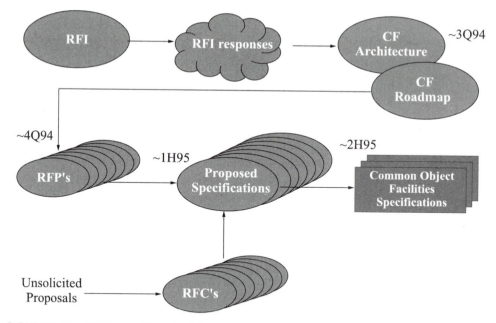

FIGURE 5.14   CORBAfacilities task force process.

5.4.4   The Request for Information Process

The RFI is a general solicitation to all members and nonmembers of the OMG to submit any kind of input that is relevant to the OMG's process in an area. The input to an RFI can include end-user requirements, descriptions of technologies and products, architectural input, and any other comments deemed relevant by the submitter. The form of an RFI submission can range from a simple E-mail submission to a formally written document. One form of submission that is encouraged is product description literature in the form of technical architecture documents that can preexist the RFI process. The submitter can make a submission package by attaching a cover letter to his or her existing documentation.

Submissions to the RFI process are reviewed by members of the OMG. The submissions are made available through the OMG's marketing capabilities, such as the OMG's World Wide Web server, as well as the file transfer protocol site. Through these public distribution capabilities, the OMG can make this submitted information available to the widest possible community and encourage further involvement by vendors and end users. Because this process is relatively mature, the OMG has been successful in creating new market areas.

Most recently, the OMG focused on the healthcare vertical market. To promote this area, the OMG created a significant liaison with the Medical

Records Institute, an organization dedicated to the resolution of interoperability needs in the healthcare market. The Institute has been tracking and facilitating standards activities in that market and is currently following more than 160 standards groups dedicated to healthcare specifications. These healthcare standards groups are pursuing more than 1,000 standards items. When the Medical Records Institute approached the OMG, it felt that at least one more standards group needed to be initiated. In particular, the OMG is able to deliver a process that converges on software interfaces and delivers commercial technology to the market, differing from most other processes in this respect.

A formal standards process, such as that of the International Standards Organization (ISO), takes from four to seven years to complete. By then, many of the original needs the market identified have evolved and changed. Because the OMG process produces specifications responsively, it is able to anticipate market needs and deliver products in a timely manner. The OMG has also been successful in keeping a future orientation so that the technologies are not easily made obsolete by future investments and innovations. In fact, the use of IDL is an important factor in isolating the specifications and technologies that depend on the underlying infrastructure of the networking software, which is undergoing constant innovation and obsolescence. In this way, specifications can outlive the product lifecycle of an infrastructure release and survive the evolution and lifecycle of end-user mission-critical applications.

The RFI process at the OMG is an important step in initiating the coordination of industry. Since the RFI is a solicitation to members and nonmembers, it represents a survey of the global-level market. Organizations that are concerned can identify what needs and technologies are related to OMG future adoptions. Once the RFI process is complete, it is the responsibility of the OMG members in the task force (and no one else) to define the architecture and begin the adoption process through RFPs and RFCs.

The RFI process has another important aspect in that once this process is initiated, the RFI notifies organizations that the OMG is at work in an area. The RFI creates a way for organizations to participate in the process in a predictable way and establishes a deadline for organizations to submit their input. The fact that there is a process in place and a deadline for response is often a critical decision factor for organizations to mobilize resources to get involved in the creation and coordination of a new market. Several areas of OMG technology went from relative inactivity to significant interest and activity through the use of a request for information process. Even if the vendors do not readily participate in the OMG process at the beginning of an RFI, it is likely they will be there at the end.

Following the deadline for the RFI is a series of one or more meetings that allow the RFI submitters to explain their input. The task force establishes an agenda in coordination with the RFI submitters that gives them a short time to present their proposals and allow for questions and discussions. These initial presentations are the first step in technology transfer among organizations, an important underlying principle in the OMG process. Without organizations understanding each other's terminology and technical approaches, at least at some fundamental level, it is impossible for them to communicate effectively and to coordinate their technologies to form cohesive markets. Because of anti-trust restrictions, the OMG cannot become directly involved in helping companies team together to create technologies. It simply facilitates the convergence of suppliers by providing a series of deadlines in a process in which they can communicate without violating anti-trust statutes.

5.4.5   Creating Architectures and Roadmaps

The RFI process, when complete, results in a brainstorming list of initial services and facilities areas that should be considered in the adoption processes of a task force. The next step is to define the architecture. The architecture uses the RFI submission as its raw materials, along with the brainstorming list of candidate facilities. The list can include some facilities not specifically documented in the RFI process because the members of the task force are responsible for defining all the areas needed for a comprehensive set of specifications.

Once these areas are organized into an architecture that includes a block diagram of categories, as well as the architecture definitions, it is important to make sure that every identified facility is well defined and agreed on. The definition of these facilities is completed by filling out the architecture template for each facility. Some proposed facilities are easily filled in by companies that are interested in those areas. In others, it is difficult for the task force to organize the resources to provide definitions of the facilities. If the task force is unable to encourage its members to define an area, the lack of interest is a legitimate reason for it to either eliminate the area from the architecture or to pursue another RFI process to help it define the technologies.

When the architecture categories are well defined, the task force can publish its architecture document for approval by the technical committee. The architecture document by itself does not identify any priorities for adoption. The definition of priorities and timeline is the role of the roadmap document (Figure 5.15), which is a list of the first few facilities that have highest priority and greatest value to the market represented by the task force. The highest priority facility in the roadmap is a candidate to be first for proposal. The request for proposal, once it is issued, initiates the adoption process. Each request for proposal adopts additional facilities to fill in the architecture areas.

For example, Figure 5.16 is a diagram of the CORBAfacilities architecture and shows the CORBAfacilities in the context of providing a layer of technologies

Cf RFP1 Compound presentation and interchange – now complete

Cf RFP2 Internationalization and time operations – 3/95 start

Cf RFP3 Data interchange and mobile agents – 11/95 start

Cf RFC1 Common management facility – 1/96 start

Cf RFP4 Business objects – 1/96 start (Note: worked by the BODTF)

Cf RFP5 Meta-object facility – 6/96 planned/designated by motion

Cf RFP6 Printing facility – 3/96 start

Cf RFP7 Asian input – 6/96 planned/designated by motion

Cf RFP8 Automation & scripting – 9/96 planned start

Cf RFC2 Workflow – 12/96 likely submission by WfMC

Cf RFP9 Rendering management – 9/96 planned start

Cf RFP10 Information storage and retrieval – 3/97 planned start

Cf RFP11 Configuration & change management – 5/97

Cf RFP12 Rule management – 8/97 planned start

Cf/ORBOS RFP Security administration – 1/98 planned start

FIGURE 5.15   CORBAfacilities roadmap.

above CORBA and the CORBAservices. CORBAfacilities provide a layer of technologies to the CORBAdomains in the applications and are organized into four facility categories: User Interface Facilities, Information Management Facilities, System Management Facilities, and Task Management Facilities. These four areas cover a universal scope of information technologies. The selection of these areas is derived from the ISO technical reference model, which is a general-purpose architecture for information technology. The facilities within CORBAfacilities are allocated to each area based on the judgment of the task force. The facilities listed include all the topics for which the task force intends to pursue adoption. It is possible that other facilities could be added to this architecture based on future need.

The Figure 5.15 roadmap is a schedule for all the facilities in the architecture, including the ones already adopted, facilities that are currently in process, and future facilities. This roadmap includes the identification of the request for comment processes, which are fast track processes. The task force does not directly control when they are initiated; they are initiated by an external unsolicited submission. However, when a task force has knowledge of an external organization, it is important to include such details in the plan. In the case of CORBAfacilities, the work flow consortium creates a set of IDL specifications for its technology area. This area was already incorporated into the facilities

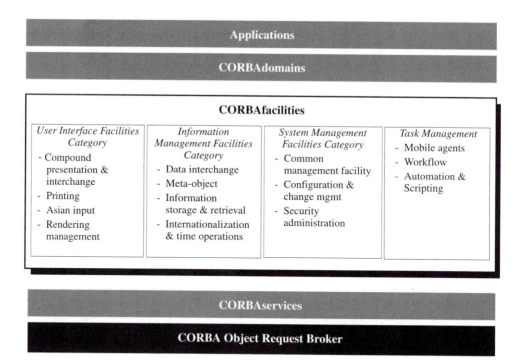

FIGURE 5.16   CORBAfacilities architecture.

architecture and will be carried forward. Because of the recent reorganization of the OMG and the addition of the CORBAdomains areas, the facilities formerly called the vertical-market facilities in the CORBAfacilities architecture have been delegated to the other technical committee, the domain technical committee. The remaining facilities in the CORBAfacilities architecture and roadmap represent the horizontal common facilities, which are generically applicable across domains.

Some of the important future facilities' adoptions are shown in the roadmap (Figure 5.15). The Automation and Scripting Facility of RFP 8 is an extension to the previous facilities for compound documents. The automation and scripting areas add electronic control of compound document applications and other objects, which is important for integrating systems and applications. The adopted technology should address the Microsoft OLE controls and Active X technologies, as well as other important technologies, such as the Component Integration Labs' OpenDoc scripting capabilities. The designation of future RFP numbers is drafted in the roadmap document, but the actual formal designation is made by decision of the task force at the time of the initiation of the process.

5.4.6   RFP Adoption Processes

The OMG adopts specifications through two processes: request for proposal (RFP) and request for comment (RFC). The RFC process is also called the fast track process and is modeled after the Internet adoption process. It is used when a specification is in an area of little controversy. The lack of controversy may be because it is a specialized area in which only a small set of organizations have strong vested interests. The other case is in an area where there is an external consensus outside the OMG with respect to a facility.

Two RFCs are the Ada95 mapping specification and the X/Open common system management specification. In the first case, the Ada95 specification was in an area of a specialized market in which there was little opportunity for controversy, given the specialty nature of the technology. The proposers were able to create a quality specification based on work by Silicon Graphics and other organizations and put together a quality binding between Ada95 and the CORBA IDL that proceeded through the RFC process without opposition. An RFC is reviewed by a task force organization and, if it is successful, is recommended to the architecture board and the technical committee for release. Once the RFC is released, there is a 90-day comment period, when anyone, including members and nonmembers of OMG, can submit comments. If significant comment, as determined by the OMG, is made on a specification, the adoption process may be derailed. Any comments are made available to the OMG membership prior to the adoption vote. The X/Open system management specification is an example of an external consensus for which another large consortium group, X/Open, created a quality specification and worked with the OMG to review this technology and adopted it through the fast track process.

Each RFP starts with an architectural description, which may be contained in the task force architecture. If this is a new facilities area, a new architectural definition needs to be created for the process to proceed. The definitions contained in the task force architecture are just the starting point for the authoring of the RFP. The actual text in the RFP is edited by members of the task force to make sure it is responsive to the current needs of the market.

For example, in the CORBAfacilities architecture and roadmap, another important RFP is RFP 9 for rendering management. Rendering management addresses the remaining interfaces for windowing and graphics not covered under the first RFP, compound document presentation. These interfaces are an important technology for portability. Current Rendering Management Interfaces are quite implementation-specific. Many programmers develop their application code in such way that it is hardwired to a hardware and operating system platform. The Rendering Management Facilities would allow the definition of efficient windowing capabilities and graphics capabilities. These capabilities would be defined in a way that is independent of any operating system, platform, or even language binding. This significance of the Rendering Management Facility is to enhance the portability of applications.

One important candidate technology discussed by the OMG is Fresco, a reference technology that is widely available through the X/Consortium's X-Windows X11R6. Fresco is being developed internally by Fujitsu Corp. for the commercial market. The technology was originally submitted as a candidate for RFP 1 but was withdrawn and reserved for a future submission.

The CORBAfacilities RFP 10 for information, storage, and retrieval is a higher-level facility for the integration and interoperation of information resources. This technology could include some current Internet technologies, such as wide-area information services and the World Wide Web. Information, storage, and retrieval could also include specializations of the OMG's query service, a fundamental set of interfaces for queryable objects that includes the definition of interfaces that support existing query languages, such as the structured query language and the object query language.

CORBAfacilities RFP 11 addresses system configuration control in the Change Management Facility. Configuration in the Change Management Facility was highly rated as important to the OMG's end users. There is an ongoing adoption for interface versioning in the ORB object services task force. The interface versioning RFP addresses the ability to store versions of the IDL in the Interface Repository. The extensions to the on-line definitions, which are introduced through RFP 5, the Meta-Object Facility, also require versioning support. The configuration in the Change Management Facility will define how the Meta-Object Facility supports version control. Many vendors are expected to work on this area and end users prefer to see the vendors coordinate their technologies through the OMG process and the definition of a standard set of interfaces. The RFP 12 is planned for rule of Management Facilities, which address the representation of knowledge, constraints, and expertise within object-oriented systems.

The final RFP on the CORBAfacilities roadmap is for security administration. The security service is an existing adopted technology at OMG and is similar to the System Management Facility in that it is only a fundamental enabling set of interfaces. Technology still needs to be added to the security service to define application architectures. The Security Administration Facility would standardize some of these additional capabilities. Because the other task force was involved in the adoption of a security service, CORBAfacilities and the ORBOS task force are expected to work together in this important area.

In this chapter, the remaining OMG specifications and activities that comprise the horizontal facilities and the vertical domains were covered. This completes the description of the OMG standards. In the following chapters we explain how to use these technologies most effectively. Most training and information teaches the mechanics of how to build simple programs using the products. The following chapters, relating more than five calendar years of CORBA applications experience that has been accumulated in management and development activities, should add to this foundation.

CORBA System Engineering

Relationships with Other Technologies

6.1 Choosing a Distributed Object Architecture

Now that the CORBA 2.0 and related standards have been covered, we return to the scenario from Chapter 1 to understand how to apply CORBA to a system development.

After reviewing the design of the legacy systems and completing the requirements for the new system, Karen's group begins to examine the options for development and integration tools. The group, however, is divided into two factions—those who want to custom build a framework for integration and development and those who prefer to use commercial products, such as OMG's CORBA, OSF's distributed computing environment (DCE) or Microsoft's distributed component object model (DCOM).

Realizing that time to market and the maintenance burden of a custom-developed framework would be detrimental to the project, Karen directs the team to assess the viability of commercial products to provide a solution. After looking at the technologies in the marketplace, the team realizes that the selection of a single solution is not a simple task. Not only do CORBA, DCE, and DCOM compete, but they also complement and integrate together at different levels. Furthermore, dependencies among related technologies in the area of compound document and frameworks require consideration. The team finally focuses on evaluating three technologies.

1. CORBA

2. DCE

3. DCOM

In addition, special consideration is given to assessing the JAVA remote method invocation (RMI) because of its similarity to the functions of the other technologies.

6.2　Analyzing the Scenario

Karen's group is faced with deciding on the best distributed architecture technology to link together the existing heterogeneous, distributed systems, as well as support rapid development of a new system. The complexity of information systems coupled with their evolutionary nature makes selecting a single approach difficult. In today's complex environment, most technologies are both competing and complementary, shown in Figure 6.1. Therefore, the focus is on selecting a primary solution but recognizing that supporting roles may be necessary.

As we examine CORBA compared with other technologies, we will examine the overlaps and the interrelationships among the technologies to establish when to select a technology and how the technologies are used in conjunction with each other.

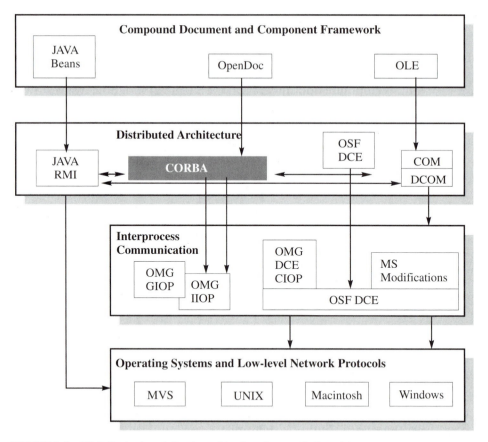

FIGURE 6.1　Distributed architectures' technology relationships.

6.3   Making an Informed Decision

CORBA provides a rich set of functionalities and capabilities. Often, the choice to use a technology is based only on these attributes. However, other considerations are equally important in the choice to deploy CORBA. Selection of CORBA should only be made after considering the following questions.

1. What does it mean when CORBA is described as a standard? The term *standard* is often used to convey openness and goodness. Unfortunately, the world of standards has become convoluted. The last 10 years has shown that there are degrees of standardization and that product availability, support, and acceptance are also important ingredients in the success of any technology.

2. How does it fit with other important technologies? No single technology can be everything to everybody. Large-scale systems require a variety of technologies working together. CORBA by its nature is an integrator of technologies and therefore addresses many issues related to integration. However, with regard to interprocess communications and compound documents, CORBA merits special attention.

3. Why was it chosen over its competitors? The two technologies typically compared to CORBA are OSF's DCE and Microsoft's DCOM. Evaluation of the technology also requires consideration of how competitive technologies are accommodated. JAVA's RMI is emerging as another potential choice for the basis of a distributed architecture.

4. Who sells and supports CORBA products? The last major consideration is product availability. Without reasonable products, selection of a technology is fruitless.

This chapter will address each of these points. Armed with this information, an organization can begin to make an informed decision about CORBA. However, because this is a book on CORBA, it will place emphasis on the comparison and selection of CORBA.

6.3.1   The Role of Standards

In Chapter 1, we introduced the role of the Object Management Group and how it is creating and evolving the CORBA standard. Standards can be used as guides in the development of information systems by organizations. With adherence to standards, products can be purchased and applications developed with confidence that hardware and software will work together for many years.

Standards are believed to improve the evolution of an organization's information systems by:

- Allowing easier change and upgrade as new technology becomes available because of their openness and availability to all participants in the marketplace

- Not locking into a vendor's proprietary products, allowing the selection of best in class because many vendors are expected to support the standard

- Limited modification or recoding of applications because of changes of standard application programmer interfaces

However, standards come in several flavors and CORBA is only one type of standard. There are two basic categories of standards.

1. Formal—A formal standard is a carefully written specification that has been adopted by a recognized standards body or an industry consortium. Participation is open to all based on some set of readily identifiable rules. The standard can be implemented by any and all.

2. De Facto, or Industry—A de facto standard is usually controlled by a vendor with significant market penetration. Product licensing is the only legitimate way to implement a product with limited input on future direction.

Both categories of standards can be acceptable to an organization, depending on their needs. However, formal standards are often viewed as the best because they provide the greater degree of openness. However, other considerations than the availability of the specification are important, including product availability, support, and acceptance. Because of the openness, formal standards are often slow in coming to market while de facto standards become so because of their ability to fill a market need. Unfortunately, de facto standards can lead to fewer choices of vendor, but they can potentially lead to greater choice of products, depending on the vendor. This is because of the nature of companies to organize their products around other successful products. Therefore, in selecting one standard versus another it is important to answer the following questions.

- What are the credentials of the organization that creates the standards?

- What organizations are involved?

- What is the state of specifications?

- What products are available and from whom?

CORBA falls within the formal standards category. Although OMG is not a government-sponsored standards organization, the breadth of membership and the openness of the offering and selection process make it a recognized entity.

Furthermore, government-sponsored standards groups are beginning to accept portions of the CORBA specifications as their own.

Standards are important to building and evolving information systems. However, even when standards are applied and enforced, problems can arise. CORBA has been fortunate in that it has seen the development of products at an accelerated rate. This required a trade-off in the lack of interoperability among products in areas in which the specification is not clear. Standards can be open to interpretation, some are intentionally left incomplete, and there are occasional conflicts among standards. CORBA has shared in this experience. Until the release of CORBA 2.0, there was no ORB interoperability, which resulted in the need for a single ORB product in an organization. Furthermore, there was no standardization on the server side of the ORB, resulting in a portability issue for server-side code. These issues have been addressed in the CORBA 2.0 release. However, constant vigilance is required in order to maintain and extend compatibility. As with all specifications, CORBA specifications comprise areas in which lack of specificity or flexibility in selection of approaches can lead to future incompatibility, especially in the areas of services and facilities.

Although there are many benefits from the application of standards, there are many things standards cannot do, including:

- Standards cannot ensure satisfactory system performance. In some cases, diversion from a standard might be necessary to achieve satisfactory performance.

- The application of standards cannot fully ensure component reliability or availability. Reliability and availability can be fully ensured only through comprehensive quality control and preventive maintenance.

- The application of standards cannot guarantee 100 percent portability of products among hardware platforms and/or operating systems. Portability problems generally arise from differing interpretations of standards.

CORBA, like all standards, shares these attributes. Care needs to be taken with the application of it or any other standard to prevent these problems.

6.4   The Underpinnings of Distributed Architectures

CORBA is a type of middleware that supports the development of applications that run in a distributed heterogeneous computing environment. It provides common services, such as communication between client and server. It is intended to insulate the application from the specifics of:

- Hardware platforms
- Operating systems

- Network protocols

- Implementation languages

The selection of these elements is based on the best combination for the organization. The selection criteria varies depending on the existing hardware and network and the knowledge level of the staff. There are CORBA implementations for all major products and standards in each area.

In the past, architects, designers, and programmers had to deal with development of distributed applications by using a variety of interprocess communication middleware. Interprocess communication is a low-level mechanism that enables application components to communicate across a heterogeneous network. CORBA also insulates the application from interprocess communication. Furthermore, it supports a variety of popular interprocess communication technologies, preserving existing usage of DCE or TCP/IP-based systems. However, where hardware, networks, operating systems, and languages are well-known elements in an organization, interprocess communications may not be as identifiable.

There is a variety of interprocess communication technologies. The most popular approach has been sockets, a low-level approach that was provided with UNIX and became the de facto standard for applications running over TCP/IP. Other technologies include message queuing and remote procedure calls.

Message queuing is often referred to as message-oriented middleware. It works by allowing applications to put messages into a queue and pull messages off a queue. It is reliable and extremely useful for asynchronous off-line processing. A variety of proprietary point solutions exist. The CORBA standard is expected to evolve to support some message queuing approaches.

Remote procedure calls have emerged as the successor to sockets as the most popular approach. However, there are a variety of implementations that do not interoperate. RPCs look like a local procedure call, a familiar paradigm for developers, but work across a network. The protocol handles the conversion and packing and unpacking of arguments and results. Some of the leading implementations in this area include the following.

- Microsoft's proprietary version, based on an extension of DCE

- OSF's DCE procedure-based functionality, which provides a rich set of services, including naming, security, and threads, and is available on a variety of platforms

- General inter-ORB protocol (GIOP) from the Object Management Group, a general mechanism optimized for ORB-to-ORB communications

When using CORBA, the architect, designer, and programmer are abstracted from the use of the interprocess communications mechanism. CORBA supports the use of either the OSF DCE through the DCE CIOP or OMG's Internet inter-ORB protocol (IIOP), an instantiation of a GIOP for TCP/IP. The selection of a vendor's ORB, the existing infrastructure, and the type of applications will dictate the use of a interprocess communication method. Ideally, the outcome at the lower levels should have little impact on applications built using CORBA. It will have impact on cost, performance, and integration with other networks. IIOP will most likely be the interprocess communications mechanism of choice in organizations.

6.5 Comparing Distributed Architectures

Selecting a product to form the basis for the organization's distributed architecture will be difficult. Fortunately, the number of choices are limited. However, no clear-cut answer exists. This section provides some guidance to help this process.

6.5.1 OSF's Distributed Computing Environment

The Open Software Foundation set out in the late 1980s to create an environment for creating heterogeneous client-server applications, shown in Figure 6.2. IBM, DEC, AT&T, Hewlett-Packard, Hitachi, Bull, Siemens, Nixdorf, and a list of others played a strong role in guiding the specifications as well as reference implementations. This led to the release of version 1.0 in 1992 and vendor products in 1993.

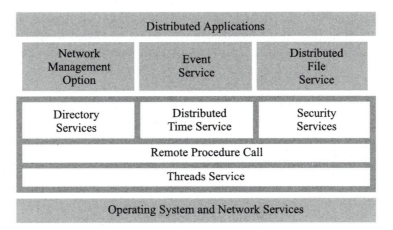

FIGURE 6.2   Distributed computing environment architecture.

DCE is a layer between the operating system/network protocols and the distributed application. DCE allows the application to view the network as a single system. Its key components are:

- Threads—Supports the management and synchronization of multiple threads of control

- Remote Procedure Call—Automated generation of code to allow procedure calls to be handled across a network; supports unique identification of resources

- Directory Service—Allows the control and management of administrative domains (or cells), including cell directory service, global directory service, and domain naming

- Distributed Time Service—Ensures the synchronization of time across computing resources

- Security Service—Maintains authentication, authorization, integrity, and privacy for all applications

- Distributed File Service—Provides the ability to access and share files without knowledge of location or local access procedures

In the future, network management and event services are intended to be offered. The network management option would allow the management of applications using the simple network management protocol (SNMP) and common management information protocol (CMIP) standard. The event service would give applications improved control over the generation and management of events on the network and among applications.

To understand the relationships between CORBA and DCE, it is important to examine the similarities and the differences. Figure 6.3 shows some of the technology interrelationships between the two distributed architectures. In general, DCE and CORBA are technologies aimed at solving similar problems using different approaches to gain acceptance in the marketplace.

Table 6.1 shows that both are on relatively similar timelines and have significant industry support.

The similarities between CORBA and DCE are striking. However, the differences shown in Table 6.2 are more striking.

DCE's roots lie in the UNIX community. It was driven by a desire to standardize the UNIX marketplace and not allow a single vendor to control its direction. CORBA came out of the object-oriented technology community, driven by the desire to have distributed interoperability of objects. The heritage of each drives the first fundamental difference—an object model (CORBA) versus a procedural model (DCE). The second fundamental difference is the scope of the services offered. DCE has chosen a focused set of services. CORBA has not only a

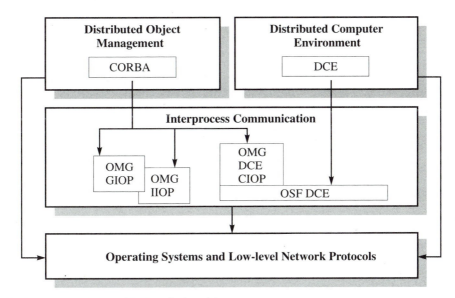

FIGURE 6.3   CORBA and DCE relationships.

broader set of services, but many are being developed at the application level. Given the breadth of this focus, CORBA has not yet reached a level of maturity in implementations that DCE has achieved, due to the scope of activity. Many services will not have implementations for several years. Recognizing the investment that organizations have in DCE, OMG specifies a DCE/CORBA gateway

Table 6.1   Similarities between CORBA and DCE

SIMILARITIES	DCE	CORBA
Problem space	Distributed, heterogeneous client-server application development	Distributed, heterogeneous client-server application development based on objects
Controlling body	Open Software Foundation —A standards-setting consortium	Object Management Group —A standards-setting consortium
Supporting organizations	Tens of vendors, including IBM, H-P, and DEC	Hundreds of vendors and users (more than 700) including IBM, H-P, DEC, and Sun
Specifications	DCE 1.0 in 1992	CORBA 1.0 in late 1991
Vendor products	Available in 1993	Available in 1993
Service similarities	Directory, time, threads, security, events, network management	Directory, time, threads, security, events, network management

Table 6.2   Differences between CORBA and DCE

DIFFERENCES	DCE	CORBA
Programming style	Procedural—can do object-oriented programming but not directly supported by DCE	Object Oriented—supports encapsulation, abstraction, polymorphism, and inheritance
Product of controlling body	Specifications, reference implementations, and validation suites	Specifications, implementation left to vendor, validation suites to be offered by X/Open
Interoperability among vendor products	DCE 1.0 in 1992	CORBA 2.0 in 1995
Data types	Handles pointers	Permits any arbitrary data type to be sent
Service differences	Provides a distributed file system	Significant number of services, including persistence, properties, query, trader, transactions, as well as facilities in the areas of user interface, information management, systems management, and task management. Lastly, services in finance, distributed simulation, and computer-integrated manufacturing
Maturity	Events and network management option under construction	Many of the services, facilities, and domain functionality are under construction
Extensible	No	Yes
Interfaces	Static invocation	Static and dynamic, invocation; IDL supports inheritance

standard. As previously discussed, CORBA already supports the lower levels of the DCE RPC through the DCE CIOP.

DCE is simpler, more mature, but more limited in scope. CORBA is complex, less mature, and virtually unlimited in scope. In some situations, it will not be either CORBA or DCE but the combination of both in the organization since CORBA can operate on top of DCE's RPC using some of the underlying functionality. However, object-oriented approaches will be the dominant method with DCE losing market share to both CORBA and DCOM, relegating DCE to a supporting role.

6.5.2   Microsoft's Distributed Component Object Model

DCOM is described as "COM with a longer wire"—an extension to the component object model (COM), as shown in Figure 6.4. COM provides operations through which a client application can connect to one or more server applications.

DCOM is the evolution of Microsoft's object technology developed in the mid-1980s.

- Dynamic Data Exchange (DDE)—A simple messaging system
- Object Linking and Embedding (OLE)—A compound document model for linking applications together
- Component Object Model (COM)—The underlying object system for OLE

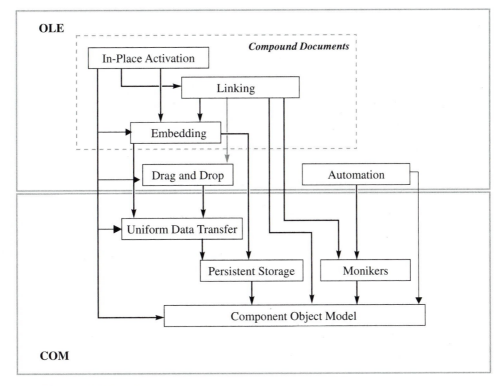

FIGURE 6.4   COM architecture.

OLE is best known as a compound document framework. Recent extensions to OLE extended this notion to a fully functional desktop integration framework. The services provided by OLE are:

- Compound Documents—The ability to link information in a document through three services.

    1. In-Place Activation—Allows container applications to display component objects, providing the user with an ability to edit component applications operations

    2. Linking—Provides access to common data with updates

    3. Embedding—Provides a separate copy of source data into container objects

- Drag-and-Drop—Adds OLE objects to Windows drag-and-drop

- Automation—A dispatch service to control applications and provide features similar to the dynamic invocation mechanism of CORBA

The component object model provides the basic communications mechanism on which all the other services rely:

- Uniform Data Transfer—Extends the clipboard to handle OLE objects

- Monikers—Naming of objects; limitations include names being server-specific

- Persistent Storage—Stores multiple objects within a container object provided by the compound files service

All of these services were designed and developed from a desktop perspective.

In addition to DCOM, Microsoft introduced ActiveX, described as "COM enabled for the Internet." ActiveX has been used to describe components used to develop Internet applications, as well as the over-arching technology that includes DCOM, COM, and OLE, also referred to as the active platform.

One of DCOM's key distinctions is its specification of a binary interface standard that is supposed to provide better portability than CORBA. However, the reliance on the WIN32 API eliminates portability in circumstances in which it is not available on UNIX or MVS.

DCOM and CORBA are similar in limited respects, described in Table 6.3. Both are integration frameworks based on object technology.

The differences, shown in Table 6.4, between the two technologies are in maturity and single vendor versus group control.

Microsoft's dominance in the personal computer industry will make DCOM a significant player in distributed object architectures. However, the focus on

Table 6.3   Similarities between CORBA and DCOM

SIMILARITIES	DCOM	CORBA
Object model	Yes	Yes
Standards body	Recently made formal; managed by the Active Group, an Open Group affiliate	Formal; managed by the Object Management Group
Interface similarities	Microsoft IDL allows for separation of interface and implementation and provides a repository for storage of interfaces (although the IDL definition is not complete).	CORBA IDL allows for separation of interface and implementation and provides a repository for storage of interfaces.
Language independence	Yes	Yes
Compound document model	Yes—object linking and embedding (OLE)	Yes—OpenDoc
Location transparency	Yes	Yes

the desktop will not be enough for most integration problems. Microsoft's ability to make DCOM an enterprise-wide solution remains questionable.

Digital Equipment Corp. (DEC), working with Microsoft, has developed an extension, DEC's common object model (COM). COM should not be confused with the component object model, also abbreviated as COM. The DEC common object model is an extension from DEC and Microsoft that allows OLE messages to be mapped into ORB messages.

DEC's COM is built on a DCE-based remote procedure call (RPC). It allows CORBA requests to be sent to OLE-based objects. Requests from OLE are also mapped into CORBA requests. However, only a subset of requests are supported.

This gateway approach has several underlying issues that need to be evaluated before using a hybrid integration framework approach, including the following.

- Performance—Gateways require a translation of requests instead of a direct request.

- Service limitations—Gateways do not allow complete utilization of all services and features.

Table 6.4 Differences between CORBA and DCOM

DIFFERENCES	DCOM	CORBA
Focus	Desktop first; enterprise second	Enterprise first; desktop second
Platforms	Windows NT; future support for Windows (all versions), Macintosh, UNIX (various), and MVS	MVS, UNIX (various), Windows (all versions), Macintosh
Availability	Single vendor; availability from other vendors expected	Multivendor
Service differences	ActiveX—interactive content standard	Significant number of additional services, including query, trader, transactions, as well as facilities in the areas of information management and systems management. Lastly, services in areas such as finance, distributed simulation, and computer-integrated manufacturing
Maturity	NT shipped in 1996; decade-long evolution of OLE and COM products; most services and facilities under construction	Products since 1992; many services and facilities under construction
Language Binding	C, C++; working on JAVA, Visual Basic, Ada	C++, Smalltalk, Ada95; JAVA and COBOL in process
Interface inheritance	Supports aggregation but not inheritance; interfaces are not classes	Multiple inheritance; interfaces are classes

- Operations and maintenance complexity—Maintaining organizational knowledge of two technologies increases the overall complexity of the system. However, gateways reduce the design complexity for the system.

In the end, both DCOM and CORBA will have to coexist. DCOM does not currently support the entire enterprise, and Microsoft's ability to deliver feasible technology across the enterprise has been marginally successful. However,

Microsoft's dominance on the desktop cannot be ignored, requiring a coexistence between the two.

6.5.3   JavaSoft's JAVA and the Remote Method Invocation (RMI)

The JAVA programming language has strengthened the World Wide Web by extending it from an environment of static content to a dynamic content and functionality environment. The standard implementation of JAVA provides the capability for JAVA objects residing on a server to be downloaded to a client for execution. This is fundamentally different from CORBA, through which a client requests service from an object in another server, shown in Figure 6.5.

The key to JAVA's success is its bytecode specification, which allows it to ship JAVA code to different platforms and guarantees it to function the same. The bytecodes ensure the binary compatibility of objects across platforms. However, note that there are some floating-point issues hampering this guarantee. Because of the nature of JAVA, software upgrade issues are significantly reduced while

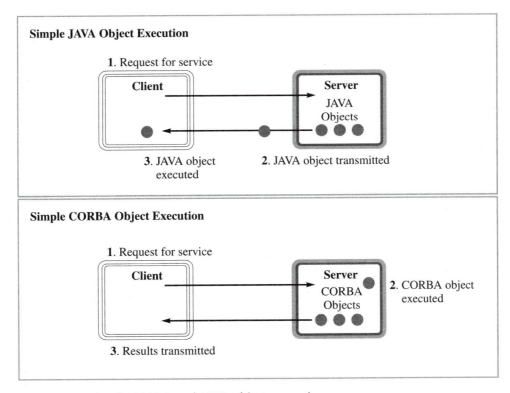

FIGURE 6.5   Simple CORBA and JAVA object execution.

allowing clients to dynamically increase functionality by downloading new classes.

However, JAVA was significantly hampered by the lack of an underlying distributed object architecture. The language did not provide any distribution services; objects from an application were required to reside on a single server. Furthermore, the objects were time-perishable and lost all state information when inactive.

The combination of JAVA and CORBA appears to be a logical choice. Unfortunately, JAVA is evolving separately from CORBA, adding in features that overlap. The JAVA RMI is the beginning of a distributed object architecture and helps to solve the two problems mentioned. It allows you to create JAVA objects whose methods can be invoked from another virtual machine.

In the end, JAVA will either have to fully develop all the capabilities of CORBA or integrate with them. One promising integration of these technologies is being accomplished through IDL. JAVA IDL allows the definition of remote interfaces that can be compiled to generate JAVA interface definitions and is based on the CORBA standard.

Independent of how JAVA evolves with CORBA, the OMG is working to integrate JAVA with CORBA. This is a good step forward but will need to be carefully considered with respect to other OMG standards. As an example, JAVA does not have a full compound document framework, but it does provide JAVA Beans, which has many of the same attributes as OpenDoc. This will require the OMG, rather than Javasoft, producer of the technology, to reconcile the overlaps.

6.6   Interworking with CORBA

Over the next years, the real competition for distributed architectures will be between CORBA and DCOM and will exist at several levels, including the ORB, OLE, and OpenDoc compound document frameworks; JAVA integration; and ActiveX. DCE will continue to lose market share to both of these competitors. The role for DCE will be relegated to the use of its RPC technology. DCOM will operate using Microsoft's derivative of the DCE RPC, and CORBA will provide direct support through the DCE CIOP.

The OMG will take a lead in standardizing the integration of JAVA and CORBA, as well as providing DCOM connectivity. This work is currently underway and should show results later in 1997. However, both JAVA and DCOM will evolve independently and, without active support for interfaces and gateways from JavaSoft and Microsoft, a long-term solution will not be provided. JAVA's independent evolution will result in instances in which the developer will have to choose between overlapping services provided by both JAVA and CORBA. This situation will occur with JAVA and DCOM as Microsoft includes support for

JAVA. The most significant manifestation of this overlap problem will be at the user interface where OpenDoc, OLE, and ActiveX will conflict with JAVA Beans.

Most organizations will need to use both CORBA and DCOM in conjunction with JAVA. The OMG task force working on the interoperability specifications between the two architectures will make this integration possible. Figure 6.6 shows a sample CORBA/JAVA configuration.

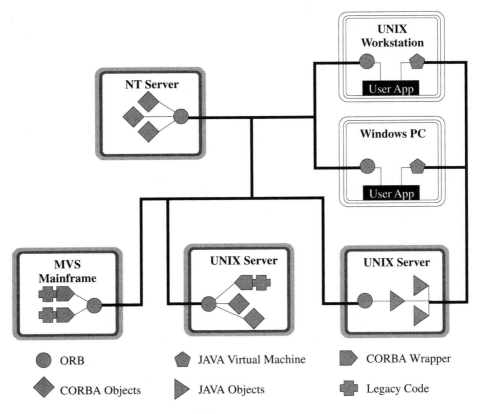

FIGURE 6.6   A CORBA and JAVA solution.

Figure 6.7 shows a CORBA/DCOM enterprise solution. CORBA's strength is the ability to combine the technologies to gain the most leverage achievable from each.

6.7   CORBA Selection and Application

Once a decision is made to use CORBA, the organization faces a variety of alternative sources from which to purchase a CORBA solution. The best vendor is one dictated by the organizations unique environment. This section provides some guidance to selecting and using a CORBA product.

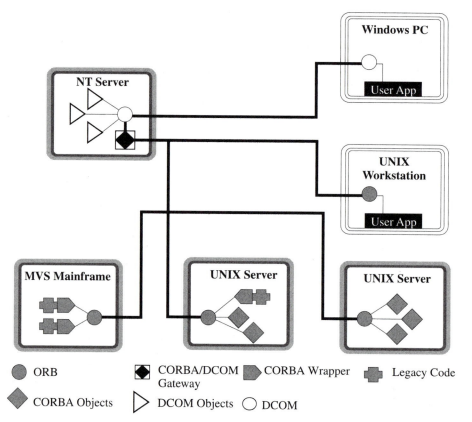

FIGURE 6.7 A CORBA and DCOM solution.

6.7.1   **CORBA Product Selection**

Distributed object management as an emerging technology has become a key component of many vendors' strategies. The OMG has created an environment in which CORBA is the solution for many vendors. Several unbundled CORBA ORB products are now available from a variety of vendors (with new vendors constantly appearing), which include:

- Visigenic
- SunSoft
- IONA
- ICL
- IBM
- Hewlett-Packard

- Expersoft
- BEA (formerly DEC's product)

Each of these vendors can supply products that are compliant with CORBA specifications, although not with all the specifications and not all with current versions of the standards. With the exception of DOS (although some vendors claim to be working on an implementation) all the major system platforms are supported—MVS, VMS, OS/400, various UNIX implementations, all Windows implementations, and Macintosh. Products that are not CORBA 2.0 compliant require that the same ORB product be used across platforms.

Selection of a product will be based on a variety of factors. Generic factors that an organization needs to consider are:

- Does it support the five basic functions of CORBA?
  1. Object request broker
  2. Basic object adapter
  3. Dynamic invocation interface
  4. Interface definition language
  5. Interface and implementation repositories
- Is it compliant with the current version of the specifications from OMG?

The product should provide all the necessary infrastructure for the ORB. Furthermore, this infrastructure must be up-to-date to ensure that it represents the latest fixes and features. Further consideration needs to be given to the richness and breadth of the product, which include asking the following questions.

- Which operating system platforms are supported?
- Which interprocess communications styles are supported?
- Which language bindings are supported?
- Which CORBAservices are supported? Special consideration should be given to support for basic services.
  — Lifecycle
  — Naming
  — Events
  — Persistent Objects
- Are key advanced services supported?
  — Transactions
  — Security
- What unique features are provided?

The widest variety of choices represents the best value for an organization, allowing it to preserve existing investment while evolving to meet new demands. Services provide productivity increases by implementing features to reduce development burdens.

In addition to the generic factors, an organization will have to consider the following requirements that influence selection.

- What are the organization's existing vendor relationships?
- Which languages does the organization use for development?
- What are the existing and future computer platforms in the organization?
- What are the organization's performance requirements?

Lastly, the organization will want a vendor that will support it over the long term. This is not to suggest that a large vendor is better than a small company. Financially sound small companies can provide high quality coupled with attention and dedication to a focused product line. The two key questions to be answered about a vendor are:

- What is the vendor's track record for delivery on promises?
- How financially sound is the vendor?

Armed with these questions and answers, a selection can be made with regard to a CORBA supplier. The most basic question that needs to be addressed is whether to support a single vendor's implementation on all platforms or use multiple vendors' implementations of CORBA. In the latter case, support for CORBA 2.0 is critical.

6.7.2 Issues in the Effective Application of CORBA

CORBA is a relatively new and promising technology that is rapidly maturing. Many benefits have been discussed, but there are a number of issues that must be addressed by an organization preparing to use CORBA for mission-critical information systems. The issues that revolve around the application of CORBA are:

- Complexity of capabilities
- Performance
- Availability

As with any complex technology, appropriate planning and budgeting for training and tool-up must be accomplished prior to taking on any significant activity. CORBA's richness of functionality requires that time be taken to understand the nuances of its capabilities. Impatience with the technology will lead to shortcuts or use of other technologies that are easy to start with but reach their limitations with a large project. The benefits of a CORBA product will accrue over time. Furthermore, because CORBA is central to the overall architecture, the entire team must be trained.

Poor performance is often a key failure point for a system. CORBA's overhead as a broker between components is relatively minimal when compared with other mechanisms and frameworks. However, performance will vary among vendor implementations. Without appropriate training and experience, a team can be expected to make some poor choices that lead to performance bottlenecks. A specific area of concern related to performance revolves around real-time systems. CORBA's focus and specifications are often in conflict with the needs of real-time system development. Therefore, in some real-time systems, CORBA may not be appropriate. However, there is a special interest group in OMG addressing this issue.

Lastly, the richness of the CORBA specifications, coupled with the speed at which these specifications are produced, leads to lags in available implementations. Some advanced services and facilities are unavailable as products. Incompleteness of some specifications can lead to differences in vendor implementations and require an organization to work around the deficiencies. OMG continues to work to resolve major problems in a timely fashion, and many of the major issues have been resolved. Small issues will continue to be identified as usage expands. The benefit to a continually expanded set of services and functions is the reduction in development time that will be seen when products are released by the domain standards groups.

The choice of using CORBA (or similar products) is not if, but when. The need is strong for reduction in the complexity of building information systems. Cleaner architectures and a move to $N + 1$ versus N-by-N interfaces is required to achieve these reductions in complexity. Furthermore, the organization must apply CORBA with broader software engineering concepts, involving analysis and design techniques, reuse and reengineering, as well as an understanding of basic object-oriented techniques to achieve full benefits.

The CORBA Migration Process

7.1 Migrating to a CORBA Architecture

During the time the team takes to select the underlying technology for the new application development, Karen contemplates the type of activity undertaken. She recognizes that the role of information systems in the organization continues to increase, yet the ability of the information staff to deliver gets increasingly difficult. The new application has become a watershed event in the information systems of the company. The role of integration has come to the forefront. Karen feels the burden of the applications that will follow, even as the pressure builds for the one in progress.

The need for an orderly migration of the current architecture to a distributed, object management-based architecture is a critical part of Karen's thinking as she refines the program plan. She is concerned over the difficulties that she will face with her team. Her biggest concern is lack of guidance for the transition. The pace of technology change rarely provides an adequate number of successful models. Furthermore, corporations able to make the change usually do not discuss their methods, preferring to keep them as a competitive advantage. Karen begins the process of trading off how much risk she can take on in this application versus positioning the company for future developments.

7.2 Analyzing the Scenario

Every major corporation will eventually be faced with the same situation Karen faces. As the Internet and electronic commerce take on larger roles in corporate business, the engines for new applications will be the old business logic and data represented in the existing information systems. Integration will be the dominant activity. Distributed object management systems like CORBA will greatly ease the burdens of the organization, but this will require fundamental change in the existing infrastructure.

The real issue for the information system groups will be how the migration process is handled. No longer can organizations start with a clean sheet of paper and completely change their information systems. Orderly migrations will be required. The best migrations will be those accomplished through the design and implementation of explicit architectures that are not embedded into the application design. The difficult chasm to be crossed by the organization will be to accept and manage the additional risk placed on the organization during the initial transition.

7.3   Enterprise Migration

One of the most important aspects of migration to CORBA is architecture, in particular, the establishment of quality interfaces at key system boundaries defined by using the IDL. In order to maximize the benefits of CORBA, designers and implementers must think differently about software interfaces, as well as change the processes and practices that define software architecture.

An IDL interface represents an opaque boundary between software modules. A boundary may be necessary because it defines the traversal of a complex barrier, such as a heterogeneous distributed network. The boundary may separate key pieces of software for reuse or other reasons.

In the following chapters, a process for migrating systems to CORBA through the design and development of quality IDL interfaces is explained. This process is based on our experience of building multiple CORBA-based systems, as well as on years of experience with successful and unsuccessful projects. The ideas are also confirmed by the guidance of leading industry thinkers for the same reason it is believed successful projects became successful: CORBA is an outstanding design and development environment. The proposed process for migration to CORBA exploits the best practices that lead to robust systems by exploiting the advantages of CORBA with a new focus on object-oriented (OO) architecture.

The migration to CORBA is a unique opportunity to improve information systems and provide many significant benefits. The benefits of migration to CORBA are primarily derived from improvements in software architecture and not from the benefits of the underlying technology. Migration to improved architecture is the most important aspect of migration to CORBA. CORBA provides significant opportunities for improving software architecture. For example, CORBA provides separation of application software from the underlying infrastructure. Much of the software that was previously required to build distributed systems is now part of stubs and skeletons that are automatically generated by the ORB. This allows developers to have a greater focus on the application-domain functionality, which is critical to business needs. An important lesson learned, through other people's experiences, is that if CORBA is adopted without changing the way information systems are built, the results of migration will not provide significant benefits. In fact, the likely outcome of migration is the same kind of brittle stovepipe system that has been the majority product of software engineering in the past.

There are many motivations and forms for migration. For example, migration can be the result of business process reengineering, a popular activity involving rethinking fundamental business assumptions and restructuring the organization. At the same time, to enable the new business processes, information technology support needs to be put in place. Firms that specialize in business process reengineering have created significant backlogs of migration work. This systems integration and information technology work results from helping numerous organizations to reengineer. Business process reengineering can be a traumatic process, particularly with respect to getting information technology to support and adapt to new business needs.

7.3.1   Architecture-Driven Migration

Software engineering is unique in that it is heavily driven by risk. About one-third of software projects result in project cancellation because the project cannot deliver the desired system [Johnson 1995]. Management loses confidence in the ability of the information systems department to deliver the desired results when they fail to deliver promised functionality on-time and on-schedule. Only about one-sixth of software projects are actually considered successful. If you undertake a software project, according to the odds, you have only one chance in six of achieving success and the other five chances are likely to be a significant disappointment. These consequences are viewed as closely related to software architecture. Architecture-driven development is the primary successful approach, according to Grady Booch's guidance in his 1996 Addison-Wesley-Longman book, *Object Solutions*. This primary role of architecture has been confirmed by the Software Engineering Institute and many other organizations [Shaw 1996].

CORBA is the technology that brings architecture issues to the foreground and is a technology for large-scale, distributed system development. Architecture comprises the technical plan for how system components are organized and interoperate. The larger the software scale, the more important planning becomes. CORBA separates interface from implementation, which allows architecture to be defined independent of how it is implemented. Many implementation decisions can be delayed to compile time and run time. CORBA introduces the IDL notation, useful for defining boundaries in software architecture.

Additional reasons for migration can include downsizing, cost reductions, and enterprise integration. All of these forms of migration are driven by business prerogatives. It is the responsibility of information technology professionals to implement support for the business decisions that lead to these types of changes. CORBA is a key technology for helping organizations to achieve these objectives.

Figure 7.1 shows one of the key paradigm shifts that needs to occur in order to survive a successful migration. From project experience, most developers are familiar with a requirements-driven development process. In this kind of development, the key drivers in the project are based on the external view of the system. Requirements-driven development focuses on externally visible attributes of the system, which are the key priorities in system development. Projects driven exclusively by external requirements often result in poor architectural solutions. A typical outcome is a system that uses many interfaces and access mechanisms, resulting in a confusing and unmanageable software structure. Emphasis on the external requirements usually leads to ad hoc internal integration approaches that result in brittle systems.

Changes in requirements are one of the key drivers in system lifecycle costs. In fact, it is estimated across all software projects that about one-third of software development costs are due to changes in requirements during development [Horowitz 1993]. About three-fourths of costs during operations and maintenance are because of system extensions. In other words, changes in requirements drive changes in the information technology. The development of

Requirements-Driven Architecture
- Different Access Mechanisms
- Ad Hoc Integration Approach
- Comingled Interfaces and Implementations
- Implementation Varies from Design

CORBA-Based Software Architecture
- Common Object Request Broker
  - Common Access Mechanisms
- Common Object Services
- Common Facilities
- Common Software Interfaces
- Common Standards

FIGURE 7.1   Requirements-driven architecture versus CORBA-based architecture.

a highly adaptable system is essential to the development of a successful system that minimizes costs. This applies to costs incurred during development and, more important, during the operations and maintenance phase of the lifecycle.

7.3.2   Conformance Between Architecture and Implementation

Other important issues in software development are projects that have intermingled designs of their software interfaces and their implementation. It is easy to define interfaces that are tightly coupled to implementations. A more challenging approach (the one that is recommended) is the design of interfaces that provide isolation between software subsystems. This book shows that it is feasible and highly beneficial to provide independence from specific implementations.

Another issue we frequently encountered is architecture and design models that vary from the implementation. This is a conformance gap between the design documentation and the actual implementation. The conformance gap begins during initial system development and increases throughout the system lifecycle. Each time a change is made, one is tempted not to modify and update the documented models of the system. Once a design specification becomes outdated and inaccurate it becomes useless. Note that only one specification is likely to be kept up to date with the system. There are no well-known examples of systems that have multiple models, such as multiple analysis and design models, that are able to keep them all up to date. It is more likely that there are systems that generate design models up front as part of the initial development. Once the system is built, documentation is reluctantly updated to reflect the implemented design.

In order to change this particular way of thinking, it is important to have a single model that provides a practical representation of the system. For example, this model should be a useful tool for the developers involved in software operations and maintenance. If the audience for the documentation continually receives benefits from it, they are more likely to consider it vital to keep that model up to date. If there are no documented models of the system other than the software itself, you have a system that has no architecture. Software systems are implementations that comprise a large number of details. No individuals can keep track of these details sufficiently to keep the original architectural vision intact. This is particularly true after multiple overlapping system modifications.

An alternative to legacy approaches to system development is the use of a CORBA-based software architecture. CORBA provides some immediate solutions to some of these issues. CORBA's ORB is a unification of all the integration mechanisms in the system. In fact, when a CORBA-based system is built, CORBA interfaces are layered over any legacy mechanisms, which leverages integration and minimizes software modification. There still may be multiple mechanisms in the system, but CORBA is used as the common backbone for all the ways of integrating within the environment. Because CORBA is the target infrastructure, new system extensions continually eliminate legacy mechanisms as migration progresses. CORBA becomes the majority infrastructure in the target architecture through direct integration of new software.

CORBA unifies multiple key capabilities within the scope of the object management architecture. For example, CORBA unifies the object services within a system through the CORBAservices interfaces. CORBAservices address many of the typical integration needs often reinvented by developer as they build systems. Other important interfaces that provide development leverage include the CORBAfacilities and the CORBAdomains, as they become available.

7.3.3   Migration to Commonality

The key concept behind successful migration, which results in sustained benefits, is a migration to commonality. Commonality includes common interfaces, common system conventions, and common standards and guidelines. It is the missing element in existing legacy systems, which inhibits enterprise benefits, interoperability and reuse. Lack of commonality is the reason why enterprises achieve limited interoperability and is also why enterprises cannot leverage existing software to build new systems in the future.

The migration to commonality does not occur overnight. Figure 7.2 represents the challenges in the migration to commonality. With current systems, the design choices of the past are analogous to separate vertically integrated pyramids of functionality in which independent technology decisions have been made at every level of system design. These independent decisions make the technology of systems highly incompatible. Examples include incompatible interfaces, incompatible tools, incompatible commercial products, incompatible software versions, and incompatible information models. With all this incompatibility, it is difficult to reuse technology and provide interoperability across systems.

Migration can begin by considering the base level of commonality (see Figure 7.2). The base level includes the selection of software standards and common operating environment technologies that allow us to gracefully migrate multiple systems to a common operating baseline.

The next step is to migrate to common services and common software interfaces. This can occur in some initial pilot systems that define a target architecture for the organizational computing environment and then, as each new capability and system extension is added, the systems can continually migrate to this target baseline, which has the commonality built in. Figure 7.3 shows that commonality actually occurs at several levels. CORBA and related stan-

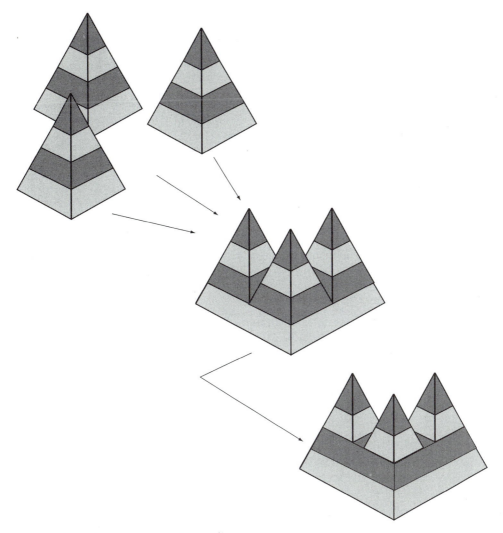

FIGURE 7.2 Migration to commonality.

dards resolve commonality issues at an intermediate level of system architecture and merge the distributed computing and application integration mechanisms, including vendor-supplied services and facilities. Other commonality issues, above and below CORBA, need to be resolved for the particular enterprise. In particular, there are numerous issues below its level that CORBA does not resolve. These issues are characterized as common system conventions.

The set of common system conventions include the choice of a standards reference model and standards profile, which define the overall migration path

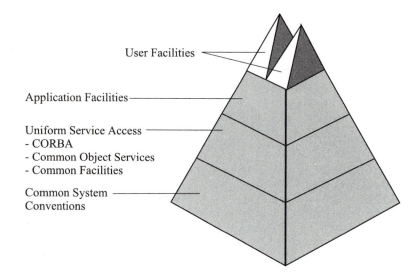

FIGURE 7.3   The need for commonality involves several levels.

for the organization. The standards reference model is the first step in defining the commonality targets for enterprise systems. Another important area of commonality conventions is the system conventions and the product selections for the operating environment. For example, it is important to define particular ranges of platforms and operating system releases that are supported in the enterprise. It is equally important to provide autonomy to organizations. It is better to provide an attractive reward than to have excessive constraining policies within an enterprise. In defining system options, it is useful to define software products that become enterprise standards, such as ORB products, database products, and development environments. There is also a need to specify which versions of these products are currently supported. Provision of training and local support for the use of these products is a key enticement to support the enterprise-operating environment. Taking these types of common operating environment steps leads to significant enterprise benefits.

Another important area of system conventions involves the way systems are installed and set up. Vendors provide ranges of options in the ways systems are configured. These conventions are significant to interoperability and technical support. Many organizations run into serious interoperability and support problems because they set up systems differently in various parts of the same enterprise. For example, the way the file system directory structures are set up on host systems, as well as end-user desktops, is an important aspect to coordinate because it can affect system management capabilities. The capability of system management software to install and maintain licenses, guarantee that software will run effectively, and providing interoperability among systems will become increasingly important as systems are distributed and decentralized.

Some key client-server set-up policies involve software allocation. Allocation decisions are enterprise-specific. Some enterprises have established policies in which virtually all software resides on host systems. End-user desktops are simply network terminals that have relatively little localized software. By allocating in this manner, the organization can economize its computing and storage resources on a number of centralized server systems. A consequence of this approach is that it centralizes coordination and IT decision making in the organization and does not efficiently use inexpensive desktop resources.

Other important areas of system set up include licensing, security, and system management. Licensing mechanisms allow enterprises to centralize some commonly used licenses. There are some significant savings and technical support advantages. Most security mechanisms cannot be feasibly adopted unless most of these issues are resolved. Common system management and administration mechanisms are desirable in a complete set of system conventions.

Finally, some important resource management issues need to be resolved. When systems integration and migration are attempted, one often encounters serious problems separate from the issues CORBA resolves. These issues can have significant impact on an organization's ability to successfully migrate and provide interoperability across the enterprise. Legacy system implementations often assume that they monopolize the desktop environment. Legacy systems built with these assumptions often monopolize memory maps, swap spaces, and other local resources.

A key decision involves support for communication layer options (Figure 7.4). CORBA is one infrastructure technology among many that may exist in most enterprises. During the lifecycle, any software system is likely to have several integration mechanisms; each will need to be supported. Most systems will need to support at least two mechanisms during the lifecycle. One of the reasons multiple mechanisms are necessary involves the use of legacy systems and commercial technology, which may come with previously selected

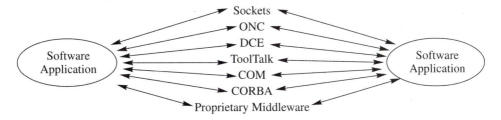

FIGURE 7.4   Communication layer options.

integration mechanisms support. Tightly coupled infrastructure mechanisms are not easy to change on preexisting software. An important strategy for surviving the migration and support of multiple mechanisms is the use of IDL, which provides a technology-neutral integration boundary. This boundary separates application software from underlying mechanisms. Many organizations have implemented this concept using both IDL and language-dependent software interfaces to achieve isolation from underlying mechanisms.

7.3.4   Migration Strategy

Migration to CORBA involves several parallel activities that may take a number of years (Figure 7.5). This time can be shortened through architecture mining and reuse of standards. The first activity that initiates migration, typically, is a business process reengineering study, which defines new information technology requirements. The definition of these requirements usually precedes the other migration activities because it sets the basic goals for information technology projects. Software architecture activities are closely aligned with business process reengineering. Architecture activities can begin soon after reengineering produces results. A periodic refinement of architectural designs should occur throughout the migration process.

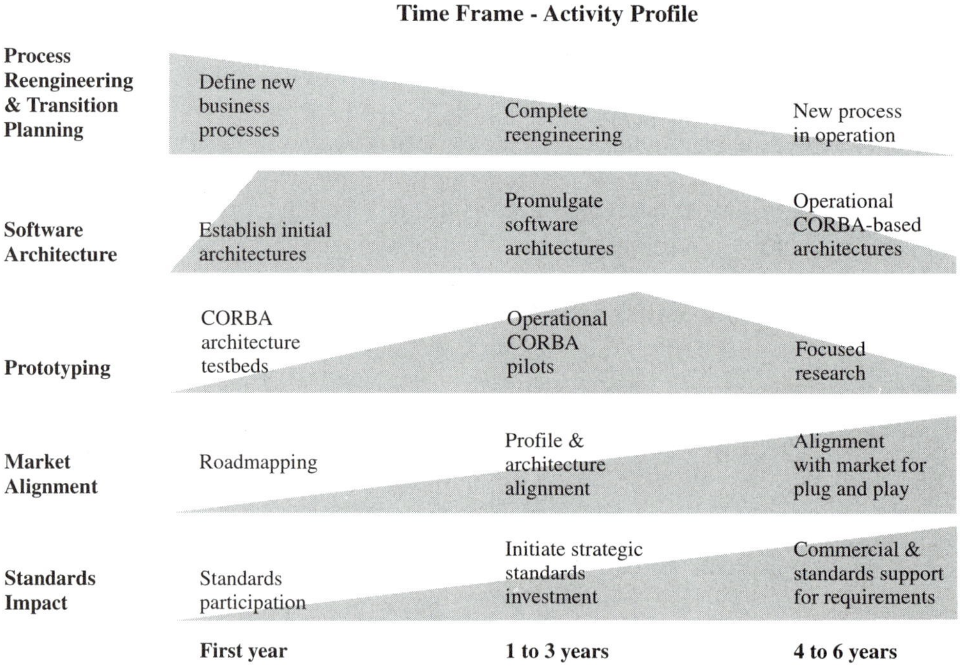

Time Frame - Activity Profile

	First year	1 to 3 years	4 to 6 years
Process Reengineering & Transition Planning	Define new business processes	Complete reengineering	New process in operation
Software Architecture	Establish initial architectures	Promulgate software architectures	Operational CORBA-based architectures
Prototyping	CORBA architecture testbeds	Operational CORBA pilots	Focused research
Market Alignment	Roadmapping	Profile & architecture alignment	Alignment with market for plug and play
Standards Impact	Standards participation	Initiate strategic standards investment	Commercial & standards support for requirements

FIGURE 7.5   Overview of migration strategy.

Design of software architecture alone will not lead to significant benefits. There needs to be concurrent prototyping activities to prove the benefits and discover the weaknesses of the architecture. Architecture and prototyping are closely aligned activities. One generates specifications; the other exercises those specifications and proves their benefits. The upcoming chapters will show that design activity and prototyping activity are intended to be coordinated but mutually exclusive. Configuration control of design during prototyping is important to providing a stable environment for developers. This enables developers to work in parallel. Evaluation of the effectiveness of architectural design can occur on only relatively stable designs. Proper configuration control enables the refinements of architecture to progress toward higher quality and increased stability.

Additional activities critical to the migration process include market alignment and standards impact. Market alignment entails an assessment of current and future technologies. To leverage commercial innovation and minimize risk, technology choices need to follow the mainstream of the technology market. Market alignment results in technology strategies, reference models, and operating environments.

Since many key forces of software engineering are driven by risk, users need to use the knowledge of the technology market to avoid risky technology choices. Any project can successfully tolerate only a small amount of technology-induced risk. It is feasible for many projects to take on only one or two bleeding-edge risk areas without creating undo risk for the entire project. Examples of risk areas include beta-test products, innovation-phase technologies, financially unstable technology suppliers, and low-volume software products. Software projects that attempt to take on half a dozen or so risk areas simultaneously usually produce negative results.

Risk areas can apply to advanced technologies, but they also apply to particular products and their releases. For any given software project, certain platform choices are better supported than others. If a software project chooses a software product release that has low support priority, this can become a significant risk area. For example, the product can be withdrawn or the product may not work at all. Experience has shown that it is important to evaluate these risks and to make project decisions based on rational decision-making processes. Subjective requirements and decisions frequently lead to choices with high technology risk.

The final migration activity involves standards impact. Every software architecture and software project has its own specifications. Because most standards are generic, most projects have a significant portion of specifications unique to those systems. As the OMG adds to its suite of adopted specifications, it expands into the vertical-market areas and the percentage of specifications unique to each system can decrease. Many organizations will be developing high-quality enterprise solutions defined in IDL. Organizations can take their designs back to the standards group or comparable enterprises and form technology agreements that change the technology markets in their favor. Vertical-market vendors can use this strategy to gain technology leadership in a market. Technology consumers can use this approach to drive the commercial markets in directions that minimize their costs and risks most effectively.

CORBA and Software Architecture

8.1   Defining a Software Architecture

After significant discussion and disagreement, Karen's team settles on using the CORBA standard as the basis for developing the new business-critical application, as well as for future development. A natural tendency of the group is to jump right into the development of the application, wrapping IDL interfaces around existing applications that will be used as components of the new application, as well as designing and implementing the required new functionality. However, the team lead for the selection process recommends that before beginning application design, the overall software architecture should be established to provide guidance, constraints, and focus to the application design and development activity.

Karen feels pressure from her corporate management team to quickly bring the new application to market. Explaining to the corporate level the benefits and necessity for a software architecture is difficult, especially when the pressure is on to develop a business-critical application. However, if she does not deal with the necessity for a software architecture, she will continually be faced with difficulties in integrating new applications. Karen balances the short- and long-term needs of the company and decides to create a software architecture team. She hires some experienced CORBA architects from a consulting firm to help the team structure the software architecture process. In addition, the team's training will be augmented through a mentoring process by these experts.

Once the design of the architecture is complete, it will be implemented through a combination of purchased software and development. The implemented architecture forms a framework for development and integration of the new application.

In conjunction with the software architecture, Karen creates a run-ahead team to look at building a prototype of the new application by creating wrappers for legacy applications and purchased software. Lessons learned from the run-ahead team will be included with the software architecture to structure the final application design and implementation. The team will be used to mitigate risks by identifying the critical threads in the new application. Furthermore, training the team is enhanced through the development of the prototype application. Karen recognizes that most, if not all, of the prototype development will be thrown out.

Finally, Karen focuses her attention on the program plan and begins to identify risk areas based on the most significant unknowns and on any lack of talent or knowledge. As the pilot and software architecture are designed and implemented, she continuously refines the estimates and risk areas. The corporate management team begins to see progress as the prototype evolves. Business and technical trade-offs are worked out with each business manager based on weighing the priority of requirements against the time to market.

8.2   Analyzing the Scenario

Karen is faced with the most complex of all development situations—trying to position the corporate information infrastructure while developing a business-critical application in a distributed environment. She develops a program plan for the new service that identifies the resources (people, computers, facilities), schedule, and costs. Without an underlying architecture and a staff experienced in its use, she will not only have to develop the new application, but develop all the underlying mechanisms to integrate the capabilities. Trying to develop a plan for the application is difficult. Trying to assess the underlying architecture adds significant complexity. The difficulty of integrating each component will not be explicitly understood until the detailed design and initial coding is completed. This places the program plan at risk.

It is difficult to be a pessimistic planner because it would be impossible to defend the levels of effort without sounding uncertain. Trying to plan resource needs is difficult because of a lack of data and tools to estimate costs coupled with a lack of a detailed knowledge of system design. Furthermore, the organization's business needs do not often line up with the time to develop complex capabilities. An optimistic plan leads to unrealistic expectations and disappointment in the application and team as the system complexities are discovered. However, Karen recognizes that the implementation of a software architecture is a necessary step to get the organization situated for the next set of application challenges.

Karen also understands that the existing schedules and constraints have been set without complete knowledge. She knows she must actively manage the program plan and ensure that the business managers are constantly kept aware of the challenges and trade-offs and allowed to participate in the selection of time to market versus functionality. Karen focuses her energy on managing the expectations and gaining support. She also brings in outside talent to complement the talents of her group, knowing that without the right mix of skills, the development will not proceed.

In making the decision to move ahead with the software architecture and prototype, Karen recognizes the importance of the software architecture. She put together a program that will allow her to achieve her goals of putting the software architecture in place while managing expectations and integrating the business stakeholders into the decision-making process. She knows that in the next application development, she will have more flexibility and increased knowledge and skills that will allow her to more accurately predict costs and manage the implementation.

8.3   The Role of Architecture in Software

System integration and the establishment of information systems that provide an open environment built for change and evolution have become the critical elements of modern information system development. The key to managing these challenges lies in how the system architect handles the design of a software architecture—reusable software components, the structure that interconnects them, and the rules by which they interact and integrate. The software architecture sets the policy for all development through the establishment of rules and components.

Until recently, software architecture and application design were heavily intertwined. The software architecture was implicitly defined into the application design. This resulted in multiple software architectures across the enterprise. CORBA separates software architecture from development. The software architecture becomes the policy for all development in the system.

The reason for this intertwining was a focus on modularity and structure of the internals of the applications—an inward-looking approach rather than a dual approach of inward to the application and outward across the system. Software components and modules were interfaced in a range of approaches, often left to a programmer to select the appropriate mechanism. This resulted in a commingling of interfaces and implementation, with the interface hidden, along with the underlying implementation, to everything but the application. Furthermore, during coding and the follow-on operations and maintenance phases, the implementation was often not well represented in the documentation, making future interfacing difficult without examination of the internal structure of the source code.

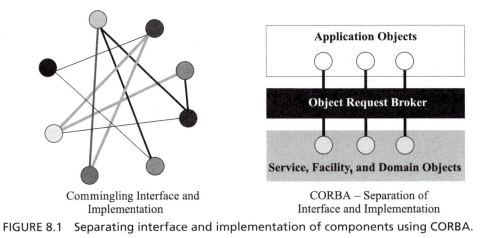

Commingling Interface and
Implementation

CORBA – Separation of
Interface and Implementation

FIGURE 8.1   Separating interface and implementation of components using CORBA.

Modularity and structure of components are necessary but not sufficient for achieving flexibility in integration. Even with modularity, it is possible to have a tightly coupled system. The structure of the interconnections and interactions is a critical element, illustrated in Figure 8.1.

Furthermore, any flexibility in integration provided by the modularity and structure of the application is often lost through the process of change when interfaces and component implementation are tightly coupled. As an example, operating system vendors have found that over time it takes increasingly longer to provide new releases of their code due to the growing complexity of the numbers of components requiring modification [Horowitz 1993]. Separating the software architecture from the application design is the key to achieving the required flexibility.

8.4   If Software Architecture Is So Important, What Is It?

The distinction between software architecture and application design is not absolute. We view software architecture as a style and method of design and construction or strategic policies and patterns that shape a system—a decoupling of access mechanisms, common services, and facilities from the application that allow an orderly arrangement of components into applications. Note that there is not one software architecture but many possibilities. Organizations need to create one based on their needs and the availability of technology in the marketplace. It is important for the organization to take control of the interfaces since the interfaces define the rules and constraints of the system.

Application design applies the rules and constraints set by the software architecture to develop an application. The application designer selects a combination of components, interfaces, and interactions from the software architecture. Application design is the work that goes on in determining the best way to build and interface a piece or component into the architecture to form an application.

Many software vendors provide the parts that form a software architecture. However, where the operating system and network software provide generic access mechanisms, services, and facilities, the software architecture we are describing provides ones that pertain to a specific enterprise. Furthermore, the software architecture owns and maintains the interfaces to each component. Finally, the software architecture supports and manages component partitioning, flow of data, flow of control, interface layering, error handling, and timing and throughput relationships.

8.4.1   The Elements of Good Software Architecture

A good software architecture for integration and evolution is one that can:

- Manage change and complexity
- Adapt to system extensions
- Minimize interdependencies among complex modules
- Allow reasonable cost estimation

In managing change and complexity, the system structure should not become so distorted that it is difficult to find where to make changes. Furthermore, designers and programmers should be able to find logical points for introducing needed extensions. The designation of components must make clear the scope of a component and relationships to other components. Finally, true reuse of services and facilities should be measurable, making it possible to accurately estimate the cost of changes or extensions.

Objects should be self-defining in the software architecture in order to support both the programmer searching for an object and a run-time client locating a service. Meta-data is the definition of the object that allows the software architecture or other objects to locate and understand its function. All too often, software architecture is thought of as an unnecessary cost. Application designers focus on making the application as efficient as possible and often do not concern themselves with the future of the application. This is a shortsighted view. Study and trend data show that the maintenance phase of an information system is two-thirds of the total system cost. Of this cost, two-thirds is spent on system improvements and one-third on defect correction and documentation. Initial design and implementation typically represents only 15 percent to 20 percent of the total cost. However, this percentage has the greatest impact on the system's ability to handle future improvements. If the architecture can allow half as much effort to modify or extend a system, it can reduce overall costs by 25 percent

[Horowitz 1993]. This does not take into account the need to connect old applications and components into new applications. Once a software architecture is in place, it is critical that everyone concerned preserve its integrity.

8.5   CORBA and Software Architecture

CORBA's specifications and resulting vendor products are based on an architectural reference model, the object management architecture (OMA), seen in Figure 8.2. This reference model is defined in such a way that it is a natural fit for defining an organization's software architecture. The essence of CORBA is to provide the starting point for an organization's software architecture.

8.5.1   Models of Use for CORBA in a Software Architecture

CORBA provides the starting point for the software architecture. Selection of a different technology would lead to a different type of software architecture.

The ORB, coupled with the IDL, provides a facility for defining component interfaces and managing the flows. The services and facilities provide a basic set of functions that can be naturally extended to form a software architecture. The domain objects are standards for specific problem areas, such as financial services, and are the beginning of a tailored software architecture. The application objects are the components that are unique to the organization and make up the information system.

There are three models of use for CORBA. The first model, the most limited, is to use CORBA only as a method of communication among application

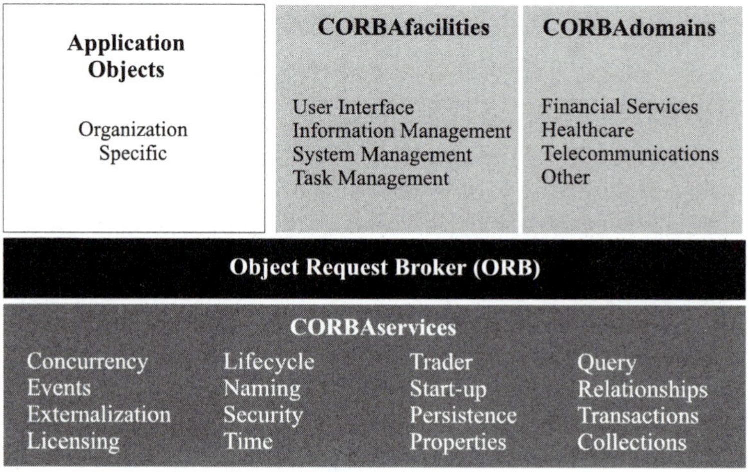

Application Objects	CORBAfacilities	CORBAdomains
Organization Specific	User Interface Information Management System Management Task Management	Financial Services Healthcare Telecommunications Other

Object Request Broker (ORB)

CORBAservices

Concurrency	Lifecycle	Trader	Query
Events	Naming	Start-up	Relationships
Externalization	Security	Persistence	Transactions
Licensing	Time	Properties	Collections

FIGURE 8.2   CORBA's architectural reference model.

objects. In this case, only the CORBA interprocess communications are used and other services are ignored. Software architecture and application design are not separated, despite our previous discussion. The rules and constraints of this model allow the architect to put all the logic into the applications and, through a trust of modularity and structure of the application components, provide a flexible system. In this instance, the benefit derived from CORBA is its ability to support integration of components, as shown in Figure 8.3, across multiple operating systems and languages. However, future changes and the ability to support these changes is based upon the implementation of the application.

In the second model, the system architect separates the software architecture and application design through the use of the CORBA generic architecture, shown in Figure 8.4, as the software architecture. To the degree that the services and facilities provided are good enough for the organization, this strategy is practical. However, in any reasonably complex system, this will not be the case. Over the long term, custom services and facilities will be developed and embedded into the application objects, leading to duplication of effort and less flexibility than required. However, this is a reasonable first step for an organization.

The last model, depicted in Figure 8.5, sees the software architect separating the design into application objects and extensions to services and facilities that are unique to the enterprise. The ORB's uniqueness in managing interfaces and component relationship, in addition to being a communication pipe, makes this not only feasible but the most desirable use of CORBA. The implementation of the software architecture through the customization and extension of CORBA provides a framework for system integration and evolution.

8.5.2   Applying CORBA to Software Architecture

In CORBA-based architecture, there is a compilable coupling between the design and implementation, as shown in Figure 8.6. As a specification notation, IDL is part of the architecture. Because it is a compilable notation, key

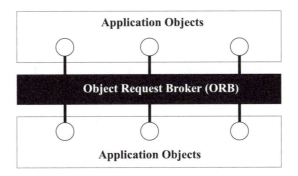

FIGURE 8.3   CORBA as a method of communication.

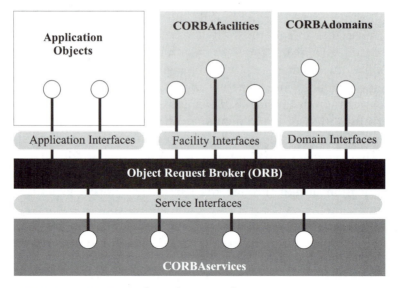

FIGURE 8.4   CORBA as the software architecture.

elements of the architecture can be automatically translated into header files, stubs, and skeleton programs. The IDL is used by programming language compilers to enforce some important architectural constraints. In particular, compilers enforce the strong typing of parameters and return values in the IDL-specified operation signatures.

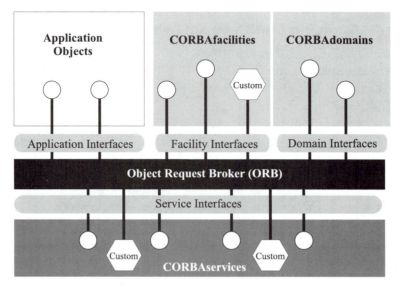

FIGURE 8.5   Customizing the CORBA generic architecture.

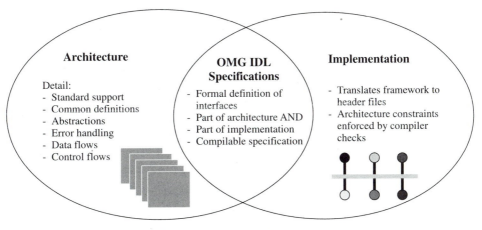

FIGURE 8.6   Coupling of architecture design and implementation.

This coupling between architecture and implementation has some important benefits. For CORBA-based architectures, it is now much easier to keep the design and the implementation synchronized. The architecture is no longer a set of separate models and design representations, but a set of tightly coupled representations that are directly utilized by developers.

Another key concept illustrated in Figure 8.6 is that the software interfaces are within the scope and responsibility of the architecture. There have been cases in which projects define architecture as relating only to the high-level concepts, such as block diagrams of the system. If the architect takes responsibility for only high-level descriptions, the design of the software interfaces is delegated to subsystem developers, who will not have the same vision for the system as the architecture intended.

Delegation of system interfaces from subsystem developers has consequences, including lack of coordination among software interfaces and a lack of effective management of complexity. Some architects assume that the details of the system and design implementation will support their architectural decisions. This assumption does not work in practice. The software interfaces for a system that are specified in IDL should be considered an important part of architecture. Someone must take direct responsibility for coordinating the details of these interfaces. By doing this, the architect begins to manage the details that are critical to the realization of architectural benefits. Through IDL, one can establish the architectural constraints and coordinate the appropriate levels of abstraction, complexity, and adaptability in the system.

The relationship of CORBA to software architecture is important to understand. CORBA enables good software architecture. For example, a single IDL specification has multiple language mappings. Regardless of the languages, platforms, or underlying mechanisms, only a single IDL specification is needed for defining the interfaces of a software architecture.

CORBA ORBs provide important implementation benefits, such as location transparency, which also benefit architecture. One can define IDL without having to detail how the software is allocated among processors. These allocation details can be changed when the system is installed or even modified on-the-fly, without affecting application software. This is an important advantage of CORBA compared with previous distributed computing technologies. With previous technologies, the choice of whether a software module was local or remote was hardcoded into the application software. In CORBA, it is possible to use IDL in places that are distributed and local. IDL should be used for all software interfaces that provide shared or reusable design interfaces. For these interfaces, the decision of whether the software objects are local or remote can then be made independently.

Location transparency is a capability that does not always have to be used (see Chapter 2). If it is desirable to provide additional knowledge of the distributed system to applications, one can always include that information in the IDL signatures. For example, one can include host machine names and Internet protocol addresses in IDL signatures, along with other information. If these types of information are included, it does have a negative impact on location transparency because it invites the participating software modules to depend on this information and to hardcode distributed system details.

Another important advantage that CORBA brings to software systems is dynamic binding. In an ORB environment, there can be many implementations of the same software interface. Each operation signature generated from IDL to a particular language binding has the ability to substitute the target object reference. By using different object references, a set of application code can reference many objects in the distributed system, including local objects and remote objects.

Objects can discover other objects through meta-data services, which are defined by OMG standards. The key meta-data services are Naming, Trader, Interface Repository, and Meta-Object Facility (see Chapter 4). The Naming service is a white-pages directory that allows applications that know the name of intended objects to discover their object references. The Naming service, Trader, and Interface Repository are some of the predefined identifiers supported by the CORBA initialization. Therefore, object references to these services are readily available to CORBA 2 applications.

The Interface Repository stores all the IDL information in the system in a form that is readily accessible to application software (see Chapter 3). By discovering interfaces in the Interface Repository, applications can use the dynamic invocation interface to construct new operation calls on-the-fly and invoke them.

The Trader service is a yellow-pages directory service that allows CORBA clients to discover a range of supporting service instances (see Chapter 4). Trader supports selection of service offers based on their qualities of service and other attributes. These attributes are included to define service discriminators. The Trader service will be one of the most frequently used and significant services in the distributed object architectures.

The Meta-Object Facility is a new facility definition, which extends the semantics of on-line descriptions beyond the Interface Repository to include relationships, constraints, and other semantics descriptions that are useful to application developers (see Chapter 5). All of the meta-data services provide important self-descriptive information for systems, which greatly increase the adaptability of implemented architectures.

The final advantage of CORBA-based architecture is abstraction of the distributed computing environment. CORBA hides the complexity of networking environments from the application software. CORBA moves many distributed system management functions into the underlying infrastructure. In effect, CORBA simplifies the client's model of the distributed system. One of the most important ways it does this is by providing a robust set of exception-handling facilities. Error reporting can be designed into the IDL of a software architecture. Another important simplification is the ability of the client to manage the service object state. CORBA automatically activates services when they are not available during a client request. The automatic activation of objects occurs transparently so that the client can depend on object availability regardless of the actual state of objects in the system. This is an important difference from previous distributed computing infrastructures, which required client dependence on service state. In fact, some existing infrastructures, such as OSF DCE, are evolving towards this capability.

CORBA provides many advantages to the designer of software architecture. But there are many issues CORBA does not address. In particular, CORBA is an infrastructure that does not define application software design. CORBA standards provide many examples of IDL designs and useful preexisting interfaces. CORBA does not select among these for any system. The design choices that comprise a software architecture remain the responsibility of application system architects and developers.

8.6   The Scope of a Software Architecture

The software architecture is the focal point for all design, development, and modification to applications. A framework is the instantiation of the software architecture as an installed base of software. The system architect is responsible for the design and enhancement of the framework; the application designer is responsible for the identification and design of components, coupled with flow of control among components, to form new applications. Components can include preexisting applications that have been wrapped for reuse.

Software architecture design starts with the system architect examining components for use and filling in with new components as necessary. This is a difficult concept to assimilate by many designers because they are usually consumed by a requirements-driven process that naturally leads to unconstrained application design. Under these rules and constraints, the software architecture becomes the focal point for fulfilling the application's requirements. This distinction is critical to exploiting CORBA.

8.6.1   The Major Entities of Software Architecture

The major entities that make up a software architecture, illustrated in Figure 8.7, are application objects; service, facility, and domain objects; interfaces; wrappers; and gateways. Application objects are the application-specific code that performs a function for another object or user. Gateways allow CORBA to interact with other distributed architectures.

Interfaces are the definition of how to request a service from an object. Wrappers are special interfaces that are used to allow existing legacy code, which is either too expensive or too difficult to fully integrate with CORBA, to integrate into the software architecture by encapsulating them through an interfacing application. This provides for interaction with other objects, applications, and data containers.

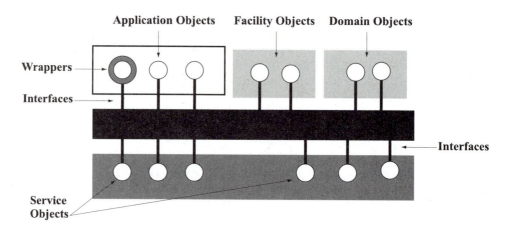

FIGURE 8.7   Services, interfaces, and wrappers.

8.6.2   Customizing the Software Architecture to the Organization

CORBA provides a variety of services and facilities. The services, described in Chapter 4, primarily provide high-level operating system and distributed computing services. CORBA's facilities and domains, described in Chapter 5, provide more application development and support services. Additional service and facility objects can be defined by the system's architect as required. The most likely types of extensions, as shown in Figure 8.8, that would be defined and customized into the organization's architecture are as follows.

- Conversion—These services ensure that data is provided to a client or server object in a form that can be accepted. An example of this would be the conversion of graphics from one format to another.

- Data Integrators—These services handle the integration of a set of data or objects so that they can be accessed as a single entity.

- Legacy Wrappers—Custom interfaces developed for legacy applications that can be reused for future application development.

The selection and implementation of any of these services depends on the needs of a software architecture. Not all software architectures require all types. In addition, some software architectures would have other specialized types that are exclusive to the needs of their business. CORBA alone cannot ensure the proper selection, design, and implementation of service objects.

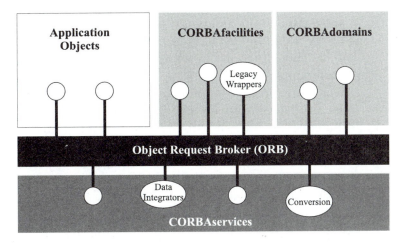

FIGURE 8.8   Adding customized services and facilities.

8.7   Software Architecture Design

Designing good software architectures comes with education and experience. For any problem, there is a broad design space. Education puts the system architect on the right vector providing some discipline and process. Experience supports the right decisions at each step.

Frequently, system architects choose to develop rich and complex software architectures. It is often believed that the more complex and complete, the more flexible the system is to change. However, study and experience has shown [Horowitz 1993] that complex software architectures are costly to learn, use, and maintain, and are brittle with regard to change. Simple architectures are easier to understand and apply and, therefore, more useable.

8.7.1   Architecture Abstraction

For any design problem, there is a broad space of design solutions. Simply distributing all the object classes in existing object-oriented programs is not sufficient to create an effective distributed software architecture. One of the most important concepts in defining good architecture is abstraction. Abstraction is also difficult to mandate, partly because it represents basic common sense. Unfortunately, few people who have been instructed in object-oriented analysis and design are able to define good abstractions. The talent for creating abstractions is different from the talent for programming. In programming, there is a variance of up to a factor of 20 in productivity among individuals with the same training. This is significant to consider in software projects because these individuals will be the key contributors in any software project. People with talent for software abstraction are not as rare—about one out of five developers. However, if four out of five people do not have abstraction skills and everyone is given an equal say in how things are done on a project, the person who sees the need for abstraction will often be overruled. This situation is a source of frustration for many competent software professionals.

An analogy to the abstraction issue is shown in Figure 8.9. The difference between an abstract software design and one that is not abstract is similar to the difference between an automatic camera and a manual camera. One can argue that a manual camera provides a richer interface that allows you to do more with it. The manual camera also requires a steeper learning curve to use it effectively. People who operate manual cameras need to be better trained because it is relatively easy to make mistakes. The type of design in software that has these hard-to-use characteristics can result from two types of individuals: those who do not have the appropriate abstraction skills and those who do not realize the importance of abstraction.

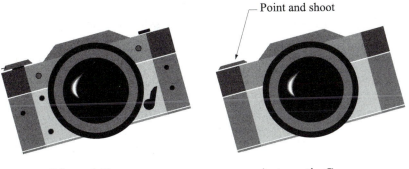

Manual Camera   Automatic Camera

FIGURE 8.9   Abstraction is a key characteristic of mature technology.

Another way to create an overly complex system is through committee design. Unfortunately, the easy resolution to design disagreements is to add features. As one continues to add features, complexity increases and the conceptual coherence of the design decreases. The automatic camera, in this analogy, represents a more mature design in which the unnecessary details have been abstracted to a simple set of interfaces. The operation of an automatic camera requires less documentation, less training, and can be performed by someone with less expertise because many errors have been extracted from the interface. The automatic camera applies to broader markets and can produce greater benefits because of this wider acceptance. Highly effective software architectures have well-defined abstractions like other mature technologies.

8.7.2   The Process for Software Architecture Design

The process for designing a software architecture requires an understanding of how to do the following.

- Identify appropriate levels for application and service objects
- Provide uniformity of interfaces
- Define meta-data for all objects

Defining objects at the appropriate levels is a subjective test. One approach that works well is to define the objects as a product that might be bought to fulfill that function. By product we mean part of a library of components or as an end-user application. If it is at too low a level, it will not be available at a commercial product level. A commercial product level would be an application, tool, or component of a code library. If it is at the product level, it will be substantive with a high probability for reuse. This is a subjective, yet practical, approach, and product levels should not be confused with lines of code.

Using the same approach for the definition and implementation of interfaces assures the uniform connection of software. With this uniformity, comes the ability to reconfigure the system, interchange the underlying object, and provide extensibility. Whether an object is a developed software component, a commercial software product, or a data source, it should be viewed through the eyes of the interface.

Meta-data provides the software architecture with the ability to dynamically bind the services or reconfigure the application. It also aids the application architect and programmers in finding and applying reusable components.

8.7.3   Defining the Software Architecture Objects and Interfaces

To define the objects, interfaces, and meta-data, the system architect must start with a good understanding of the following.

- IDL and the object request broker
- Services and facilities objects

Therefore, the first step in using CORBA as the basis of the software architecture is to understand its functions and services. Then an analysis of the system is conducted with emphasis on the following components.

- Types of applications to be developed
- Existing legacy applications or systems
- Commercial applications to be purchased

Examples that might be identified during component analysis are shown in Figure 8.10.

The system architect should develop a set of system conventions and standards for the system. Guidance on constraints for design, implementation, and criteria for product selection should be completed. In addition, standards should be selected in the areas of communications, data management, user interface, and operating system to aid in the selection of compatible products and code libraries. This would include the specification of APIs, protocols, and data formats, including information on how and when to use them. Extensions to the services and facilities can then be identified and designed using these conventions.

With this knowledge, the system architect develops an object model for the system. Application objects are kept at a high level. Later, the application designers will work to break down these objects into fine-grained detail where required. The system architect, using analysis and design techniques, identifies the components and flows. The system should be understood from the broadest sense. Major functions and flows are critical items. Distinctions between

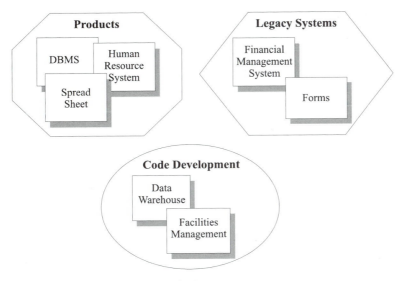

FIGURE 8.10   Component analysis.

developed and commercial applications to fulfill needs of the system should be completed. Coupling this with knowledge of the existing applications and systems completes the picture. Knowledge of the system implies the need for domain experts to assist the architect. Existing applications or systems should be viewed as components where possible. Figure 8.11 shows an example of what might be identified during this step.

Interfaces can be defined based on the identification of the high-level objects. For each application object, the types of interactions are discovered. The

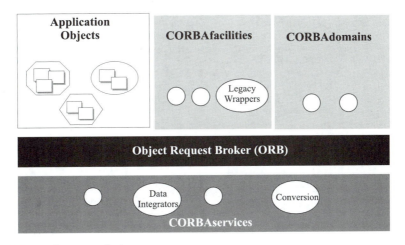

FIGURE 8.11   Object analysis.

interactions are analyzed, and IDL is created for each object. No consideration is given to formats, location, or detailed design. During the definition of IDL, the system architect will learn a lot about the nature of each object. At this point, extended services and facilities should become visible. Interactions among components will drive out those that fall into the conversion and fusion categories.

Definition of the interactions should focus on the following three areas.

1. Interaction model

2. Style of communications

3. Inheritance of interfaces

The interaction model is the manner in which an object will expect to handle interactions. Specific considerations are:

- Is the object a client, server, or both?
- Are the interactions RPC-like or peer-to-peer?

An RPC-like approach is a simple request-reply model, while the peer-to-peer approach allows for a dialogue between the objects during the processing. The object as client, server, or both and the interaction styles are illustrated in Figure 8.12.

The communication style is the manner in which an object sends or receives a request. The four types, depicted in Figure 8.13, are:

1. Synchronous

2. Deferred synchronous

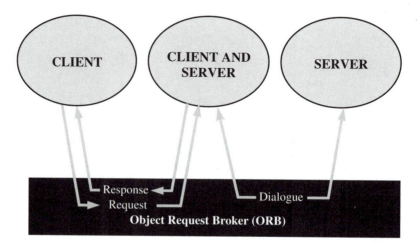

FIGURE 8.12   Interaction models.

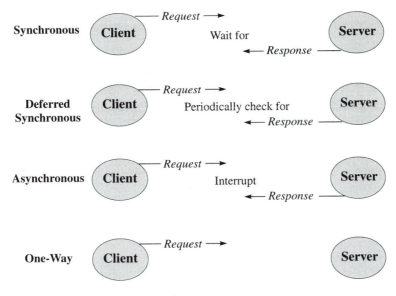

FIGURE 8.13 Communication styles.

3. One-way

4. Asynchronous

Synchronous communication puts the client into a state of suspension until the request is complete. Deferred synchronous allows the client to continue processing after the request is sent. However, the client must poll the system to see if the request is complete. One-way lets the client send a request without expecting a reply. Asynchronous supports the client's ability to continue processing and be interrupted by the server when the request is complete.

CORBA does not support true asynchronous communication. Using threads combined with synchronous communications, asynchronous communications can be achieved. In this case, the client and server must also support reverse roles so that the server can call to the client when necessary. This is referred to as a call back. In the future, CORBA will be extended to handle true asynchronous communications.

8.7.4   Other Software Architecture Considerations

When objects can share or reuse an interface, inheritance of the interfaces is important. An object might share similar interface requirements with several objects. CORBA allows for multiple inheritance. However, the system architect needs to evaluate the benefit of inheriting from multiple objects with the complexity that is incurred.

Establishing the software architecture also includes determining the distribution of the objects and completion of interface definitions, shown in Figure 8.14. The allocation of objects to processing resources affects the performance of the overall system. As a result, the system architect should employ either a distributed-system modeling technique or generate the IDL and build out stubs for the objects with varying performance attributes and perform tests. By building out the stubs, the architect can iteratively develop the architecture, constantly refining the design by stubbing additional interfaces as necessary.

Through either mechanism, the system architect will be able to examine strategies for distribution of the objects. Flow of control and data can be monitored and accessed. The system architect can also evaluate the utility of the Interface and Implementation Repositories in the context of the software architecture. Conversion and data integrator services can be identified at this stage. Definition will be dependent on the interactions established and the performance characteristics desired. Especially important is the use of this prototype code as a specification for the system.

It is important to examine the objects and interfaces, as well as establish the context objects and meta-data. The object meta-data will describe the object and can be placed into the repositories, as well as represented in the definition of the interface. The CORBA context object can be used for the implementation of the meta-data on a client, environment, or other unique circumstance of a request.

After the software architecture is defined, it can be implemented. The extended services and facilities should be built and the software architecture provided to the application designers and programmers. The application inter-

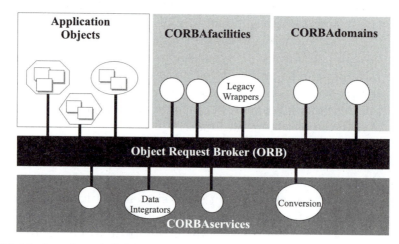

FIGURE 8.14   Interface definition.

faces that were defined can be used by the application designers as a starting point for the applications.

Having completed the design of the software architecture, attention can be focused on the task of implementation.

8.8   Software Architecture Conclusions

Software architecture is important because it provides a framework that ensures the proper mix of constraints and flexibility for an organization during implementation. It should also reduce the burden on the organization in new application development. The selection of CORBA as the basis of a software architecture indicates a focus on system integration. The constraints imposed on the interfaces ensures improved integration while the flexibility exists to extend the CORBA environment to include local, reusable services. IDL is the key to this flexibility since it is a public interface.

System integration and the need to manage future integration have become the drivers in the development of new applications. This requires a software architecture that focuses on the design of components, where custom development is required, but more important, on the consistency of communications and interfaces in the software architecture. CORBA supports a variety of programming languages and includes a significant selection of services and facilities for improved development of applications.

CORBA's genesis and continued focus has been as the broker of components and technology across the enterprise based on object technology. It provides a model and implementation that can be used as the basis of an organization's unique software architecture. Using CORBA in this manner provides the greatest benefit to an organization.

9

Application Design Using Software Architecture

9.1 Designing the Application

Now that Karen's team has completed the requirements for the application, the inventory of existing systems and applications, and the software architecture, they are ready to begin application design. The design team focuses on reusing or buying as many components as it can and is supported by the lead software architect in deciding how to fit each into the architecture.

The run-ahead team results are critical to the design decisions. The most critical issue they raise is the complexity of bringing in a new financial system in conjunction with the application. At this point, the early decision to rewrite the financial management system is reconsidered in light of the time-to-market constraints, and the decision is made to handle the replacement as a follow-on activity. It is decided to provide a limited interface to a minimal set of data from the existing financial system and not to create business objects from the logic.

A few components are to be developed from scratch, mainly converters and data integrators. The conversion routines will be used to convert data elements, such as the customer identification numbers, which are in different formats across the data sources, into a consistent form. The data integrators will be used to combine data and logic from the multiple data sources into a single customer business object that will be the primary source for the new on-line reports that will be available to customers. Once this is complete, use cases are developed to help identify the flow of data and control across the components and to ensure that all components have been properly identified. The software architect continues to be the guide on how to place the components into the architecture, as well as which components might be tailored. After a lot of haggling over the right components and the use cases, the team is satisfied that it can meet the requirements.

The final stage of the application design begins with the definition of the interfaces, including the identification of potential error conditions and the appropriate mechanisms for their handling. In conjunction with this activity, Karen asks a small group to determine the performance characteristics of the system and ensure that the design will support their needs. Models and prototypes are developed to help to predict the performance. It is discovered that for a particular function, the number of components and their sequencing leads to an unacceptable performance measurement. The design team is sent to look into how to shorten the sequence or install parallel, rather than sequential, activities.

After a final design review and approval, the IDL specifications are compiled, changes are made in the existing legacy applications, and coding begins for the new components. Several of the new products selected use IIOP and are quickly integrated into the system. The software architecture is modified as the real needs are discovered. Karen continues to update the program plan and begins to build confidence as the amount of new code is reduced and existing applications are given IDL interfaces.

9.2   Analyzing the Scenario

Karen's confidence in the team's ability to build the system increases with each identification of an existing component. Although the first version of the application will not be perfect, they will be able to build the new application and provide a sophisticated capability. Furthermore, the follow-on activities will include a continually evolving set of interfaces. With this plan, she will be able to replace old components, such as the financial management system, at a more reasonable pace, taking the biggest risk out of the new application.

The application design phase has gone well only because her team had:

- The appropriate knowledge of the requirements and existing applications

- An open mind to the reuse of existing code

- A tenacious attitude in looking for the points of integration

- Identified the key risk areas and were willing to change or limit expectations

- Training and mentoring

- Support from the software architect

Given these traits, the team was able to conduct this portion of the activity in a quick and effective manner. The key for Karen was having a program plan that was continually refined with experience, appropriate training and skills for the team, and a design process focused on integration.

9.3   The Relationship of Architecture to Program Planning

Arguably, the most difficult area in the development of any new application or system is the development of the program plan. It is common for information system projects to be years behind schedule and two to three times over budget before completion or cancellation [Standish 1994]. CORBA and a software architecture are not the silver bullet to solve this problem. However, they will help in providing an improved structure in partitioning the development and integration for more-accurate cost estimation. This is true only when a significant amount of logic and data containers can be identified from legacy or a commercial product and the IDL interfaces can be reasonably designed. If the system is entirely custom developed, traditional program planning problems will still prevail.

9.3.1   Recognizing the Learn-as-You-Go Process

While a variety of factors are responsible for excessive optimism in program plans, a lack of knowledge about the complexity of the undertaking is typically central to this problem [Horowitz 1993]. Rarely is an information system developed for the second time with the same technology. Projects usually try to do something new, either with the technology or for the team involved. Most information system projects are a learn-as-you-go process.

Traditional structured development activities emphasized the analysis and design phases as the method to understanding all aspects of a development. Unfortunately, experience gained in the code and test phases related to performance, technology limitations, and incompleteness of design often leads to significant changes in the original plans. Modifications made to the structured development process to accommodate this phenomenon have been to perform iterative development of an application, allowing experience to be folded into the planning of a system. However, without a commonly understood framework, the system begins to become incoherent, making further changes impossible. Specification of an architecture has further enhanced the process to ensure an overall structure holding the iterations together. A properly designed architecture remains coherent to the architect as the design changes.

Therefore, it is important for the program planning effort to be done with an understanding of the architecture and application design (components, data flow, control, interface definitions, error handling, timing, and mechanisms for tying them together) and experimentation with interfacing and integrating the more complex components through prototyping or run-ahead teams.

9.3.2 Prototype Development Using CORBA

If CORBA already underlies the architecture and IDL interfaces exist to most components, the planning effort can be done in a short time, based on real experience in developing wrappers. If the development of the application is done in conjunction with putting in place a CORBA architecture, the team will be required to design and prototype a number of interfaces before a solid plan can be established. Each component that needs to be developed from scratch can be estimated using traditional techniques.

Two techniques will help in the planning activity.

- Rapidly develop the IDL and stub the components.

- Integrate existing components into a prototype model.

In the first case, a quick analysis is done to identify the components and their interactions, and the IDL is completed for core interfaces. The components are stubbed and a test application developed. This technique is useful for understanding the complexity of the application, as well as the depth of IDL required. Early performance tests can be conducted to understand the potential bottlenecks with respect to flow of control and data.

In cases in which the components to be integrated exist and can be readily equipped with IDL interfaces either directly or through a wrapper, a rapid prototype of the core components and their IDL is highly desirable. This effort will lead to the understanding of the complexity of the integration effort. The IDL and interfaces developed at this point should be planned to be replaced in the code phase of the development.

9.3.3 Creating a Successful Environment

Probably the most important factor in the planning is the availability of experienced personnel and the learning curve associated with CORBA. Without a core of trained and experienced personnel, the application of new technology has significant risk. Experience should center around how to develop the architecture and modeling of object-oriented systems. The effort to inject the core technology of the software architecture into the system while developing a major application imposes another key risk. Both situations should be avoided when introducing new technology into an organization. However, it is recognized that for most organizations, the software architecture will need to be done in conjunction with an application as a starting point. The most important rule is to ensure that trained and experienced personnel are involved throughout the process.

Organizations should plan for the architecture as a separate activity. This planning should be focused around:

- Training
- Product selection
- Pilot activity
- Architecture design
- IDL definitions
- Core component integration

Especially important is organizational buy-in. All levels of staff should be included in these activities.

Any significant project will require an experienced CORBA team member. Several other team members should have been trained by giving them a few months of experience. Early selection of CORBA products will make the application development effort simpler since product intricacies will have been discovered. Picking a pilot application that is important to the organization but not the central business application is the best approach and will help to begin the process of developing the architecture. IDL can be developed for components, and real experience with control and flow of requests, combined with performance evaluations, will help in future planning activities.

With these activities completed, future program planning can be accomplished based on real experience. As system development has become an integration activity, the more that is understood about the architecture, the more integration is accomplished with the architecture, and the more that people are trained in the architecture, the better the analysis will be for new application development. If Karen had the foresight to put time and energy into developing an architecture before the need for the new application, she would have been better able to develop the plan for the integration of the new application. The result was that she needed to continuously update the plan based on experiences.

9.4 Applying the Software Architecture to Application Design

The process of applying a CORBA-based software architecture to an application design includes the following essential steps for the application architecture.

1. Defining the level of application components. The granularity of components is often the most difficult aspect of design. Often, there is a tendency to make the components too fine grained. This is a natural outgrowth of our

training to develop modular applications. Note that each module of an application is not a component. In addition, each component that is developed should be done in a modular and structured fashion. It is a good rule of thumb to make components of the highest granularity equivalent to that which can be purchased from software vendors as component libraries, tools, or applications. Success in this will be based on the experience and ability of the designer.

2. Establishing the flow of data. The flow and handling of data is often embedded into an application. An application is required to establish what data is to be sent in what form and to fuse data from multiple sources into a unified form. However, when changes occur, the cascading effects are often impossible to manage. The software architecture should provide the necessary services to manage data flow. Components should provide the data in the format most suitable to its needs and should expect to receive data in the correct form. Providing conversion and data integrator services in the software architecture is critical. Success will be based on the designer's ability but the Externalization Service, Compound Interchange, and Data Interchange Facilities will be helpful.

3. Establishing flow of control. Traditionally, execution sequences are embedded directly into modules. Documentation provides the only macro-level view of this flow but is never complete or up to date. Handling the flow of data should not require the flow of control to be embedded into the components. Rather, the software architecture should handle the complexity. In addition, Trader and Naming services should handle the selection of the appropriate component required to handle requests that require decisions, such as load balancing or data-driven design. Finally, location transparency should underlay the flow of control. The ORB itself will be supportive of this activity. The Events service can also be useful.

4. Providing interface layering. Components at the macro level often provide a large array of capabilities with multiple entry points. The software architecture should allow a component to have multiple interfaces that allow everything from simple services that use only a small, localized function to highly complex services that use the complete suite of functionality of a component. Experience and ability with IDL is important to this activity.

5. Handling of error conditions. Most large systems are abysmal at error handling. Error conditions are not only undetected but, when detected, are often ignored, sent to the wrong modules, or mishandled. Embedding these into the application makes fixing this problem or extending the system untenable. The software architecture should provide a robust capability to manage error conditions. Error handling should be implemented as a service. The use of the exception-handling capabilities of the ORB are critical skills.

6. Managing timing and throughput attributes. Shortcuts are often made for good reasons—for example, a design does not provide adequate performance where required and making the required changes is too difficult when discovered. The software architecture should ensure that the time to handle any request is not a bottleneck. Performance should be related to the design of a component or service, giving the programmer the ability to change a component to improve performance. Success here is based on good designers, early modeling and testing, and proper allocations.

9.4.1   Selection of Application Components

The software architecture represents the customization of CORBA software to the needs of the enterprise. It changes the role of software architecture from an application-specific functional design to a service-based object design. With the right service and facility extensions, the application architect can concentrate on the application level components.

Selection of application components will depend on a variety of factors.

- Existing systems and applications
- Availability of products in the commercial market
- Unique algorithmic or processing functions

Examples of these components are shown in Figure 9.1.

9.4.2   Designing Application Component Interfaces

IDL is the tie that binds the application components to the software architecture. IDL provides the mechanism to create interfaces in a variety of manners that can utilize the software architecture.

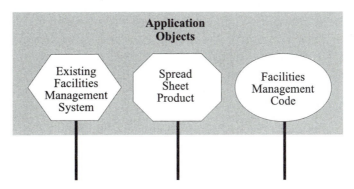

FIGURE 9.1   Example application objects.

Interfaces provide access to the objects. Independent of the type of object and how it behaves, all objects must have a CORBA interface. The interface is designed using the IDL described in Chapter 2. Consideration must be given to the style of invocation to be made to the object. As we have seen, CORBA provides a rich set of mechanisms for invoking an object. Consideration must be given to static versus dynamic invocation, use of stubs and skeletons, and inheritance of the interface by other objects.

Unfortunately, not every application can be directly fitted with a CORBA interface. If this is the case and the code is too difficult or expensive to rewrite, it requires a wrapper. A wrapper is an application object that handles the communication and management of requests to legacy code. It often interfaces to the legacy code through crude mechanisms such as files. Typical interfaces, from most desirable but least likely to least desirable and most likely, are done through the following.

- Application Program Interfaces—This can be performed if the application was designed with the goal of allowing external interfacing.

- Pipes and Streams—In some cases, the application can be either modified or have input and output redirected so that it appears to come from the keyboard or sent to the screen.

- Clipboards—Applications written to provide user interfaces on a personal computer or workstation can have input or output redirected through the operating system clipboard.

- Files—In most cases, information can be passed to and from files used by the legacy application.

Figure 9.2 illustrates each of these interfaces.

Since most code in the past was written without thought to future integration, the most likely scenario for wrapping legacy code is the file interface. In many cases, the legacy code does not require modification. However, if absolutely no mechanism exists, the legacy code will have to be changed.

Once all components have interfaces, the flow of control can be established. Because much of the complexity of interactions has been reduced, the time to develop these systems can be reduced for each succeeding application.

CORBA provides many of the tools necessary to manage these interfaces and their associated objects. In addition to IDL, the Interface and Implementation Repositories are key to supporting the management of interfaces for both the programmer and run-time objects. In the future, the Meta-Object Facility should further improve these activities. Finally, the Naming and Trader services are important services for locating objects.

Application Objects

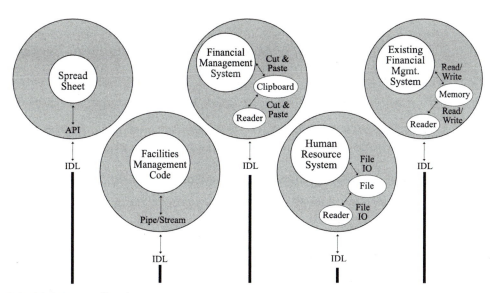

FIGURE 9.2   Application wrappers.

9.4.3   Defining Component Relationships

A considerable amount of the application architect's time will be spent in determining the relationships among components. There are three levels the application architect needs to consider. A component might have one or all of these relationships.

1. Coincidental Components. This is the lowest level of interaction, in which the components do not interact with each other without direct manipulation by the user. An example of this would be a word processor and spreadsheet component, where the user transfers information between the two through a mechanism like a clipboard. CORBA's existing services and facilities provide everything required to support this with only modest IDL.

2. Cooperating Components. This level of interaction provides automatic data transfer and reformatting. Active links are supported. An example of this would be the integration of a spreadsheet, forms manager, and a database management system. Every time a new form was filled out and entered into the database, a spreadsheet would be automatically updated to reflect the change. CORBA's existing services and facilities provide most that is required here. Moderate IDL would be required, along with attention to flow of control.

3. Cohesive Components. This is the highest level of interaction. Automatic correlation and database management, active queries, and triggers make up the kinds of required tools. An example here would be the integration of a spreadsheet, database management system, and a custom stock trading application that was executed when a spreadsheet analysis that uses real-time data feeds from the database management system indicated it was time to buy or sell a stock. Extensions to the existing services and facilities would be required, along with extensive IDL and flow of control.

With the completion of the definition and design of components, interfaces, and relationships, the application can be implemented.

9.4.4 Designing for Interoperability

Object interoperability is the ability to communicate a request between two components and have the components understand the format and semantics of the request and the attendant results, shown in Figure 9.3. One of the driving factors that lead to the development of the CORBA standard and continues to be a driving force is interoperability. CORBA was designed to ensure that a request and response between components could be generated and communi-

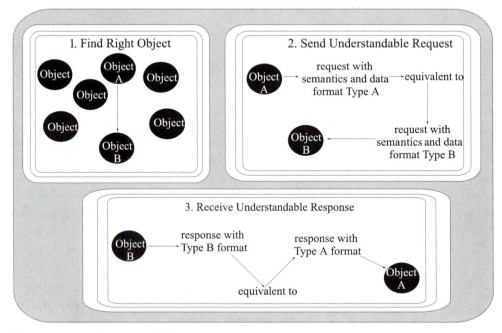

FIGURE 9.3 Definition of object interoperability.

cated. CORBA provides this as a fundamental capability. Other than using IDL and the object request broker as the core of the architecture, there is nothing the architect, designer, or programmer need do with respect to request and response handling. Chapter 3 describes how this is accomplished.

However, CORBA cannot guarantee interoperability in the areas of data format and semantics. These are left to the architect, designer, and programmer to provide in the definition and implementation of the architecture and applications.

CORBA's services and facilities provide a set of functionality to support interoperability at the data format and semantics level, as described in Chapters 4 and 5. The key functionality to support interoperability are:

- ORB
  - Interface Repository
- Services
  - Externalization
  - Trader
  - Naming
- Facilities
  - Compound Interchange
  - Data Interchange
  - Meta-Object

The Interface Repository allows for the creation and storage of interfaces. These can be utilized at development or run time to determine the needs of the object with respect to the interface. Unfortunately, the Interface Repository does not contain semantic information, reducing its potential role in interoperability. Externalization allows data to be formatted to the needs of the receiving object. Compound Interchange, as well as Data Interchange, will further enhance this service to provide additional functionality to ensure data consistency and conversion among objects. Taken together, these provide abilities to understand differences, act on the understanding, and provide anticipated format or action to an object. Figure 9.4 further illustrates CORBA's interoperability support.

Full interoperability is based on the application of these services and facilities by the architect, designer, and programmer. Three types of strategies can be employed, as shown in Figure 9.5.

1. The first is to use these on a case-by-case basis in the implementation. The programmer is responsible for ensuring that the correct format is used to access any object through detailed knowledge of the interfaces.

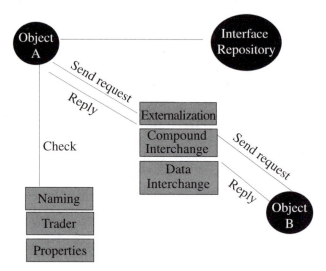

FIGURE 9.4   CORBA interoperability support.

2. The second method is to have a component provide a capability to convert the request dynamically, using predefined information or information from one of the services, facilities, or the Interface Repository. Then the component would perform a conversion on the data and send an appropriate request.

3. The final method would be to use the Externalization service, as well as the Compound and Data Interchange Facilities. In addition, the software architecture could be extended to support a set of custom facilities to automatically handle the data conversion service with each request or at the request of the client component.

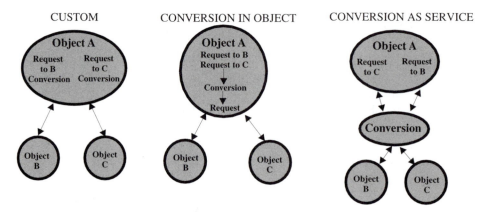

FIGURE 9.5   Interoperability strategies.

Each of these has different implications for the architecture in terms of resources and performance. The last method eases the future interoperability problems by ensuring data format interoperability. However, data semantic interoperability is only partially addressed by CORBA. Even customization of the architecture will not fully address this problem. Data semantics are also embedded in each application component and must be addressed inside of the component.

CORBA and a well-defined architecture will address communications, request generation, and data formats. It will support data semantics interoperability, but the programmer carries the burden of ensuring interoperability at this level.

9.4.5   Increasing Reuse

CORBA provides a set of services that aid in the reuse of components. However, in the end, reuse is a decision that will primarily rest with the architect, designer, and programmer. If the architect and designer are aware of the existence of a component, they identify the component in the design of the architecture or application. However, the distance the architect and designer have from the system make it impossible for them to see all the opportunities. Therefore, having the programmer involved with the development of the architecture or application during the design phase provides the best opportunity to identify reusable components.

Two aspects of reuse need to be addressed. The first is the implementation of reusable components. The second is finding reusable components. Higher-level components that could be described as in the class of commercial products are the most likely reusable components. In addition, the specification of the interface, coupled with how it was layered, further improve the chance of being reused. Specification of the name and the properties of a component further improve the chance of reuse.

The programmer has the greatest ability to affect the discovery process for reusable components because of their closeness to the code. Knowledge of the architecture plays a large role. However, CORBA provides several services that can be valuable.

- Naming
- Trader
- Meta-Object
- Relationships
- Properties

Each of these services can be used to find components or discover information about an object, either by finding components by name or type, meta-data descriptions, or the relationship between like components (This component is similar to the one I am building. Which components does it use?). Once a component is located, it can be used or changes made to the interface to fit the needs of the system.

The Interface Repository also can play a role in the discovery process. All the IDL that exists in a system is in the Interface Repository. CORBA specifications define a comprehensive schema for the IDL. Unfortunately, the Interface Repository does not provide for the storage of semantic information. This limits the ability to browse and discover objects through their interface definitions to cases in which the interface is descriptive enough for the programmer.

CORBA provides one unique form of reuse that can play a large part in reuse and system evolution: An interface can be reused by another component. Reuse is achieved through inheritance. A component has the ability to inherit interfaces from several other components. This is known as multiple inheritance.

9.4.6   Making the Most of Inheritance

Inheritance is one of the key features provided by CORBA. In general, inheritance is the ability to pass attributes or behaviors among objects or components. The ability to inherit interfaces provides significant benefits.

- Similar services can be developed by utilizing an existing interface, reducing complexity and chance of error.

- Old functionality can be replaced by new in an evolutionary process.

- Components can be combined when required.

Figure 9.6 illustrates CORBA inheritance. CORBA supports a special kind of inheritance, known as multiple inheritance. Multiple inheritance is the ability to pass along the attributes or behaviors from multiple objects to a single object. In the case of CORBA, a single component can inherit the interfaces from multiple components, creating a single interface. Interface inheritance allows new components to be quickly and easily integrated into a system either as extensions or replacements for existing components.

Inheritance is defined by using IDL for the component to be integrated. The programmer describes the component or components from which to inherit, as well as new operations and attributes.

When applying inheritance, the programmer should exercise extreme caution. Inheritance implies a detailed understanding by the programmer of the existing interface. If the inherited interface is not well understood, the pro-

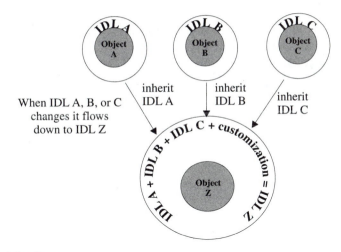

FIGURE 9.6   Inheritance.

grammer could misapply the behavior or misunderstand the data semantics. Multiple inheritance further complicates the situation. The programmer's understanding of the interfaces has to go beyond the application to resolving any discrepancies or conflicts. Furthermore, the programmer must track the family tree of interfaces and understand the lineage. The use of inheritance and its effect is in the hands of the programmer. Once again, training and experience are critical to success.

9.4.7   Providing Good Exception Handling

CORBA provides the supporting infrastructure for handling errors that result from an invocation, as described in Chapter 3. Two types of exceptions, shown in Figure 9.7, are defined for the programmer.

- Standard exceptions that are defined by CORBA and can be set by either the ORB or the object implementation
- User-defined exceptions that are set by the object implementation

The exceptions functionality of CORBA allows the programmer to identify and handle both system-level and application-specific errors. The exception arguments in CORBA can quickly be checked by the client for either system or user exception. Standard routines allow for accessing the information about the exception and clearing exception information.

The uniformity of the interface and access to exception handling in CORBA allows for standard exception-handling code to be written and provided in every client object. Furthermore, a set of standard routines for every

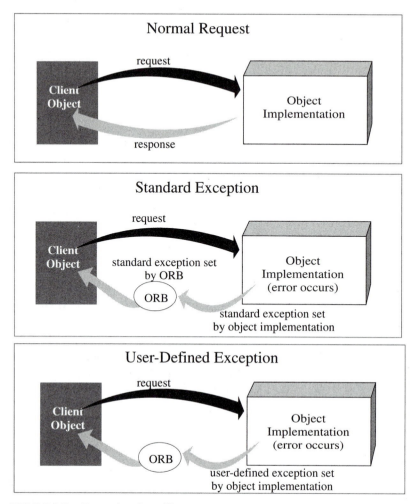

FIGURE 9.7   Exception handling.

user-specific error can be developed and used by all objects. However, exception handling requires active participation by the programmer. Standard exceptions will only be identified by the ORB if the programmer does not explicitly implement the logic in the object implementation. User-defined exceptions require additional thought and actions by the programmer, above and beyond the standard exception. In addition, the client will not check for and handle an exception unless explicitly coded.

The architecture design should incorporate a philosophy and design for the implementation of exception handling, and the programmer should provide a standard implementation for clients to test and handle exceptions.

9.4.8   Test and Evaluation of the System

Test and evaluation need to be conducted on the architecture, as well as on the application. The focus of test and evaluation should be on the completeness of the interfaces and the error handling. Architecture testing is a component-oriented test since the architecture does not dictate a control of flow but is a capability on which an application is built.

Testing of the architecture is conducted in two stages.

1. Early testing of individual interfaces, interface layers, and error handling by developing test drivers in place of component software

2. Final testing of completed component and associated interfaces

Once completed, the architecture is ready for application development. An application will go through four stages of test and evaluation.

1. Early testing of individual interfaces, interface layers, and error handling by developing test drivers in place of component software

2. Mid-term testing of data and control flow among components, using test driver software

3. Mid-term testing of performance and throughput attributes

4. Final testing of completed components and associated interfaces, using test driver software

Final testing should be done independent of the developer of the interface or code.

9.4.9   CORBA in the Operations and Maintenance Phase

Development of new and improved capabilities often occurs during the operations and maintenance phase of an information system. A well-designed CORBA architecture will improve the quality of the operations and maintenance phase by providing:

- Architecture for integrating components
- Tools for the management of components
- Services and facilities to change and add capabilities

Documentation that is incomplete or inaccurate in the operations and maintenance of a system can be a problem with CORBA. However, the IDL for the interfaces exists and provides a mechanism to understand the function of every component. The Interface Repository will be a key resource to be managed by the operations and maintenance staff.

Given the amount of development in this phase, it is important that the operations and maintenance staff be trained in the use of CORBA and the architecture. Skills in the areas of inheritance and reuse should be emphasized. The operations and maintenance phase will provide the greatest opportunity for increased productivity and reuse.

9.5 Measuring Progress

Once a CORBA-based architecture is in place with its attendant components—devices, facilities, interfaces, and meta-data—the measurement of progress in the development of a new application into the architecture can be a quantifiable activity. Using CORBA, the bulk of any integration effort is in the complexity of the interfaces. Each interface needs to be analyzed and assessed separately. Each interface should be assigned to a single individual, with a review by the most experienced individuals. Interfaces will require from a few days to a few months, depending on the answers to the following questions.

- What kind of interface is required?
- How much interface layering is required?
- Are the other components known beforehand?
- Will data formats be compatible?
- What kind of wrapping will be required?
- Are these existing APIs?

The second area to be measured in the development of the application is the flow of data, control, and timing. Each flow should be identified and developed. The more complicated the combination of flow, control, and performance, the more time will be required in development. Specific areas of complexity are:

- The number of data flows
- The number of control points
- The real-time requirements
- The performance characteristics of an ORB and supporting services
- The number of concurrent activities

The progress on each of these should be measured. Code will be required to implement these activities. Each will be different, based on the definitions of these terms. Finally, each component that needs to be developed from scratch will need to be measured for progress.

9.5.1 Measuring the Progress of the Software Architecture

If the CORBA software architecture is not in place, a plan is required to develop the architecture in conjunction with the first application. Measurement of this has many of the same attributes as application measurement. Some major differences are:

- Number of unique services and facilities
- Configuration complexity of CORBA and its services and facilities
- Meta-data complexity

While CORBA defines a significant set of services and facilities, an organization will define a unique set based on their business and needs. These are similar in nature to components that are developed from scratch but may be a combination of existing services and facilities. Like any system software, CORBA and its services and facilities require set up and configuration. The complexity of this needs to be considered in any planning effort. The number of products and the use of repositories and databases will have an impact on the resources and time to implement. One area of special consideration is the establishment of meta-data standards. Meta-data standards will be locally defined by the organization and often take a significant time to identify and agree on.

9.6 Tying It All Together: Architecture and Application Design Processes

The following CORBA-based development approaches are ways to create new systems or migrate to CORBA-based systems. Our approach focuses on the definition of the system-level architecture and its realization. A system is realized by the integration of several subsystems. Each subsystem may be new software, migrated software from legacy systems, or software from commercial products. This approach works synergistically with popular methods [Booch 1994]. These methods are highly applicable to definitions of the subsystem objects and classes. The CORBA-based development approach applies to the definition of larger-scale software interfaces, such as class categories.

In order to create a CORBA-based system (using the recommended approach), there are two parallel activities: (1) the definition of the architecture and (2) the integration of subsystem implementations. The software interfaces are part of both architecture and implementation (Figure 9.8). The definition of the system-level software interfaces is the responsibility of the architects. Their ultimate product is used by the implementers as the blueprint for system integration and extension. The pairing of architecture and implementation can apply at multiple scales of software design [Mowbray 1997].

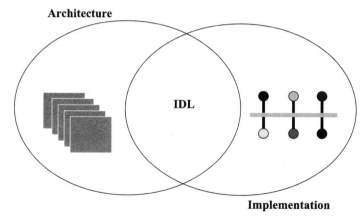

FIGURE 9.8   Interfaces are part of architecture and implementation.

9.6.1   Collaborative Processes for Architecture and Application Development

Figure 9.9 is an overview of the CORBA architecture and development process, which comprises two incremental cycles of design and development. The CORBA architecture cycle starts with the collection of information. The goal of architecture data collection is an understanding of the application domain. The architecture cycle also builds an understanding of existing systems and standards that are relevant to so-called architecture mining. The study of existing systems and standards can yield some important benefits and risk reductions

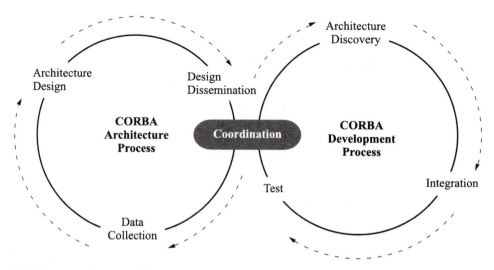

FIGURE 9.9   CORBA architecture and subsystem development process.

by reusing design ideas that were proven in previous software systems. In general, the data collection process is important because it educates the architects about the problem and, therefore, reduces risks.

After data collection, a design process produces the key architectural abstractions. From these abstractions and data collections come the IDL descriptions of the software boundaries. Once the design is drafted, it is not sufficient to simply produce a written specification. It is also essential to consciously disseminate the design information through meetings, tutorials, discussions, and mentoring. This assures that the developers gain a comprehensive understanding of the design and its intentions. It is important to reinforce the design vision continually during the development process. The architecture team provides a resource to the developers to help them to shorten their need for system discovery.

Running in parallel with the architecture process is the CORBA development process. The development process focuses on creation of subsystems and subsystem integration. The architecture and development cycles operate concurrently. However, we recommend that the architecture design remain stable during active development. Design changes in the architecture or IDL should be made infrequently. After changes, existing code should be migrated as soon as possible to the new design. In this way, the architecture and IDL provide a stable basis for subsystem development during most of the time the system is under construction. Configuration control of the architecture and interfaces allows developers to work more efficiently because they can rely on a high-quality set of stable abstractions. This approach also provides isolation among subsystems: Developers do not directly integrate with other subsystems; instead they integrate to the architecture design.

The CORBA development process initiates with design review and discovery. There is a learning curve the developers need to experience to gain sufficient understanding of the architecture. Ideally, developers can program with confidence, not based on guess-work (as is the case in many software projects). After discovery, there is an integration process, which involves the developers integrating their subsystem implementations and providing interoperability with the other subsystems in the architecture. Integration is a test phase in which the subsystem integration and the design itself are proven.

Following the development process cycle, there is need for further coordination between the two processes for the architects to understand the consequences of their design choices and to fine-tune the architecture and its benefits. In our experience, about three major iterations of these cycles are necessary to mature and validate a new software architecture.

At all times, a goal of the process is to define the highest-quality architecture possible, given knowledge of the domain, preexisting systems, standards, and development experience. Architecture quality and stability should increase substantially with each iteration of the cycle. As the process progresses, the need for major architecture revision should become unnecessary. The resulting architecture becomes the stable basis for the balance of the software system lifecycle.

9.6.2 CORBA Architecture Process—The Analysis Steps

Figure 9.10 is a more detailed view of the CORBA architecture process. In the first step, the architects gain an understanding of the domain and the problem specifics from subject matter experts. There are several forms of domain analysis. For example, this process can take the form of a business object analysis, using class-responsibility-collaborator (CRC) cards [Taylor 1995].

An important assumption in this analysis is of a well-defined architecture scope. The scope provides a focus for the analysis on issues that are bounded. In practice, we found that the results of the domain analysis are usually higher-level abstractions than are needed to define detailed software interfaces. A top-down process that begins with the end-user domain can drive out only a rough

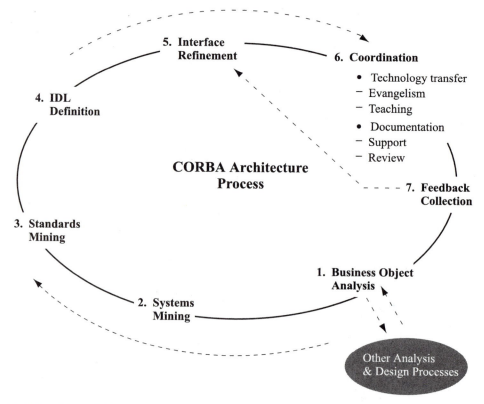

FIGURE 9.10 CORBA architecture process.

set of interface details that are insufficient to define a high-quality architecture and its interfaces.

The second step in the CORBA architecture process is to discover interface and design details through an analysis of existing systems. This is called a system mining process. For any design, there are several previous systems that can provide useful design information. For example, the systems may be legacy systems within your enterprise. They may be systems you can discover in the published literature or on the Internet. It is important to recognize the similarity between previous system solutions and new problems that are addressed.

Ideally, the mining study is an interview process that involves legacy system architects and developers. A suitable interface specification is selected. The mining team may prepare for the interview by converting the legacy interface to IDL as an exercise. The interview includes a walk-through of the legacy system documentation. The focus of the questions should be to increase understanding of each legacy operation and parameter. Important discussions involve how the system differs from the documentation and what the rationales are for the changes. A typical mining interview focuses solely on software interfaces and takes less than a day to complete. Subsequent to the interview, the mining team can update its IDL models to reflect the information revealed in the meeting.

Mining can also be conducted without interviews, based solely on documentation. Construction and validation of IDL models of the interfaces is an important part of documentation studies.

The system mining process helps to extend the range of available knowledge and expertise that can be applied to problem. System mining reveals design details and forces that occur only through practice and experience. A key benefit of system mining is a concrete knowledge of previous solutions that can provide a rationale for current design choices. By explaining how existing systems successfully solve problems, one can justify architecture decisions confidently.

The third step is similar to system mining. It is also important to do mining studies of available standards. Usually, standards are not as specific as the information you can find in system mining studies, but standards mining is still useful. It allows discovery of potential design reuse that may exist in commercial technologies. This potential reuse is often not readily recognized because key standards may not be fully understood without explicit mining studies.

A comprehensive set of mining studies leads to a mature understanding of relevant architectural solutions and provides a solid basis for architectural decision making. Risk areas are exposed when comprehensive mining yields no applicable guidance. Since the majority of systems are designed without explicit mining, most legacy system architects know of few system implementations. Mining studies expand the breadth and depth of architectural knowledge rapidly.

Architectural mining is similar in some respects to the documentation of design patterns. Design patterns convey recurring solutions used by expert architects and developers [Mowbray 97]. Both mining and design patterns are studies of existing solutions. In architecture mining, a single occurrence of a discovered solution may be useful to support design decisions. Mining knowledge may be gathered for only one reuse. It is usually not important to generate permanent documentation of architecture mining studies. Patterns are intended for multiple reuses, therefore, the selection and documentation of design patterns is more stringent. At least three occurrences of the pattern are the customary criteria for identifying a pattern. Design patterns should also be carefully reviewed and edited before dissemination. This step is important to assure clarity of documentation [Mowbray 1997].

9.6.3   CORBA Architecture Process—The Definition Steps

The first three steps of the CORBA architecture process provide essential background information to help the architect define an effective solution. The fourth step is the definition of the IDL interfaces. With the knowledge acquired in the previous steps, the architect is in a good position to define a proper solution to the architecture problem. The initial IDL interfaces can be based on some previous design or on a new design invented for this purpose.

Once the draft IDL is created, the architect can pursue a process of refinement. The purpose of a fifth step is to improve the quality of the interface definitions. This process of refinement continues throughout the development process. The architect continually searches for ways to improve the architecture to provide more benefits throughout the system lifecycle. Improvements are integrated into the design here in step five or in future iterations of the architecture cycle.

The first steps of refinement can be performed by the architects in relative isolation. Initial refinement allows the architects to make sure the design makes sense to the development team. Refinement continues through review processes, starting with smaller groups and proceeding to larger groups and higher-level management. The refinement review process evolves into a technology transfer process.

In step six, the architecture is conveyed to the full staff of developers and maintainers of the system. An important goal is the creation of a quality design for the long-term lifecycle of the system. Many projects do not share this perspective and, therefore, make decisions that are short-term in nature. This attitude usually results in poor-quality designs and design instability.

Step six in the architecture process involves coordination with the development process. The architect's role includes evangelism of the architecture vision. A tutorial is an appropriate format for teaching the developers about the architectural details. Documentation and support is necessary as the architecture is reviewed and communicated to the development team. This communication step is essential to an effective architecture.

An effective strategy to retain the investment in this step is to make a videotape training course of the architecture presentation. The project can make this videotape available or mandatory for new persons joining the development team. It is also important to keep the architecture design information up to date throughout the lifecycle of the system. The architecture tutorial can be a key tool in eliminating system discovery costs that are significant as the system matures.

After the design is tutorialized and conveyed to the development team in step six, it is appropriate to freeze the design to allow the development team to gain some prototyping experience. When the design is frozen, there may still be unknowns and gaps in communication regarding the intended benefits of architectural design choices. For example, these intentions can include (1) how the designs can save development costs, (2) how the designs provide interoperability, and (3) how the designs provide for adaptability in system extension. These intentions are not proven until they are actually experienced in the development process. Regardless of the architectural intentions, if the developers are unable to experience the benefits, it is more than likely the benefits do not exist.

In step seven, the architecture team collects feedback from the development process. This may take the form of an interview similar to system mining. In this step, it is essential to make a determination about which benefits were realized. It is also important to identify which changes and upgrades may need to be done to the architecture to improve it.

In practice, there is usually a variance between how designs are intended to be used with how the designs are actually used. Some parts of designs are used as intended, with the intended benefits. In the same project, elements of the design can be misused. For example, developers can misuse a design to provide features that were not designed into the original architecture. Developers can invent ways of using operation signatures that were not intended in order to provide for missing functionality. It is commonplace for designs to be misused because they are not sufficiently understood. Often, there are intended ways of using the design that were not exploited because the developers did not have sufficient information about the architecture. After the feedback collection that occurs in step seven, step five (refinement) can be repeated to bring the architecture back into alignment with its actual usage.

9.6.4   CORBA Application Development Process

Figure 9.11 is the CORBA development process, which begins with the review process for the architecture. The developers review and assimilate the design information in the architecture to understand how the subsystems work together to achieve the system functionality.

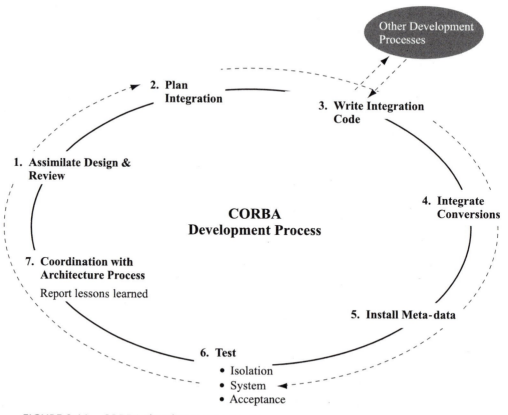

FIGURE 9.11   CORBA development process.

Once this design is understood, developers can proceed to the next step, which is integration planning. In this step, developers determine how to provide interoperability between subsystem implementations and the balance of the system (represented by the architecture).

Table 9.1 is an example of the integration planning that occurs during step two. Target IDL operations are associated with the available integration mechanisms. One or more mechanisms may be present in existing software. We have found that few legacy-integration-tasks software involve clean coding of IDL interfaces directly into application code. Often, it is more effective to reuse existing mechanisms to build application object wrappers than to recode [Mowbray 1995]. When one reuses mechanisms, one can take advantage of existing interfaces that have been proven and tested. The alternative would be to modify existing code. Code modification involves significant cost and risk.

Table 9.1   Integration strategy matrix.

INTEGRATION WRAPPING MECHANISMS	TARGET FRAMEWORK INTERFACE 1	TARGET FRAMEWORK INTERFACE 2	TARGET FRAMEWORK INTERFACE 3	OTHER INTERFACES
CORBA ORB	X			
Other Middleware				
Remote Procedure Call		X		
Library Function Call		X		
Application Program Interface				X
Scripting Interface			X	
Socket Interface				
File Interface	X			

Figure 9.12 is an example of an integration control flow that corresponds to the integration strategy defined in Table 9.1. We note that there are several mechanisms used to achieve integration. This is typical of system integration. A key role of the development team is to provide the impedance match between existing interfaces and the target architecture environment. It is important to achieve integration expediently, at least for initial prototyping. There may be advantages to later providing tighter coupling in the integration software. This can eliminate some implied costs for maintenance that result from maintaining legacy integration mechanisms in the wrapping code. More direct coupling may be necessary to provide a more seamless user interface.

In the third step, the developers write the integration code. The primary purpose of this code is to provide subsystem interoperability. Other key capabilities of object wrappers include system management, security, conversions, and metadata [Mowbray 1995].

An important addition to any basic wrapping code is the inclusion of format translations. Most subsystem applications and commercial software packages have unique data formats. It is essential to provide conversions among native

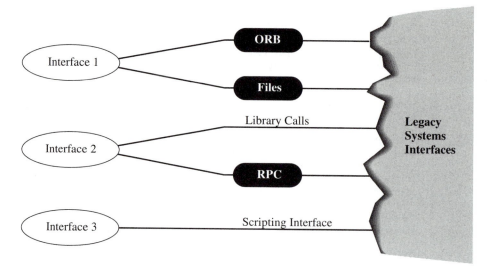

FIGURE 9.12   Integration control flow.

application formats and interchangeable formats. Interchangeable formats can include either formats that are defined for an architecture or commonly accepted industry formats (HTML, TIFF, GIF).

In step five, the developers install any appropriate meta-data that allows the system dynamic characteristics and configurations in various installation environments.

The sixth step is testing, which can occur at several levels. Testing is not critical in the early iterations of prototype development. Isolation testing of each subsystem is important and necessary prior to interoperability testing between subsystems. As the system progresses toward operational deployment, testing plays an increasingly important role. If an architecture or its interfaces are reused in multiple systems, testing is essential to assure architecture compliance, specification conformance, and interoperability. The strategy for the creation of stable architecture is supportive of the testing process. Relatively few upgrades of the subsystem test suite will be required due to changes to the system-level architecture.

The seventh step provides feedback to the architecture process. In this step, the developers reveal how the architecture and its interfaces were used to achieve the system integration. At this point, there may be architecture upgrades. Following any architecture changes, the system implementation should be upgraded to support the modifications. An effective system development process includes several cycles of architecture and development.

CORBA Migration Case Study: The Information Access Facility

10.1 Problem and Objective

In many organizations, there are a number of existing legacy systems that have overlapping functionality. Each system serves the needs of a department or function and provides some unique capabilities. Reuse of this functionality is difficult. When new systems are developed, it is likely the new system is developed independently of legacy. Usually, there are a few capabilities that can be reused for the new system. It is also difficult to make existing legacy systems interoperable. Each legacy system has an integration solution that provides interoperability among subsystems. Because their integration solutions were developed independently, there is little commonality between legacy systems.

In the case study system, the problem of providing interoperability across an enterprise of 5,000 end users and more than a dozen overlapping legacy systems was explored. In the course of the project, the software architecture solution for this enterprise's migration was defined and its integration and migration mentored. This process involved a set of prototyping and testing that provided some important lessons and demonstrated the interoperability potential of CORBA migration.

Figure 10.1 is a diagram of the legacy system environment (prior to CORBA migration), showing a handful of the systems encountered. In the case of System One, the applications were coded as single-tier programs that performed all information access as simply disk file access. Disk files were the only way of interoperating with other information access systems. There was more than one system of this type and initiatives were underway to merge some of these highly overlapping systems without changing the underlying integration and data access approach.

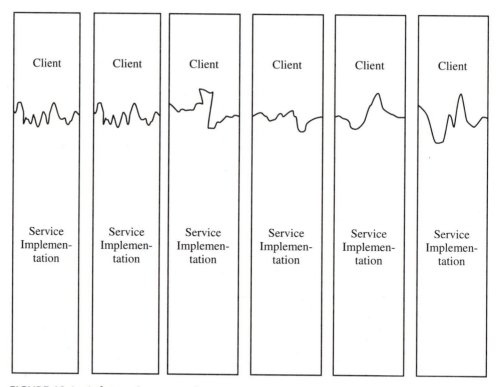

FIGURE 10.1   Information access legacy systems.

In another system, an interface control document (ICD) defined the information access interface at a wire protocol, or bit, level. The ICD was a relatively accurate representation of the solution. However, several of its areas were not completely defined—for example, how to handle error conditions. This solution was a two-tier architecture with a unique back-end solution. This unique ICD provided access to the back-end definition.

A third system that was encountered also had a wire protocol ICD definition. In this case, the ICD varied significantly from the implemented system design. In all the system mining studies conducted to understand these solutions, no systems had updated their documentation to represent the implemented system. All these design documents were created before implementation began. In this system, additional capabilities were constructed for World Wide Web (WWW) access. The WWW interface was the result of a rapid prototyping activity that did not generate any design documentation. The only model was the actual code. The WWW extension had unique ways of using Internet technologies—for example, the representation of the universal resource locators that caused problems on some Internet browsers.

The fourth system type encountered involved a two-tier architecture that had an undocumented interface description based on a proprietary prototype development. This is an example of a non-decomposable system [Brodie 1995]. In particular, there were no defined boundaries between subsystems that could be analyzed or utilized for system migration.

In the definition of the target architecture solution, system mining from the CORBA-based architecture migration process was used to analyze each existing system. System mining showed how each system had resolved design issues and what their needs were, in terms of the target architecture interfaces.

Figure 10.2 is the vision for a common interface solution to provide interoperability among all the legacy systems and to define this common interface so that new system extensions could be added. It was found that with the existing legacy systems, there was a lot of overlap in functionality. Each system stored similar information, but all performed information access differently. This prevented interoperability. The fact that each system used unique solutions also

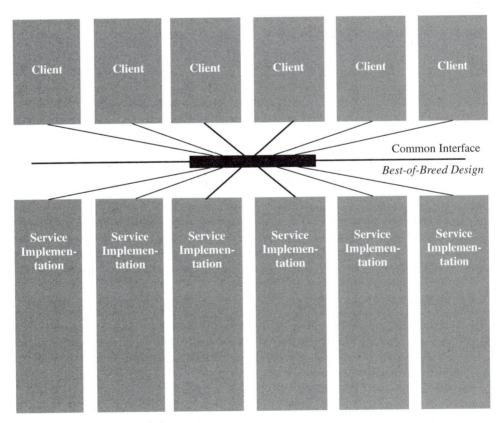

FIGURE 10.2   Common information access.

prevents the enterprise from gaining any leverage to add capabilities to more than one system at a time.

Another interesting discovery encountered during architecture mining was that each legacy system performed some function well in advance of any other system studied. In fact, some of these capabilities were beyond the state of the art. By studying the advanced capabilities of individual systems, the-best-of-breed interoperability solution was defined. This solution incorporates advanced capabilities that should be part of the common target architecture so that clients can exploit the special capabilities of implementations and encourage other implementations to adopt these capabilities by defining a common enterprise interface.

In this section, the legacy system problem of information access was described. The vision for legacy migration to an extensible common interface architecture was also described. The next section covers profiling, a key approach for using standards and technologies. Profiling supports effective use of standards and common interfaces for interoperability and reuse.

10.2 Standards-Based Profiles

Essential to the use of CORBA and related standards is the definition of profiles. Figure 10.3 shows how standards are typically used. In terms of the case study example, this is how the CORBA migration would evolve if a centralized architecture activity was not provided to coordinate the use of the technology. Figure 10.3 shows a standards reference model in a number of industry standards that are going to be applied across multiple application systems. Application system development is quite independent and many decisions are made locally about how to apply the standards and technologies that each system uses.

Standards are inherently generic and flexible so that they can be applied across a range of application system needs. When a generic standard is applied within an application system environment, there are many decisions to be made about how the standards are utilized to provide their inherent benefits. If each application system makes those decisions independently, the resulting solutions will vary significantly from each other, with the result that the standards will not provide benefits of interoperability or reuse. This is an important lesson that many organizations should learn.

Figure 10.4 shows how standards are intended to be used. In this case, there are application systems, reference models, and standards (as in Figure 10.3), but in the middle is a set of profiles, which capture the commonality conventions for how the generic standards are used in multiple application systems.

There are two levels of profiles. One type, a functional profile, defines how standards are used across a broad industry area, such as healthcare and finan-

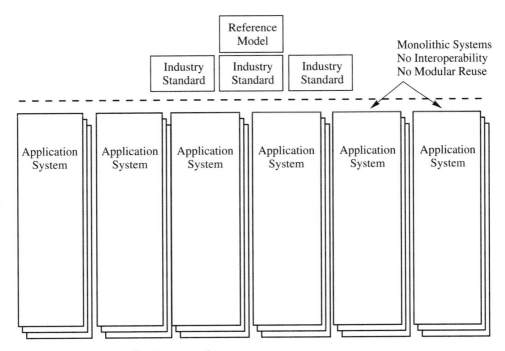

FIGURE 10.3   Vertically integrated systems.

cial services. Functional profiles are created through technology agreements among enterprises in the same domain and provide the first level of conventions for how the standards are used and constrained to provide benefits. Some functional profiles are defined by technology suppliers who have interests in vertical-market and domain areas. The majority of profiles need to be defined by the consumers of technology, the only organizations with sufficient understanding of their domains to define the profiles that meet their industry and enterprise needs.

The other type of profile, the system profile, is usually specific to an enterprise and defines the conventions for use of standards within that enterprise. The system profile is the commonality definition that provides for interoperability and reuse of technology based on standards. This profile captures the commonality among application systems. When the CORBA migration solution is defined across the case study enterprise, a system profile for a range of similar overlapping systems is defined.

In this section, the concept of profiles was described. Profiles are essential for realizing the benefits of standards and also for realizing interoperability and reuse. In the next section, the way IDL definitions requiring profiling are used in the context of this case study is described.

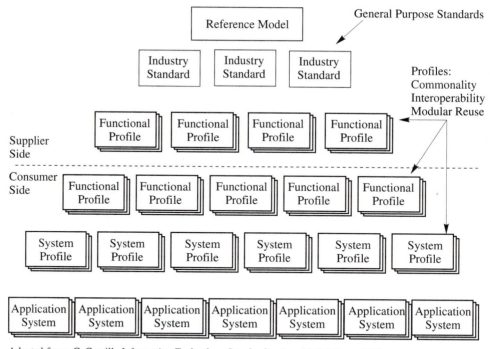

Adapted from: C. Cargill, *Information Technology Standardization,* Digital Press, 1989.

FIGURE 10.4   Commonality profiles.

10.3   Project Context

The CORBA migration activity was part of a larger reengineering project that redefined business processes and architectural models for the entire enterprise (see Figure 10.5). The CORBA migration required detailed interoperability definitions, compared with the reengineering that occurred. The definition of software interfaces is a drill-down exercise. In order to feasibly define these interfaces, one needs to define the scope within the architecture that each interface satisfies. The scope of each interface must be relatively narrow to allow interface definers to proceed to the level of detail necessary to define a quality solution. Many organizations make architectural errors when they expand the scope of interfaces beyond what is feasible.

The IDL definition process focused on the interoperability needs of the organization. The software interfaces comprise an internal model of the system elements considered in the reengineering (see Figure 10.6). The top-level architecture focuses on external requirements and categorizes them in ways that are meaningful to the external users of the system. The IDL definition process needs to focus on linkages among major components of the architecture. The

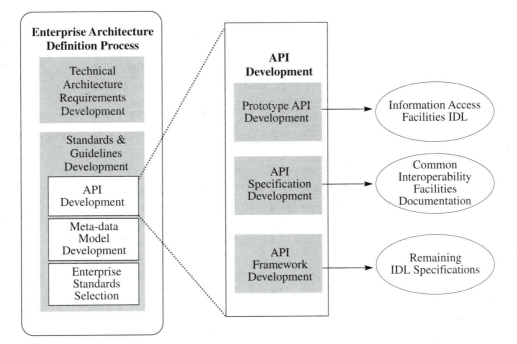

FIGURE 10.5   Architecture and IDL definition process.

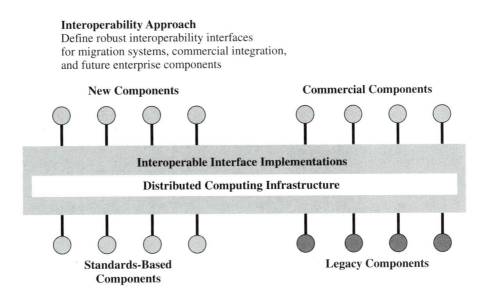

FIGURE 10.6   Interoperability-based approach.

partitioning, defined by IDL interfaces, may bundle the functionality in ways that are different from the logical bundling of requirements.

Key products of the IDL definition process are the facilities architecture and the IDL specifications. These products parallel what is done in the OMG in the definition of commercial standards. The first product is a facilities definition that identifies areas of interface definitions to be undertaken as coordinated, but separate, architecture initiatives. This is similar in many respects to the CORBAfacilities architecture, which was discussed in Chapter 5. In fact, the form and outline were reused from that earlier commercial architecture to define the architecture for this enterprise.

The other types of architecture products are the actual IDL specifications, which include IDL definitions, as well as definitions of their sequencing and semantics. In addition to these elements that appear in OMG specifications, there needs to be some definition of system profiles. The profiles include how the specifications are used in the systems and also list multiple scenarios supported in the operation of the system. Use-case definitions can be an effective way to represent these scenarios.

In addition, IDL definitions may contain places where flexibility is designed into the architecture. In each of these places, there also needs to be profile conventions that define how the flexible definitions are used. For example, if there is a string definition in the IDL to allow extensible representation of names, the names that are used in the development process need to be specified in the profile documentation. Figure 10.7 shows how the facilities defined

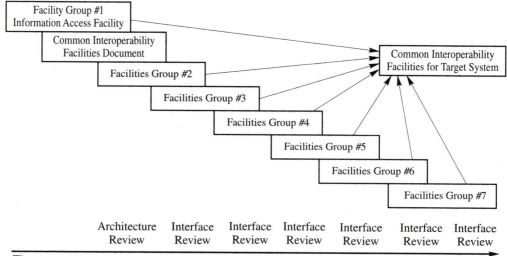

FIGURE 10.7 IDL facilities timeline.

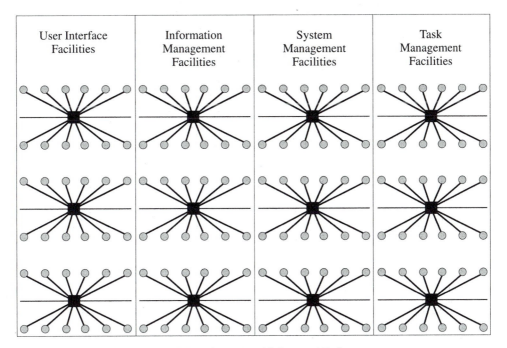

Commercial Services, Facilities and Infrastructure

FIGURE 10.8   Information access facilities architecture.

in the architecture converge to support the target architecture goal. The ordering of these facilities is based on priorities for interoperability in the environment and on the resources of the organization to conduct the architecture and development migration studies to allow the systems to migrate.

Figure 10.8 is a representation of the architecture categories identified in this case study and the initial categories that were addressed in the specification. These initial interface definitions were selected to address the majority of interoperability needs for the community. The other areas included in the architecture could be defined locally for projects in the initial migration. Later, it could be determined if coordination was necessary across the enterprise systems.

In this section, the high-level architecture for IDL-based facilities was described. In the next section, the process for discovering business objects that prepare for the IDL definition will be described.

10.4   Business Objects and Process

One of the important aspects of this case study is defining how IDL designs are traceable from the system requirements. In a traditional development process, requirements and implementations are at different levels of specialization and traceability is not apparent, although it is tracked to conform to the policy and procedures of the enterprise. In the CORBA-based development process, the business object analysis allows the requirements to focus on the drilled-down areas where IDL will be specified (Figure 10.9). In this way, architects can obtain buy-in from the requirements' authors and the requirements' authors can explain the business object model that defines the traceability between the requirement and the drilled-down capabilities captured in the IDL definitions.

A key requirement of the design exercise was to show a relationship to the existing requirements. This was challenging for several reasons. The requirements were global in scope and high-level. The interoperability problems to solve were more focused and required a detailed low-level design. The requirements represented an external model of the system that included both end-user and architectural requirements. The interoperability solution needed to reflect an extensible internal model of the system—one that solves a fundamental horizontal infrastructure problem not directly related to observable external requirements.

In the business object modeling process, a team of domain experts helped to define the high-level objects for information access. The domain experts

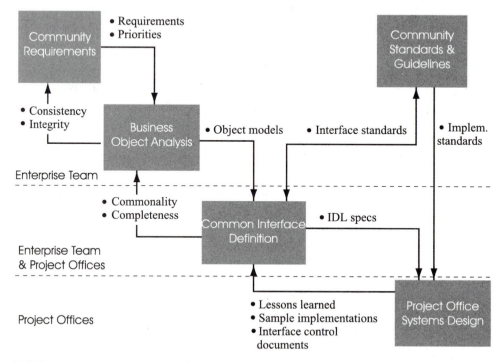

FIGURE 10.9 Business process for interoperability definition.

were from the staff of requirements writers for the enterprise systems. In the object modeling process, the requirements writers became familiar with the information access problem. They learned that the design issues of image-access were at a significantly greater level of detail than had previously been addressed in requirements' definitions. This realization helped to address concerns about the requirements' traceability and architecture coordination that had arisen earlier in the project. Since the resulting object model could be explained and defended by the domain experts, it was easy to obtain management buy-in for the next phase of design and development.

The IDL interface definition process proceeds in conjunction with the system design processes, including the system mining studies and prototyping activities. Common interfaces can be based on several standards selected through standards reference models. The common interface definitions are completed when they are used to migrate the enterprise systems to the desired standards. Profiles provide the integration plan that describes how the IDL specifications are used.

In this section, business object modeling is described as part of the IDL definition process. Business objects provide a top-down perspective on the definition of the IDL, leaving significant interface detail undefined. In the next section, the bottom-up approach for providing interface details is described.

10.5   Interface Migration

Figure 10.10 is a typical example of a legacy system integration based on an ICD. In this case, the ICD defines the integration solution at a low level. When the system is implemented, some libraries are created that map the low-level interface documentation to higher-level software interfaces. Because these new software interfaces are generally not part of the original design, they are often not well documented. If someone wanted to reuse the design, they would need access to these interfaces. The ICD varies from what is actually implemented.

Figure 10.11 shows how IDL supports the definition of interfaces. In this case, a single IDL interface defines both the client and the server interface definitions and the networking solution is isolated from the application software and can be replaceable.

Interface details were extracted from the study of multiple legacy systems and from standards that address the information access problem (architecture mining). In this mining process, the development teams rarely communicated with each other. Thus, the lack of commonality among systems was easy to explain. In the mining study, information was gathered to define a generalized interface for the information-access systems. This was not a lowest-common-denominator interface. Each legacy system had some unique capability that was significantly ahead of other systems. By combining the best ideas from the

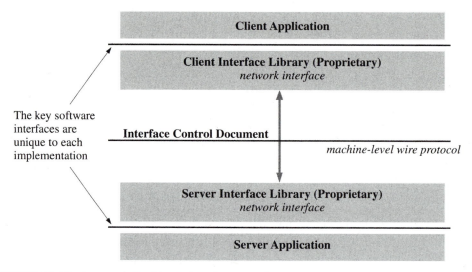

FIGURE 10.10   Legacy interface control approach.

legacy, a best-of-breed interoperability solution was defined. Since the common interface was based on real systems, the risk was reduced. In many cases, it was also clear how to wrap the legacy based on its relationship to the common interface definition.

In our prototyping activity, the common IDL specification for the systems was refined and an intensive training course to educate developers throughout

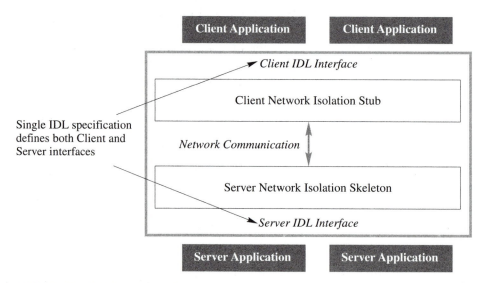

FIGURE 10.11   IDL-based interface control.

the enterprise was conducted. Ten development teams were attracted into the training course. Many of these groups provided their own funding. By attracting this diverse expertise, some additional insights were gathered into the effective design of the target solution. When conducting the prototyping, three of these organizations volunteered their own resources to participate in improving the design. In this first experiment, the three development teams migrated their legacy systems to adopt the target architecture interfaces and then proved interoperability with the other development teams' solutions. This occurred over the course of several months and provided us with important lessons. These prototypes proved to management that the integration approach could achieve the desired results inexpensively.

In the second iteration of the IDL specifications, the scope of the architecture and the number of organizations that directly participated in the review, specification, and prototyping processes were expanded.

This section described architecture mining, training, and prototyping used to create and refine the IDL design. In the next section, some lessons learned are provided.

10.6   Conclusions

Within a year, an enterprise interoperability solution was defined. An important lesson was that the enterprise must define priorities for its interoperability needs. In addition, the enterprise needs to carefully scope each interoperability need. Some interoperability problems needed to be coordinated and resolved in common, compared with other issues that could be resolved independently within each system.

Many organizations run into problems because they do not define priorities for interoperability. They assume that for any migration solution to be attractive it needs to resolve all perceived interoperability needs, as well as other issues. The potential list of add-on requirements, such as security, system management, reliability, and fault tolerance, can quickly become intractable. By defining the priorities effectively with well-defined scopes for interface definitions, it is possible to come up with good, high-quality architecture designs that resolve the key interoperability problems. Because development skills are highly transferable, it is possible to guide developers (given target IDL) to rapidly migrate to the new designs and to build confidence in the target architecture solutions. The follow-up includes migration of the bulk of the legacy systems for operational usage. This is an ongoing process that will occur throughout the lifecycles of the systems.

10.6.1 Do Not Design in a Vacuum

The most common mistake that was encountered with people building CORBA-based systems was designing the system in a knowledge vacuum. This means that many systems are designed without considering the relationship of the design to similar and potentially cooperating systems—a key reason why there is general lack of interoperability and reuse among application systems.

Designers often operate in a knowledge vacuum. The way to address this is through communication, awareness, and architecture mining. Awareness can be obtained through training, including vendor-product training, and more-general educational programs and conferences. Monitoring or participation in standards activities, such as the OMG, is also valuable. Communication among developers of enterprise systems is the other missing ingredient and can be addressed by management. The following list describes typical failure modes based on knowledge vacuums.

- An organization makes an implicit or explicit assumption that no external R&D is relevant. There is an implicit assumption that the group will create a new custom design for every new system, and this new design will naturally be a stovepipe system.

- Systems are constructed incrementally by programmers, without a focus on architecture. Often, these designers do not have a good understanding of their system's relationship to the needs of end users.

- The system is designed in isolation from similar systems. These other systems are often located in the same organization, but no one considers the potential value of technology transfer among projects. This lack of communication guarantees that the systems will not be interoperable, that the systems will not benefit from reuse, and that there will be much reinvention of capabilities. Reinvention initially results in designs and implementations of inferior quality.

- The organization makes an assumption that the new system is so unique that there are no other systems or technologies that are relevant or should be studied through architecture mining.

- Due to organizational restrictions imposed by management, system design occurs without technical exchanges with internal or external groups or consultants.

- Ignorance of available standards can cause systems to be built in a knowledge vacuum. The assumption that no standard is relevant is another cause. It may be believed that it is easier to build new custom capabilities than to learn about and reuse existing capabilities. This belief may be due to a lack of understanding of how to use standards effectively through standards profiles.

10.6.2 Design for Quality

In this book, we advocate the use of OMG IDL interfaces at all system-level software boundaries and reusable software boundaries. It is critical to have quality designs in these places, and the benefits of IDL enhance the benefits of interoperability, decoupling, and reuse.

We are aware of many software efforts that take the opposite approach. When a project is interested in short-term results, such as a demonstration, the project will often generate throwaway code. More often than not, a successful demonstration leads to follow-on development and evolution toward an operational system. The investment in throwaway code then becomes problematic because lack of design and poor quality implementation will not be extensible. Throwaway code has the unfortunate ability to find its way into operational systems because it is a working implementation. To the external observer, there is little difference between a demonstration of a quality design and a throwaway design. The right thing to do with throwaway code is to throw it away. It is even better to not have throwaway code as a goal in the first place.

Experience indicates that the choice between design for quality and design for throwaway does not have a significant cost differential in the prototype system. The results of these two approaches can vary greatly in the follow-on implementations. Of course, design for quality does not mean that the system must solve all previously intractable problems or require extensive documentation. Quality design means that the designers have a vision (that they can defend) for how the design evolves into expanded capabilities.

In conclusion, the principal benefit of CORBA is the migration to improved software architecture. Coordination and reuse of design across multiple systems in an enterprise leads to ease of interoperability and reuse.

Epilogue

By using CORBA and an integration approach, Karen is able to deliver a capability after nine months of effort. The system is then evolved over periods of four to six months in a two-year period. Paul, the CEO, is satisfied with the progress, although he would like to see things more quickly. However, the evolving capability is better able to be embraced by the organization because it involves a series of small changes to the way it does business, rather than a single leap.

As the organization and customers interact with the system, they begin to ask for new capabilities never envisioned by the design team. The architecture quickly pays for itself by boosting the productivity of the development team at each new iteration. Karen's ability to quickly respond to new corporate needs and provide new and innovative services makes her one of the most critical cogs in the organization.

The company's ability to rapidly adapt old systems to new processes makes the organization increasingly efficient. The business process reengineering teams find that implementation of many of their recommendations is easier because the systems are not required to be rewritten.

While Karen is a fictional character, the situations and events are based on new developments encountered by the authors over the past five years. Karen's success is not in the selection of CORBA per se, but in its application to leveraging the old and new technology and applications.

CORBA's success is directly tied to the way it is applied to any application of system development. In the end, we believe that the use of object management technology will become mandatory in every organization. CORBA is a technology whose time has come and can help organizations in fulfilling the needs of business by improved leveraging of information technology.

OMG IDL Grammar

Conventions

The syntactic conventions for OMG IDL are expressed in an extended Backus-Naur Form (BNF) notation. As used in the CORBA specification, this BNF notation uses quotes (" ") to denote literals and angle brackets (<>) to denote nonterminals. Curly brackets ({}) are used to group tokens for alternation (|) or repetition, plus (+) for one-or-more times, and asterisk (*) for zero-or-more times. Also, the square brackets ([]) are used for grouping optional items, that is, items repeated zero or one time.

OMG IDL Grammar

```
<specification>        ::= <definition>+
<definition>           ::= <type_dcl> ";"
                         |  <const_dcl> ";"
                         |  <except_dcl> ";"
                         |  <interface> ";"
                         |  <module> ";"
<module>               ::= "module" <identifier>
                               "{" <definition>+ "}"
<interface>            ::= <interface_dcl>
                         |  <forward_dcl>
<interface_dcl>        ::= <interface_header> "{"
                           <interface_body> "}"
<forward_dcl>          ::= "interface" <identifier>
<interface_header>     ::= "interface" <identifier>
                           [ <inheritance_spec> ]
```

```
<interface_body>      ::= <export>*
<export>   :          ::= <type_dcl> ";"
                       |   <const_dcl> ";"
                       |   <except_dcl> ";"
                       |   <attr_dcl> ";"
                       |   <op_dcl> ";"
<inheritance_spec>    ::= ":" <scoped_name> { "," <scoped_name> }*
<scoped_name>         ::= <identifier>
                       |   "::" <identifier>
                       |   <scoped_name> "::" <identifier>
<const_dcl>           ::= "const" <const_type> <identifier> "="
                          <const_exp>
<const_type>          ::= <integer_type>
                       |   <char_type>
                       |   <boolean_type>
                       |   <floating_pt_type>
                       |   <string_type>
                       |   <scoped_name>
<cont_exp>            ::= <or_expr>
<or_expr>             ::= <xor_expr>
                       |   <or_expr> "|" <xor_expr>
<xor_expr>            ::= <and_expr>
                       |   <xor_expr> "^" <and_expr>
<and_expr>            ::= <shift_expr>
                       |   <and_expr> "&" <shift_expr>
<shift_expr>          ::= <add_expr>
                       |   <shift_expr> ">>" <add_expr>
                       |   <shift_expr> "<<" <add_expr>
<add_expr>            ::= <mult_expr>
                       |   <add_expr> "+" <mult_expr>
                       |   <add_expr> "-" <mult_expr>
<mult_expr>           ::= <unary_expr>
                       |   <mult_expr> "*" <unary_expr>
                       |   <mult_expr> "/" <unary_expr>
                       |   <mult_expr> "%" <unary_expr>
<unary_expr>          ::= <unary_operator> <primary_expr>
                       |   <primary_expr>
<unary_operator>      ::= "-"
                       |   "+"
                       |   "~"
<primary_expr>        ::= <scoped_name>
```

```
                                      |    <literal>
                                      |    "(" <const_exp> ")"
<literal>                     ::=  <integer_literal>
                                      |    <string_literal>
                                      |    <character_literal>
                                      |    <floating_pt_literal>
                                      |    <boolean_literal>
<boolean_literal>      ::=  "TRUE"
                                      |    "FALSE"
<positive_int_const>   ::=  <const_exp>
<type_dcl>                   ::=  "typedef" <type_declarator>
                                      |    <struct_type>
                                      |    <union_type>
                                      |    <enum_type>
<type_declarator>       ::=  <type_spec> <declarators>
<type_spec>                 ::=  <simple_type_spec>
                                      |    <constr_type_spec>
<simple_type_spec>    ::=  <base_type_spec>
                                      |    <template_type_spec>
                                      |    <scoped_name>
<base_type_spec>        ::=  <floating_pt_type>
                                      |    <integer_type>
                                      |    <char_type>
                                      |    <boolean_type>
                                      |    <octet_type>
                                      |    <any_type>
<template_type_spec>  ::=  <sequence_type>
                                      |    <string_type>
<constr_type_spec>     ::=  <struct_type>
                                      |    <union_type>
                                      |    <enum_type>
<declarators>               ::=  <declarator> { "," <declarator> }*
<declarator>                 ::=  <simple_declarator>
                                      |    <complex_declarator>
<simple_declarator>    ::=  <identifier>
<complex_declarator>  ::=  <array_declarator>
<floating_pt_type>       ::=  "float"
                                      |    "double"
<integer_type>             ::=  <signed_int>
                                      |    <unsigned_int>
<signed_int>                ::=  <signed_long_int>
```

```
                                  |    <signed_short_int>
<signed_long_int>      ::= "long"
<signed_short_int>     ::= "short"
<unsigned_int>             ::=  <unsigned_long_int>
                                  |    <unsigned_short_int>
<unsigned_long_int>    ::= "unsigned" "long"
<unsigned_short_int>   ::= "unsigned" "short"
<char_type>            ::= "char"
<boolean_type>         ::= "boolean"
<octet_type>           ::= "octet"
<any_type>             ::= "any"
<struct_type>          ::= "struct" <identifier>
                               "{" <member_list> "}"
<member_list>              ::=  <member>+
<member>                   ::= <type_spec> <declarators> ";"
<union_type>           ::= "union" <identifier> "switch"
                                        "(" <switch_type_spec> ")"
                                        "{" <switch_body> "}"
<switch_type_spec>     ::= <integer_type>
                               |    <char_type>
                               |    <boolean_type>
                               |    <enum_type>
                               |    <scoped_name>
<switch_body>              ::=  <case>+
<case>                 ::= <case_label>+<element_spec> ";"
<case_label>           ::= "case" <const_exp> ":"
                               |    "default" ":"
<element_spec>             ::=  <type_spec> <declarator>
<enum_spec>            ::= "enum" <identifier> "{" <enumerator>
                                        { "," <enumerator> }* "}"
<enumerator>           ::= <identifier>
<sequence_type>        ::= "sequence" "<" <simple_type_spec> ","
                                        <positive_int_const> ">"
                               |    "sequence" "<" <simple_type_spec>
                                   ">"
<string_type>          ::= "string" "<" <positive_int_const> ">"
                               |    "string"
<array_declarator>     ::= <identifier> <fixed_array_size>+
<fixed_array_size>     ::= "[" <positive_int_const> "]"
<attr_decl>            ::= [ "readonly" ] "attribute"
                               <simple_type_spec> <declarators>
```

```
<except_dcl>            ::=  "exception" <identifier>
                            "{" <member>* "}"
<op_dcl>                ::=  [ <op_attribute> ] <op_type_spec>
                                    <identifier>
                                    <parameter_dcls>
                                    [ <raises_expr> ]
                                    [ <context_expr> ]
<op_attribute>          ::=  "oneway"
<op_type_spec>          ::=  <simple_type_spec>
                        |    "void"
<parameter_dcls>        ::=  "(" <param_dcl> { "," <param_dcl> }* ")"
                        |    "(" ")"
<param_dcl>             ::=  <param_attribute> <param_type_spec>
                            <declarator>
<param_attribute>       ::=  "in"
                        |    "out"
                        |    "inout"
<raises_expr>           ::=  "raises" "(" <scoped_name>
                            { "," <scoped_name> }* ")"
<context_expr>          ::=  "context" "(" <string_literal>
                            { "," <string_literal> }* ")"
<param_type_spec>       ::=  <base_type_spec>
                        |    <string_type>
                        |    <scoped_name>
<multi_line_comment>    ::=  "/*" <text> "*/"
<single_line_comment>   ::=  "//" <text>
```

OMG IDL Definitions From CORBA 2

Introduction

This appendix is an extraction of the OMG IDL definitions contained in the CORBA 2.0 specifications. By default, these specifications are defined within module CORBA.

Language-specific definitions are denoted with a comment, such as /* C */ for a definition that relates to the C binding or //PIDL for a definition in pseudo-IDL.

Standard Exceptions

```
#define ex_body {unsigned long minor; completion_status completed;}

enum completion_status {COMPLETED_YES, COMPLETED_NO,
COMPLETED_MAYBE};
enum exception_type {NO_EXCEPTION, USER_EXCEPTION,
SYSTEM_EXCEPTION};

exception UNKNOWN ex_body;
exception BAD_PARAM ex_body;
exception NO_MEMORY ex_body;
exception IMP_LIMIT ex_body;
exception COMM_FAILURE ex_body;
exception INV_OBJREF ex_body;
exception INTERNAL ex_body;
```

```
exception MARSHAL ex_body;
exception INITIALIZE ex_body;
exception NO_IMPLEMENT ex_body;
exception BAD_TYPECODE ex_body;
exception BAD_OPERATION ex_body;
exception NO_RESOURCES ex_body;
exception NO_RESPONSE ex_body;
exception PERSIST_STORE ex_body;
exception BAD_INV_ORDER ex_body;
exception TRANSIENT ex_body;
exception FREE_MEM ex_body;
exception INV_IDENT ex_body;
exception INV_FLAG ex_body;
exception INTF_REPOS ex_body;
exception BAD_CONTEXT ex_body;
exception OBJ_ADAPTER ex_body;
exception DATA_CONVERSION ex_body;
exception OBJECT_NOT_EXIST ex_body;
// Standard Exceptions Supporting Transactions
exception TransactionRequired {};
exception TransactionRolledBack {};
exception InvalidTransaction {};
exception WrongTransaction {};
```

Dynamic Invocation Interface

The Named Value Structure

```
typedef unsigned long Flags;
struct NamedValue {
  Identifier name;
  any argument;
  long len;
  Flags arg_modes;
};


CORBA_NamedValue *CORBA_NVList; /* C */
```

The Status Return Value

```
typedef unsigned long Status;
```

Request Objects

```
module CORBA {
  interface Request {                    //PIDL
    Status add_arg (
       in Identifier name,
       in TypeCode arg_type,
       in void *value,
       in long len,
       in Flags arg_flags);
    Status invoke (in Flags invoke_flags);
    Status delete();
    Status send (in Flags invoke_flags);
    Status get_response (in Flags response_flags);
  };
};
Status create_request(                   //PIDL
  in Context ctx,
  in Identifier operation,
  in NVList arg_list,
  inout NamedValue result,
  out Request request,
  in Flags req_flags);
```

Multiple Requests

```
/* C */

CORBA_Status CORBA_send_multiple_requests (
  CORBA_Request reqs{},
  CORBA_Environment *env,
  CORBA_long count,
  CORBA_Flags invoke_flags);


CORBA_Status CORBA_get_next_response (
  CORBA_Environment *env,
  CORBA_Flags response_flags,
  CORBA_Request *req);
```

Named Value Lists

```
interface NVList {                       //PIDL
  Status add_item (
```

```
      in Identifier item_name,
      in TypeCode item_type,
      in void *value,
      in long value_len,
      in Flags item_flags);
    Status free();
    Status free_memory();
    Status get_count(out long count);
};


Status create_list (in long count,    //PIDL
  out NVList new_list);


Status create_operation_list (
  in OperationDef oper,
  out NVList new_list);
```

Context Objects

```
module CORBA {
  interface Context{                    //PIDL
    Status set_one_value (
      in Identifier prop_name,
      in string value);
    Status set_values (
      in NVList values);
    Status get_values (
      in Identifier start_scope,
      in Flags op_flags,
      in Identifier prop_name,
      out NVList values);
    Status delete_values (
      in Identifier prop_name);
    Status create_child (
      in Identifier ctx_name,
      out Context child_ctx);
    Status delete (
      in Flags del_flags);
  };
};


Status get_default_context (out Context ctx);
```

Dynamic Skeleton Interface

Server Request Pseudo Object

```
module CORBA {

  pseudo interface ServerRequest{    //PIDL
    Identifier op_name();
    Context ctx();
    void params (inout NVList params);
    Any result();
  };
};
```

Registering Dynamic Implementation Routines

```
/* C */
BOA_setimpl (BOA, ImplementationDef, MethodList, skeleton);
```

Interface Repository

Supporting Type Definitions

```
module CORBA {
  typedef string Identifier;
  typedef string ScopedName;
  typedef string RepositoryId;

  enum DefinitionKind {
    dk_none, dk_all,
    dk_Attribute, dk_Constant, dk_Exception, dk_interface,
    dk_Module, dk_Operation, dk_Typedef,
    dk_Alias, dk_Struct, dk_Union, dk_Enum,
    dk_Primitive, dk_String, dk_Sequence, dk_Array,
    dk_Repository };
};
```

The Interface Repository Object Interface

```
module CORBA {
  interface IRObject {
    readonly attribute DefinitionKind def_kind;
    void destroy();
  };
};
```

The Contained Interface

```
module CORBA {
  typedef string VersionSpec;

  interface Contained {
    attribute RepositoryId id;
    attribute Identifier name;
    attribute VersionSpec version;

    readonly attribute Container defined_in;
    readonly attribute ScopedName absolute_name;
    readonly attribute Repository containing_repository;

    struct Description {
      DefinitionKind kind;
      any value; };

    Description describe();

    void move (
      in Container new_container,
      in Identifier new_name,
      in VersionSpec new_version);
  };
};
```

The Container Interface

```
module CORBA {
  typedef sequence<Contained> ContainedSeq;

  interface Container: IRObject {

    Contained lookup (in ScopedName search_name);

    ContainedSeq contents (
      in DefinitionKind limit_type,
      in boolean exclude_inherited);

    ContainedSeq lookup_name (
      in Identifier search_name,
      in long levels_to_search,
      in DefinitionKind limit_type,
```

```
      in boolean exclude_inherited);

struct Description {
  Contained contained_object;
  DefinitionKind kind;
  any value; };

typedef sequence<Description> DescriptionSeq;

DescriptionSeq describe_contents (
    in DefinitionKind limit_type,
    in boolean exclude_inherited,
    in long max_returned_objs);

ModuleDef create_module (
    in RepositoryId id,
    in Identifier name,
    in VersionSpec version);

ConstantDef create_constant (
    in RepositoryId id,
    in Identifier name,
    in VersionSpec version,
    in IDLType type,
    in any value);

StructDef create_struct (
    in RepositoryId id,
    in Identifier name,
    in VersionSpec version,
    in StructMemberSeq members);

UnionDef create_union (
    in RepositoryId id,
    in Identifier name,
    in VersionSpec version,
    in IDLType discriminator_type,
    in UnionMemberSeq members);

 EnumDef create_enum (
    in RepositoryId id,
    in Identifier name,
```

```
         in VersionSpec version,
         in EnumMemberSeq members);

      AliasDef create_alias (
         in RepositoryId id,
         in Identifier name,
         in VersionSpec version,
         in IDLType original_type);

      InterfaceDef create_interface (
         in RepositoryId id,
         in Identifier name,
         in VersionSpec version,
         in InterfaceDefSeq base_interfaces);
   };
};
```

The IDL Type Interface

```
module CORBA {

   interface IDLType: IRObject {
     readonly attribute TypeCode type;
   };
};
```

The Repository Interface

```
module CORBA {

   interface Repository: Container {

     Contained lookup_id (in RepositoryId search_id);

     PrimitiveDef get_primitive (in PrimitiveKind kind);

     StringDef create_string (in unsigned long bound);

     SequenceDef create_sequence (
        in unsigned long bound,
        in IDLType element_type);

     ArrayDef create_array (
```

```
      in unsigned long length;
      in IDLType element_type);
  };
};
```

The Module Definition Interface

```
module CORBA {

  interface ModuleDef: Container, Contained {};

  struct ModuleDescription {
    Identifier name;
    RepositoryId id;
    RepositoryId defined_in;
    VersionSpec version; };
};
```

The Constant Definition Interface

```
module CORBA {

  interface ConstantDef: Contained {
    readonly attribute TypeCode type;
    attribute IDLType type_def;
    attribute any value;
  };

  struct ConstantDescription {
    Identifier name;
    RepositoryId id;
    RepositoryId defined_in;
    VersionSpec version;
    TypeCode type;
    any value; };
};
```

The Typedef Definition Interface

```
module CORBA {

  interface TypedefDef: Contained, IDLType {};

  struct TypeDescription {
```

```
        Identifier name;
        RepositoryId id;
        RepositoryId defined_in;
        VersionSpec version;
        TypeCode type; };
   };
```

The Structure Definition Interface

```
module CORBA {

  struct StructMember {
    Identifier name;
    TypeCode type;
    IDLType type_def; };
  typedef sequence<StructMember> StructMemberSeq;

  interface StructDef: TypedefDef {
    attribute StructMemberSeq members;
  };
};
```

The Union Definition Interface

```
module CORBA {

  struct UnionMember {
    Identifier name;
    any label;
    TypeCode type;
    IDLType type; };
  typedef sequence<UnionMember> UnionMemberSeq;

  interface UnionDef: TypedefDef {
    readonly attribute TypeCode discriminator_type;
    attribute IDLType discriminator_type_def;
    attribute UnionMemberSeq members;
  };
};
```

The Enumeration Definition Interface

```
module CORBA {
  typedef sequence<Identifier> EnumMemberSeq;

  interface anInterface {
```

```
      attribute EnumMemberSeq members;
   };
};
```

The Alias Definition Interface

```
module CORBA {

  interface AliasDef: TypedefDef {
    attribute IDLType original_type_def;
  };
};
```

The Primitive Definition Interface

```
module CORBA {

  enum PrimitiveKind {
    pk_null, pk_void, pk_long, pk_ushort, pk_ulong,
    pk_float, pk_double, pk_boolean, pk_char, pk_octet,
    pk_any, pk_TypeCode, pk_Principal, pk_string, pk_objref };

  interface anInterface {
    readonly attribute PrimitiveKind kind;
  };
};
```

The String Definition Interface

```
module CORBA {

  interface StringDef: IDLType {
    attribute unsigned long bound;
  };
};
```

The Sequence Definition Interface

```
module CORBA {

  interface SequenceDef: IDLType {
    attribute unsigned long bound;
    readonly attribute TypeCode element_type;
    attribute IDLType element_type_def;
  };
```

```
};
```

The Array Definition Interface

```
module CORBA {

  interface ArrayDef: IDLType {
    attribute unsigned long length;
    readonly attribute TypeCode element_type;
    attribute IDLType element_type_def;
  };
};
```

The Exception Definition Interface

```
module CORBA {

  interface ExceptionDef: Contained {
    readonly attribute TypeCode type;
    attribute StructMemberSeq members;
  };

  struct ExceptionDescription {
    Identifier name;
    RepositoryId id;
    RepositoryId defined_in;
    VersionSpec version;
    TypeCode type; };
};
```

The Attribute Definition Interface

```
module CORBA {

  enum AttributeMode {ATTR_NORMAL, ATTR_READONLY};

  interface AttributeDef: Contained {
    readonly attribute TypeCode type;
    attribute IDLType type_def;
    attribute AttributeMode mode;
  };

  struct AttributeDescription {
    Identifier name;
```

```
        RepositoryId id;
        RepositoryId defined_in;
        VersionSpec version;
        TypeCode type;
        AttributeMode mode; };

    };
```

The Operation Definition Interface

```
module CORBA {

    enum OperationMode {OP_NORMAL, OP_ONEWAY};

    enum ParameterMode {PARAM_IN, PARAM_OUT, PARAM_INOUT};
    struct ParameterDescription {
        Identifier name;
        TypeCode type;
        IDLType type_def;
        ParameterMode mode; };
    typedef sequence<ParameterDescription> ParDescriptionSeq;

    typedef Identifier ContextIdentifier;
    typedef sequence<ContextIdentifier> ContextIdSeq;

    typedef sequence<ExceptionDef> ExceptionDefSeq;
    typedef sequence<ExceptionDescription> ExcDescriptionSeq;

    interface OperationDef: Contained {
        readonly attribute TypeCode result;
        attribute IDLType result_def;
        attribute ParDescriptionSeq params;
        attribute ContextIdSeq contexts;
        attribute ExceptionDefSeq exceptions;
    };

    struct OperationDescription {
        Identifier name;
        RepositoryId id;
        RepositoryId defined_in;
        VersionSpec version;
        TypeCode result;
        OperationMode mode;
```

```
          ContextIdSeq contexts;
          ParDescriptionSeq parameters;
          ExcDescriptionSeq exceptions; };
      };
```

The Interface Definition Interface

```
      module CORBA {

        interface InterfaceDef;
        typedef sequence<InterfaceDef> InterfaceDefSeq;
        typedef sequence<RepositoryId> RepositoryIdSeq;
        typedef sequence<OperationDescription> OpDescriptionSeq;
        typedef sequence<AttributeDescription> AttrDescriptionSeq;

        interface InterfaceDef: Container, Contained, IDLType {
          attribute InterfaceDefSeq base_interfaces;
          boolean is_a (in RepositoryId interface_id);

          struct FullInterfaceDescription {
            Identifier name;
            RepositoryId id;
            RepositoryId defined_in;
            VersionSpec version;
            OpDescriptionSeq operations;
            AttrDescriptionSeq attributes;
            RepositoryIdSeq base_interfaces;
            TypeCode type; };

          FullInterfaceDescription describe_interface();

          Attribute create_attribute (
            in RepositoryId id,
            in Identifier name,
            in VersionSpec version,
            in IDLType type,
            in AttributeMode mode );

          OperationDef create_operation (
            in RepositoryId id,
            in Identifier name,
            in VersionSpec version,
            in IDLType result,
```

```
            in OperationMode mode,
            in ParDescriptionSeq params,
            in ExceptionDefSeq exceptions,
            in ContextIdSeq contexts);
    };

    struct InterfaceDescription {
        Identifier name;
        RepositoryId id;
        RepositoryId defined_in;
        VersionSpec version;
        RepositoryIdSeq base_interfaces; };
    };
```

The TypeCode Interface

```
module CORBA {

    enum TCKind {
        tk_null, tk_void,
        tk_short, tk_long, tk_ushort, tk_ulong,
        tk_float, tk_double, tk_boolean, tk_char,
        tk_octet, tk_any, tk_TypeCode, tk_Principal, tk_objref,
        tk_struct, tk_union, tk_enum, tk_string,
        tk_sequence, tk_array, tk_alias, tk_except };

    interface TypeCode {
        exception Bounds {};
        exception BadKind {};

        boolean equal (in TypeCode tc);
        TCKind kind ();

        RepositoryId id () raises(BadKind);

        Identifier name () raises(BadKind);

        unsigned long member_count () raises(BadKind);
        Identifier member_name (in unsigned long index)
            raises(BadKind, Bounds);

        TypeCode member_type (in unsigned long index)
```

```
          raises(BadKind, Bounds);
      any member_label(in unsigned long index)
        raises(BadKind, Bounds);
      TypeCode discriminator_type () raises(BadKind);
      long default_index () raises(BadKind);

      unsigned long length () raises(BadKind);

      long param_count ();
      any parameter (in long index) raises(Bounds);
  };
};
```

Creation of Typecodes

```
module CORBA {
  interface ORB {
    // other operations...

    TypeCode create_struct_tc (
      in RepositoryId id,
      in Identifier name,
      in StructMemberSeq members );

    TypeCode create_union_tc (
      in RepositoryId id,
      in Identifier name,
      in TypeCode discriminator_type,
      in UnionMemberSeq members );

    TypeCode create_enum_tc (
      in RepositoryId id,
      in Identifier name,
      in EnumMemberSeq members );

    TypeCode create_alias_tc (
      in RepositoryId id,
      in Identifier name,
      in TypeCode original_type );

    TypeCode create_exception_tc (
      in RepositoryId id,
      in Identifier name,
```

```
          in StructMemberSeq members );

    TypeCode create_interface_tc (
      in RepositoryId id,
      in Identifier name );

    TypeCode create_string_tc (
      in unsigned long bound );

    TypeCode create_sequence_tc (
      in unsigned long bound,
      in TypeCode element_type );

    TypeCode create_recursive_sequence_tc (
      in unsigned long bound,
      in unsigned long offset );

    TypeCode create_array_tc (
      in unsigned long length,
      in TypeCode element_type );
  };
};
```

Object Request Broker Interfaces
Converting Between Object References and Strings

```
module CORBA {

  interface ORB {                      //PIDL

    string object_to_string (in Object obj);
    Object string_to_object (in string str);

    Status create_list (
      in long count,
      out NVList new_list );

    Status create_operation_list (
      in OperationDef oper,
      out NVList new_list );
  };
  Status get_default_context (out Context ctx);
```

```
        };
```

Object Reference Operations

```
module CORBA {

  interface Object {                    //PIDL

    ImplementationDef get_implementation ();
    InterfaceDef get_interface ();
    boolean is_nil();
    Object duplicate ();
    void release ();
    boolean is_a (in string logical_type_id);
    boolean non_existent ();
    boolean is_equivalent (in Object other_object);
    unsigned long hash (in unsigned long maximum);

    Status create_request (
       in Context ctx,
       in Identifier operation,
       in NVList arg_list,
       inout NamedValue result,
       out Request request,
       in Flags req_flags);
  };
};
```

ORB Initialization Operations

```
module CORBA {                         //PIDL
  typedef string ORBid;
  typedef sequence<string> arg_list;
  ORB ORB_init (
    inout arg_list argv,
    in ORBid orb_identifier);
};
```

Object Adapter Initialization Operations

```
module CORBA {
  interface ORB {                      //PIDL

    typedef sequence<string> arg_list;
```

```
    typedef string OAid;
    // Template for OA initialization operations
    // <OA> <OA>_init (
    //          inout arg_list argv,
    //          in OAid oa_identifier);

    BOA BOA_init (
      inout arg_list argv,
      in OAid boa_identifier);
  };
};
```

Obtaining References to Primal Objects

```
module CORBA {

  interface ORB {                         //PIDL
    typedef string ObjectId;
    typedef sequence<ObjectId> ObjectIdList;
    exception InvalidName {};

    ObjectIdList list_initial_services ();

    Object resolve_initial_references (in ObjectId identifier)
      raises(InvalidName);
  };
};
```

Basic Object Adapter

Basic Object Adapter Interface

```
module CORBA {                          //PIDL

  interface InterfaceDef;
  interface ImplementationDef;
  interface Object;
  interface Principal;
  typedef sequence<octet, 1024> ReferenceData;

  interface BOA {
```

```
Object create (
   in ReferenceData id,
   in InterfaceDef intf,
   in ImplementationDef impl );

void dispose (in Object obj);
ReferenceData (in Object obj);

void change_implementation (
   in Object obj,
   in ImplementationDef impl );

Principal get_principal (
   in Object obj,
   in Environment ev );

void set_exception (
   in exception_type major,
   in string userid,
   in void *param );
};
};
```

IDL for CORBAservices

Naming Service

The CosNaming Module

```
module CosNaming {
  typedef string Istring;
  struct NameComponent {
    Istring id;
    Istring kind;
  };

  typedef sequence <NameComponent> Name;

  enum BindingType {nobject, ncontext};

  struct Binding {
    Name binding_name;
    BindingType binding_type;
  };

  typedef sequence <Binding> BindingList;

  interface BindingIterator;

  interface NamingContext {

    enum NotFoundReason {missing_node, not_context, not_object};

    exception NotFound {
```

```
          NotFoundReason why;
          Name rest_of_name;
        };

        exception CannotProceed {
          NamingContext cxt;
          Name rest_of_name;
        };

        exception InvalidName {};
        exception AlreadyBound {};
        exception NotEmpty {};

        void bind(in Name n, in Object obj)
          raises(NotFound, CannotProceed, InvalidName, AlreadyBound);
        void rebind(in Name n, in Object obj)
          raises(NotFound, CannotProceed, InvalidName);
        void bind_context(in Name n, in NamingContext nc)
          raises(NotFound, CannotProceed, InvalidName, AlreadyBound);
        void rebind_context(in Name n, in NamingContext nc)
          raises(NotFound, CannotProceed, InvalidName);
        Object resolve(in Name n)
          raises(NotFound, CannotProceed, InvalidName);
        void unbind(in Name n)
          raises(NotFound, CannotProceed, InvalidName);
        NamingContext new_context();
        NamingContext bind_new_context(in Name n)
          raises(NotFound, CannotProceed, InvalidName, AlreadyBound);
        void destroy( )
          raises(NotEmpty);
        void list(in unsigned long how_many,
            out BindingList bl, out BindingIterator bi);
      };
```

The Names Library

```
    interface LNameComponent {              //PIDL
      exception NotSet{};
      string get_id()
        raises(NotSet);
      void set_id(in string i);
      string set_kind()
        raises(NotSet);
```

```
    void set_kind(in string k);
    void destroy();
};


interface LName {                         //PIDL
  exception NoComponent{};
  exception OverFlow{};
  exception InvalidName{};
  LName insert_component(in unsigned long i, in LNameComponent n)
    raises(NoComponent, OverFloat);
  LNameComponent get_component(in unsigned long i)
    raises(NoComponent);
  LNameComponent delete_component(in unsigned long i)
    raises(NoComponent);
  unsigned long num_components();
  boolean equal(in LName ln);
  boolean less_than(in LName ln);
  Name to_idl_form()
    raises(InvalidName);
  void from_idl_form(in Name n);
  void destroy();
};


LName create_lname();                         // C/C++
LNameComponent create_lname_component();     // C/C++
```

Relationship Service

The CosIdentity Module

```
module CosObjectIdentity {

  typedef unsigned long ObjectIdentifier;

  interface IdentifiableObject {
    readonly attribute ObjectIdentifier constant_random id;
    boolean is_identical {
      in IdentifiableObject other_object);
    };
  };
```

The CosRelationships Module

```
module CosRelationships {

  interface RoleFactory;
  interface RelationshipFactory;
  interface Relationship;
  interface Role;
  interface RelationshipIterator;

  typedef Object RelatedObject;
  typedef sequence<Role> Roles;
  typedef string RoleName;
  typedef sequence<RoleName> RoleNames;

  struct NamedRole {RoleName name; Role aRole;};
  typedef sequence<NamedRole> NamedRoles;

  struct RelationshipHandle {
    Relationship the_relationship;
    CosObjectIdentity::ObjectIdentifier constant_random_id;
  };
  typedef sequence<RelationshipHandle> RelationshipHandles;

  interface RelationshipFactory {
    struct NamedRoleType {
    RoleName name;
     ::CORBA::InterfaceDef named_role_type;
  };
  typedef sequence<NamedRole> NamedRoleTypes;
  readonly attribute ::CORBA::InterfaceDef relationship_type;
  readonly attribute unsigned short degree;
  readonly attribute NamedRoleTypes named_role_types;
  exception RoleTypeError {NamedRoles culprits;};
  exception MaxCardinalityExceeded {
    NamedRoles culprits;};
  exception DegreeError {unsigned short desired_degree;};
  exception DuplicateRoleName {NamedRoles culprits;};
  exception UnknownRoleName {NamedRoles culprits;};

  Relationship Create (in NamedRoles named_roles)
    raises(RoleTypeError,
```

```
        MaxCardinalityExceeded,
        DegreeError,
        DuplicateRoleName,
        UnknownRoleName);
};


interface Relationship :
    CosObjectIdentity::IdentifiableObject {
  exception CannotUnlink {
    Roles offending_roles;
  };
  readonly attribute NamedRoles named_roles;
  void destroy () raises(CannotUnlink);
};


interface Role {
    exception UnknownRoleName {};
    exception UnknownRelationship {};
    exception RelationshipTypeError {};
    exception CannotDestroyRelationship {
      RelationshipHandles offenders;
    };
    exception ParticipatingInRelationship {};
      RelationshipHandles the_relationships;
    };
  RelatedObject get_other_related_object (
      in RelationshipHandle rel,
      in RoleName target_name)
    raises (UnknownRoleName,
      UnknownRelationships);
  Role get_other_role (in RelationshipHandle rel,
      in RoleName target_name)
    raises (UnknownRoleName, UnknownRelationships);
  void get_relationships (
      in unsigned long how_many,
      out RelationshipHandles rels,
      out RelationshipIterator iterator);
  void destroy_relationships()
    raises(CannotDestroyRelationship);
  void destroy() raises(ParticipatingInRelationship);
  boolean check_minimum_cardinality ();
  void link (in RelationshipHandle rel,
```

```idl
      in NamedRoles named_roles)
    raises (RelationshipFactory::MaxCardinalityExceeded,
      RelationshipTypeError);
  void unlink (in RelationshipHandle rel)
    raises (UnknownRelationship);
  };


  interface NoFactory {
  exception NilRelatedObject {};
  exception RelatedObjectTypeError {};
  readonly attribute ::CORBA::InterfaceDef role_type;
  readonly attribute unsigned long max_cardinality;
  readonly attribute unsigned long min_cardinality;
  readonly attribute sequence
      <::CORBA::InterfaceDef> related_object_types;
    Role create_role (in RelatedObject related_object)
      raises (NilRelatedObject, RelatedObjectTypeError);
  };


  interface RelationshipFactory {
    boolean next_one(out RelationshipHandle rel;);
    boolean next_n (in unsigned long how_many,
      out RelationshipHandles rels);
    void destroy ();
  };
};
```

The CosGraphs Module

```idl
#include <Relationships.idl>
#include <ObjectIdentity.idl>

module CosGraphs {

  interface TraversalFactory;
  interface Traversal;
  interface TraversalCriteria;
  interface Node;
  interface NodeFactory;
  interface Role;
  interface EdgeIterator;
```

```
struct NodeHandle {
  Node the_node;
  ::CosObjectIdentity::ObjectIdentifier constant_random_id;
};
typedef sequence<NodeHandle> NodeHandles;

struct NamedRole {
  Role the_role;
  ::CosRelationships::RoleName the_name;
};
typedef sequence<EndPoint> EndPoints;

struct Edge {
  NodeHandle the_node;
  NamedRoles the_role;
};
typedef sequence<Edges> EndPoints;

enum PropagationValue {deep, shallow, none, inhibit};
enum Mode {breadthFirst, bestFirst};

interface TraversalFactory {
  Traversal create_traversal_on {
    in NodeHandle root_node,
    in TraversalCriteria the_criteria,
    in Mode how);
};

interface Traversal {
  typedef unsigned long TraversalScopeId;
  struct ScopedEndPoint {
    EndPoint point;
    TraversalScopedId id;
  };
  typedef sequence<ScopedEndPoint> ScopedEndPoints;
  struct ScopedRelationship {
    ::CosRelationships::RelationshipHandle
      scoped_relationship;
    TraversalScopedId id;
  };
  struct ScopedEdge {
```

```
      ScopedEndPoint from;
      ScopedRelationship the_relationship;
      ScopedEndPoints relatives;
    };
    typedef sequence<ScopedEdge> ScopedEdges;
    boolean next_one (out ScopedEdge the_edge);
    boolean next_n (in short how_many,
      out ScopedEdges the_edges);
    void destroy ();
  };


  interface TraversalCriteria {
    struct WeightedEdge {
      Edge the_edge;
      unsigned long weight;
      sequence<NodeHandle> next_nodes;
    };
    typedef sequence<WeightedEdge> WeightedEdges;
    void visit_node(in NodeHandle a_node,
      in Mode search_mode);
    boolean next_one (out WeightedEdge the_edge);
    boolean next_n (in short how_many,
      out WeightedEdges the_edges);
    void destroy();
  };


  interface Node: ::CosObjectIdentity::IdentifiableObject {
    typedef sequence<Role> Roles;
    exception NoSuchRole {};
    exception DuplicateRoleType {};

    readonly attribute ::CosRelationships::RelatedObject
      related_object;
    readonly attribute Roles roles_of_node;
    Roles roles_of_type (
      in ::CORBA::InterfaceDef role_type);
    void add_role (in Role a_role)
      raises (DuplicateRoleType);
    void remove_role (in ::CORBA::InterfaceDef of_type)
      raises (NoSuchRole);
  };
```

```
interface NodeFactory {
  Node create_node (in Object related_object);
};

interface Role {
  void get_edges (in long how_many,
    out Edges the_edges,
    out EdgeIterator the_rest);
};

interface EdgeIterator {
  boolean next_one (out Edge the_edge);
  boolean next_n (in unsigned long how_many,
    out Edges the_edges);
  void destroy ();
};
};
```

The CosContainment Module

```
#include <Graphics.idl>

module CosContainment {

  interface Relationship:
    ::CosRelationships::Relationship {};

  interface ContainsRole: ::CosGraphs::Role {};

  interface ContainedInRole: ::CosGraphs::Role {};
};
```

The CosReference Module

```
#include <Graphics.idl>

module CosReference {

  interface Relationship:
    ::CosRelationships::Relationship {};

  interface ReferencesRole: ::CosGraphs::Role {};
```

```
      interface ReferencedByRole: ::CosGraphs::Role {};
};
```

Transactions Service

The CosTransactions Module

```
module CosTransactions {

  // DATATYPES
  enum Status {
    StatusActive,
    StatusMarkedRollback,
    StatusPrepared,
    StatusCommitted,
    StatusRolledBack,
    StatusUnknown,
    StatusNoTransaction,
    StatusPreparing,
    StatusCommitting,
    StatusRollingBack
  };

  enum Vote {
    VoteCommit,
    VoteRollback,
    VoteReadOnly
  };

  // Heuristic exceptions
  exception HeuristicRollback {};
  exception HeuristicCommit {};
  exception HeuristicMixed {};
  exception HeuristicHazard {};

  // Other transaction-specific exceptions
  exception SubtransactionsUnavailable {};
  exception NotSubtransaction {};
  exception Inactive {};
  exception NotPrepared {};
  exception NoTransaction {};
```

```
      exception InvalidControl {};
      exception Unavailable {};

      // Forward references
      interface Control;
      interface Terminator;
      interface Coordinator;
      interface Resource;
      interface RecoveryCoordinator;
      interface Synchronization;
      interface SubtransactionAwareResource;
      interface TransactionFactory;
      interface TransactionalObject;
      interface Current;

  };
```

The Current Interface

```
  module CosTransactions {              // Continued

    interface Current : CORBA::ORB::Current {
      void begin ()
        raises (SubtransactionsUnavailable);
      void commit (in boolean report_hueristics)
        raises (
          NoTransaction,
          HeuristicMixed,
          HeuristicHazard
        );
      void rollback ()
        raises (NoTransaction);
      void rollback_only ()
        raises (NoTransaction);

      Status get_status ();
      string get_transaction_name ();
      void set_timeout (in unsigned long seconds);

      Control get_control ();
      Control suspend ();
      void resume (in Control which)
```

```
                              raises (InvalidControl);
                      };
                };
```

The TransactionFactory Interface

```
module CosTransactions {                    // Continued

interface TransactionFactory {
  Control create (in unsigned long time_out);
  Control recreate(
    in CosTSInteroperation::PropagationContext ctx;
  };
};
```

The Control Interface

```
module CosTransactions {                    // Continued


    interface Control {
      Terminator get_terminator ()
        raises (Unavailable);
      Coordinator get_coordinator ()
        raises (Unavailable);
    };
};
```

The Terminator Interface

```
module CosTransactions {                    // Continued


    interface Terminator {
      void commit (in boolean report_heuristics)
        raises {
          HeuristicMixed,
          HeuristicHazard
        );
      void rollback ();
    };
};
```

The Coordinator Interface

```
module CosTransactions {                    // Continued


    interface Coordinator {
```

```
Status get_status ();
Status get_parent_status ();
Status get_top_level_status ();

boolean is_same_transaction (in Coordinator tc);
boolean is_related_transaction (in Coordinator tc);
boolean is_ancestor_transaction (in Coordinator tc);
boolean is_descendant_transaction (in Coordinator tc);
boolean is_top_level_transaction ();

unsigned long hash_transaction ();
unsigned long hash_top_level_tran ();

RecoveryCoordinator register_resource (in Resource r);
  raises (Inactive);

void register_synchronization(
  in synchronization sync) raises ( Inactive );

void register_subtran_aware (in SubtransactionAwareResource r)
  raises (Inactive, NotSubtransaction);

void rollback_only ()
  raises (Inactive);

string get_transaction_name ();

Control create_subtransaction ()
  raises (SubtransactionsUnavailable, Inactive);

CosTSInteroperation::PropagationContext
  get_context() raises ( Inactive );
};
};
```

The Recovery Coordinator Interface

```
module CosTransactions {                    // Continued

  interface RecoveryCoordinator {
    Status replay_completion (in Resource r)
      raises (NotPrepared);
```

```
        };
    };
```

The Synchronization Interface

```
module CosTransactions {              // Continued


    interface Synchronization: TransactionalObject {
      void before_completion();
      void after_completion(in Status status);
    };
```

The Resource Interface

```
module CosTransactions {              // Continued

   interface Resource {
     Vote prepare ();
     void rollback ()
       raises (
         HeuristicCommit,
         HeuristicMixed,
         HeuristicHazard
       );
     void commit ()
       raises (
         NotPrepared,
         HeuristicRollback,
         HeuristicMixed,
         HeuristicHazard
       );
     void commit_one_phase ()
       raises (
         HeuristicHazard
       );
     void forget ();
   };
  };
```

The Subtransaction Aware Resource Interface

```
module CosTransactions {              // Continued

    interface SubtransactionAwareResource: Resource {
```

```
        void commit_subtransaction(in Coordinator parent);
        void rollback_subtransaction();
    };
};
```

The Transactional Object Interface

```
module CosTransactions {              // Continued

  interface TransactionalObject {
  };

};
```

The CosTSInteroperation Module

```
module CosTSInteroperation {          //PIDL
  struct otid_tid {
    long formatID;
    long bequal_length;
    sequence<octet> tid; };
  struct TransIdentity {
    CosTransactions::Coordinator coordinator;
    CosTransactions::Terminator terminator;
    otid_t otid; };
  struct PropagationContext {
    unsigned long timeout;
    TransIdentity current;
    sequence<TransIdentity> parents;
    any implementation_specific_data; };
};
```

The CosTSPortability Module

```
module CosTSPortability {             //PIDL
  typedef long ReqId;

  interface Sender {
    void sending_request (in ReqId id,
      out CosTSInteroperation::PropagationContext ctx);
    void received_reply (in ReqId id,
      out CosTSInteroperation::PropagationContext ctx,
      in CORBA::Environment env);
  };
```

```
interface Receiver {
  void receiver_request (in ReqId id,
    out CosTSInteroperation::PropagationContext ctx);
  void sending_reply (in ReqId id,
    out CosTSInteroperation::PropagationContext ctx);
};
};
```

Lifecycle Services

The CosLifeCycle Module

```
#include "Naming.idl"
module CosLifeCycle {

  typedef Naming::Name Key;
  typedef Object Factory;
  typedef sequence<Factory> Factories;
  typdef struct NVP {
    Naming::Istring name;
    any value;
  } NamedValuePair;
  typedef sequence<NamedValuePair> Criteria;

  exception NoFactory {
    Key search_key;
  };
  exception NotCopyable { string reason; };
  exception NotMovable { string reason; };
  exception NotRemoveable { string reason; };
  exception InvalidCriteria {
    Criteria invalid_criteria;
  };
  exception CannotMeetCriteria {
    Criteria unmet_criteria;
  };
```

The FactoryFinder Interface

```
module CosLifeCycle {                    // Continued

  interface FactoryFinder {
```

```
        Factories find_factories (in Key factory_key)
           raises (NoFactory);
      };

   };
```

The Generic Factory Interface

```
      module CosLifeCycle {                        // Continued

        interface GenericFactory {
          boolean supports (in Key k);
          Object create_object (
               in Key k,
               in Criteria the_criteria)
             raises (NoFactory, InvalidCriteria,
               CannotMeetCriteria);
        };
      };
```

The Compound Lifecycle Module

```
      #include <Lifecycle.idl>
      #include <Relationships.idl>
      #include <Graphs.idl>

      module CosCompoundLifeCycle {
        interface OperationsFactory;
        interface Operations;
        interface Node;
        interface Role;
        interface Relationship;
        interface PropagationCriteriaFactory;

        enum Operation (copy, move, remove);

        struct RelationshipHandle {
          Relationship the_relationship;
          ::CosObjectIdentity::ObjectIdentifier constant_random_id;
        };
      };
```

The Compound Lifecycle Operations Factory Interface

```
module CosCompoundLifeCycle {          // Continued


  interface OperationsFactory {
    Operations create_compound_operations ();
  };
};
```

The Compound Lifecycle Operations Interface

```
module CosCompoundLifeCycle {          // Continued


  interface Operations {
    Node copy (
        in Node starting_node,
        in ::CosLifeCycle::FactoryFinder there,
        in ::CosLifeCycle::Criteria the_criteria)
      raises (::CosLifeCycle::NoFactory,
        ::CosLifeCycle::NotCopyable,
        ::CosLifeCycle::InvalidCriteria,
        ::CosLifeCycle::CannotMeetCriteria
        );
    void move (
        in Node starting_node,
        in ::CosLifeCycle::FactoryFinder there,
        in ::CosLifeCycle::Criteria the_criteria)
      raises (::CosLifeCycle::NoFactory,
        ::CosLifeCycle::NotMoveable,
        ::CosLifeCycle::InvalidCriteria,
        ::CosLifeCycle::CannotMeetCriteria
        );
    void remove (in Node starting_node)
      raises (::CosLifeCycle::NotRemoveable);
    void destroy ();
  };
};
```

The Compound Lifecycle Node Interface

```
module CosCompoundLifeCycle {          // Continued


  interface Node: ::CosGraphs::Node {
```

```
        exception NotLifeCycleObject {};
        Node copy_node (in ::CosLifeCycle::FactoryFinder there,
            in ::CosLifeCycle::Criteria the_criteria,
            out Node new_node,
            out Roles roles_of_new_node)
          raises (::CosLifeCycle::NoFactory,
            ::CosLifeCycle::NotCopyable,
            ::CosLifeCycle::InvalidCriteria,
            ::CosLifeCycle::CannotMeetCriteria
          void move_node (in ::CosLifeCycle::FactoryFinder there,
            in ::CosLifeCycle::Criteria the_criteria)
          raises (::CosLifeCycle::NoFactory,
            ::CosLifeCycle::NotMoveable,
            ::CosLifeCycle::InvalidCriteria,
            ::CosLifeCycle::CannotMeetCriteria
          );
      void remove_node ()
        raises (::CosLifeCycle::NotRemoveable);
      ::CosLifeCycle::LifeCycleObject get_life_cycle_object ()
        raises (NotLifeCycleObject);
    };
  };
```

The Compound Lifecycle Role Interface

```
    module CosCompoundLifeCycle {        // Continued

    interface Role: ::CosGraphs::Role {
      Node copy_role (in ::CosLifeCycle::FactoryFinder there,
          in ::CosLifeCycle::Criteria the_criteria,
          out Node new_node,
          out Roles roles_of_new_node)
        raises (::CosLifeCycle::NoFactory,
          ::CosLifeCycle::NotCopyable,
          ::CosLifeCycle::InvalidCriteria,
          ::CosLifeCycle::CannotMeetCriteria
        );
      void move_role (in ::CosLifeCycle::FactoryFinder there,
          in ::CosLifeCycle::Criteria the_criteria)
        raises (::CosLifeCycle::NoFactory,
          ::CosLifeCycle::NotMoveable,
          ::CosLifeCycle::InvalidCriteria,
```

```
                ::CosLifeCycle::CannotMeetCriteria
            );
        ::CosGraphs::PropagationValue life_cycle_propagation (
            in Operation op,
            in RelationshipHandle rel,
            in ::CosRelationships::RoleName to_role_name,
            out boolean same_for_all);
    };
};
```

The Compound Lifecycle Relationship Interface

```
    module CosCompoundLifeCycle {        // Continued

    interface Relationship:
        ::CosRelationships::Relationship {
        Relationship copy_relationship (
            in ::CosLifeCycle::FactoryFinder there,
            in ::CosLifeCycle::Criteria the_criteria,
            in ::CosGraphs::NamedRoles new_roles)
          raises (::CosLifeCycle::NoFactory,
            ::CosLifeCycle::NotCopyable,
            ::CosLifeCycle::InvalidCriteria,
            ::CosLifeCycle::CannotMeetCriteria
            );
        void move_relationship (
            in ::CosLifeCycle::FactoryFinder there,
            in ::CosLifeCycle::Criteria the_criteria)
          raises (::CosLifeCycle::NoFactory,
            ::CosLifeCycle::NotMoveable,
            ::CosLifeCycle::InvalidCriteria,
            ::CosLifeCycle::CannotMeetCriteria
            );
        ::CosGraphs::PropagationValue life_cycle_propagation (
            in Operation op,
            in ::CosRelationships::RoleName from_role_name,
            in ::CosRelationships::RoleName to_role_name,
            out boolean same_for_all);
    };
};
```

The Compound Lifecycle Propagation Criteria Factory Interface

```
module CosCompoundLifeCycle {          // Continued

  interface PropagationCriteriaFactory {
    ::CosGraphs::TraversalCriteria create (in Operation op);
  };
};
```

The Lifecycle Containment Module

```
#include <Containment.idl>
#include <CompoundLifeCycle.idl>

module CosLifeCycleContainment {

  interface Relationship:
    ::CosCompoundLifeCycle::Relationship,
    ::CosContainment::Relationship {};

  interface ContainsRole:
    ::CosCompoundLifeCycle:Role,
    ::CosContainment::ContainsRole {};

  interface ContainedInRole:
    ::CosCompoundLifeCycle:Role,
    ::CosContainment::ContainedInRole {};
};
```

The Lifecycle Reference Module

```
#include <Reference.idl>
#include <CompoundLifeCycle.idl>

module CosLifeCycleReference {

  interface Relationship:
    ::CosCompoundLifeCycle::Relationship,
    ::CosReference::Relationship {};

  interface ReferencesRole:
    ::CosCompoundLifeCycle:Role,
    ::CosReference::ReferencesRole {};

  interface ReferencedByRole:
```

```
        ::CosCompoundLifeCycle:Role,
        ::CosReference::ReferencedByRole {};
    };
```

Event Service

The Event Communication Module

```
module CosEventComm {

   exception Disconnected {};

   interface PushConsumer {
     void push (in any data) raises (Disconnected);
     void disconnect_push_consumer();
   };

   interface PushSupplier {
     void disconnect_push_supplier();
   };

   interface PullSupplier {
     any pull () raises (Disconnected);
     any try_pull (out boolean has_event)
       raises(Disconnected);
   };

   interface PullConsumer {
     void disconnect_pull_consumer();
   };

};
```

The Event Channel Administration Module

```
#include "CosEventComm.idl"

module CosEventChannelAdmin {

   exception AlreadyConnected {};
   exception TypeError {};

   interface ProxyPushConsumer: CosEventComm::PushConsumer {
```

```
      void connect_push_supplier {
          in CosEventComm::PushSupplier push_supplier)
        raises(AlreadyConnected);
    };

    interface ProxyPullSupplier: CosEventComm::PullSupplier {
      void connect_pull_consumer(
          in CosEventComm::PullConsumer pull_consumer)
        raises(AlreadyConnected);
    };

    interface ProxyPullConsumer: CosEventComm::PullConsumer {
      void connect_pull_supplier(
          in CosEventComm::PullSupplier pull_supplier)
        raises(AlreadyConnected, TypeError);
    };

    interface ProxyPushSupplier: CosEventComm::PushSupplier {
      void connect_push_consumer(
          in CosEventComm::PushConsumer push_consumer)
        raises(AlreadyConnected, TypeError);
    };
};
```

The Typed Event Communication Module

```
    #include "CosEventComm.idl"

module CosTypedEventComm {

    interface TypedPushConsumer: CostEventComm::PushConsumer {
      Object get_typed_consumer();
    };

    interface TypedPullSupplier: CosEventComm::PullSupplier {
      Object get_typed_supplier();
    };
};
```

The Typed Event Channel Administration Module

```
    #include "CosEventChannel.idl"
    #include "CosTypedEventChannel.idl"
```

```
module CosTypedEventChannelAdmin {

  exception InterfaceNotSupported {};
  exception NoSuchImplementation {};
  typedef string Key;

  interface TypedProxyPushConsumer:
    CosEventChannelAdmin::ProxyPushConsumer,
    CosTypedEventComm::TypedPushConsumer { };

  interface TypedProxyPullSupplier:
    CosEventChannelAdmin::ProxyPullSupplier,
    CosTypedEventComm::TypedPullSupplier { };

  interface TypedSupplierAdmin:
      CosEventChannelAdmin::SupplierAdmin {
    TypedProxyPushConsumer obtain_typed_push_consumer(
        in Key supported_interface)
      raises(InterfaceNotSupported);
    ProxyPullConsumer obtain_typed_pull_consumer (
        in Key uses_interface)
      raises(NoSuchImplementation);
  };

  interface TypedConsumerAdmin:
      CosEventChannelAdmin::ConsumerAdmin {
    TypedProxyPullSupplier obtain_typed_pull_supplier(
        in Key supported_interface)
      raises(InterfaceNotSupported);
    ProxyPushSupplier obtain_typed_push_supplier(
        in Key uses_interface)
      raises(NoSuchImplementation);
  };

  interface TypedEventChannel {
    TypedComsumerAdmin for_consumers();
    TypedSupplierAdmin for_suppliers();
    void destroy();
  };
};
```

Persistent Object Service

The Persistent Identifier Module

```
module CosPersistencePID {

  interface PID {
    attribute string datastore_type;
    string get_PIDString();
  };
};
```

Examples of Persistent Identifier Specializations

```
#include "CosPersistencePID.idl"

interface PID_DB: CosPersistencePID::PID {
  attribute string database_name; // name of database
};

interface PID_SQLDB: PID_DB {
  attribute string sql_statement; // SQL statement
};

interface PID_OODB: PID_DB {
  attribute string segment_name; // segment within database
  attribute unsigned long oid; // object id within a segment
};
```

An Example Persistent Identifier Factory Interface

```
interface PIDFactory {
  CosPersistencePID::PID create_PID_from_key(in string key);
  CosPersistencePID::PID create_PID_from_string(
    in string pid_string);
  CosPersistencePID::PID create_PID_from_string_and_key(
    in string pid_string, in string key);
};
```

The Persistent Object Module

```
#include "CosPersistencePDS.idl"
// CosPersistencePDS.idl #includes CosPersistencePID.idl

module CosPersistencePO {
```

```
interface PO {
  attribute CosPersistencePID::PID p;
  CosPersistencePDS::PDS connect (
    in CosPersistencePID::PID p);
  void disconnect (in CosPersistencePID::PID p);
  void store (in CosPersistencePID::PID p);
  void restore (in CosPersistencePID::PID p);
  void delete (in CosPersistencePID::PID p);
};


interface SD {
  void pre_store();
  void post_restore();
};
};
```

The Persistent Object Manager Module

```
#include "CosPersistencePDS.idl"
// CosPersistencePDS.idl #includes CosPersistencePID.idl

module CosPersistencePOM {
  interface Object;
  interface POM {
    CosPersistencePDS::PDS connect (
      in Object obj,
      in CosPersistencePID::PID p);
    void disconnect (
      in Object obj,
      in CosPersistencePID::PID p);
    void store (
      in Object obj,
      in CosPersistencePID::PID p);
    void restore (
      in Object obj,
      in CosPersistencePID::PID p);
    void delete (
      in Object obj,
      in CosPersistencePID::PID p);
  };
};
```

The Persistent Data Service Module

```
#include CosPersistencePID.idl

module CosPersistencePDS {

  interface Object;
  interface PDS {
    PDS connect (in Object obj,
      in CosPersistencePID::PID p);
    void disconnect (in Object obj,
      in CosPersistencePID::PID p);
    void store (in Object obj,
      in CosPersistencePID::PID p);
    void restore (in Object obj,
      in CosPersistencePID::PID p);
    void delete (in Object obj,
      in CosPersistencePID::PID p);
  };
};
```

The Direct Access Persistent Data Service Module

```
#include "CosPersistencePDS.idl"
// CosPersistencePDS.idl #includes CosPersistencePID.idl

module CosPersistencePDS_DA {

  typedef string DAObjectID;
  interface PID_DA: CosPersistencePID::PID {
    attribute DAObjectID oid;
  };

  interface DAObject {
    boolean dado_same(in DAObject d);
    DAObjectID dado_oid();
    PID_DA dado_pid();
    void dado_remove();
    void dado_free();
  };
```

```
interface DAObjectFactory {
  DAObject create();
};

interface DAObjectFactoryFinder {
  DAObjectFactory find_factory(in string key);
};

interface PDS_DA: CosPersistencePDS::PDS {
  DAObject get_data();
  void set_data(in DAObject new_data);
  DAObject lookup(in DAObjectID id);
  PID_DA get_pid();
  PID_DA get_object_pid(in DAObject dao);
  DAObjectFactoryFinder data_factories();
};

typedef sequence<string> AttributeNames;
interface DynamicAttributeAccess {
  AttributeNames attribute_names();
  any attribute_get(in string name);
  void attribute_set(in string name, in any value);
};

typedef string ClusterID;
typedef sequence<ClusterID> ClusterIDs;
interface PDS_ClusteredDA: PDS_DA {
  ClusterID cluster_id();
  string cluster_kind();
  ClusterIDs clusters_of();
  PDS_ClusteredDA create_cluster(in string kind);
  PDS_ClusteredDA open_cluster(in ClusterID cluster);
  PDS_ClusteredDA copy_cluster(in PDS_DA source);
};
};
```

The Persistent Dynamic Data Object Module

```
#include "CosPersistencePID.idl"

module CosPersistenceDDO {

  interface DDO {
    attribute string object_type;
```

```
      attribute CosPersistencePID::PID p;
      short add_data();
      short add_data_property (in short data_id);
      short get_data_count();
      short get_data_property_count (in short data_id);
      void get_data_property (in short data_id,
         in short property_id,
         out string property_name,
         out any property_value);
      void set_data_property (in short data_id,
         in short property_id,
         in string property_name,
         in any property_value);
      void get_data (in short data_id,
         out string data_name,
         out any data_value);
      void set_data (in short data_id,
         in string data_name,
         in any data_value);
   };
};
```

The Persistent Data Store Call Level Interface Module

```
#include "CosPersistenceDDO.idl"
// CosPersistencePDS.idl #includes CosPersistencePID.idl

module CosPersistenceDS_CLI {

  interface UserEnvironment {
    void set_option (in long option, in any value);
    void get_option (in long option, out any value);
    void release();
  };

  interface Connection {
    void set_option (in long option, in any value);
    void get_option (in long option, out any value);
  };

  interface ConnectionFactory {
    Connection create_object (
```

```
          in UserEnvironment user_envir);
};

interface Cursor {
  void set_position (in long position, in any value);
  CosPersistenceDDO::DDO fetch_object();
};

interface CursorFactory {
  Cursor create_object (
    in Connection connection);
};

interface PID_CLI: CosPersistencePID::PID {
  attribute string datastore_id;
  attribute string id;
};

interface Datastore_CLI {
  void connect (in Connection connection,
    in string datastore_id,
    in string user_name,
    in string authentication);
  void disconnect (in Connection connection);
  Connection get_connection (
    in string datastore_id,
    in string user_name);
  void add_object (in Connection connection,
    in CosPersistenceDDO::DDO data_obj);
  void delete_object (in Connection connection,
    in CosPersistenceDDO::DDO data_obj);
  void update_object (in Connection connection,
    in CosPersistenceDDO::DDO data_obj);
  void retrieve_object (in Connection connection,
    in CosPersistenceDDO::DDO data_obj);
  Cursor select_object (in Connection connection,
    in string key);
  void transact (in UserEnvironment user_envir,
    in short completion_type);
  void assign_PID (in PID_CLI p);
  void assign_PID_relative (
    in PID_CLI source_pid,
    in PID_CLI target_pid);
```

```
     void is_identical_PID (
       in PID_CLI pid_1,
       in PID_CLI pid_2);
     string get_object_type (in PID_CLI p);
     void register_mapping_schema (in string schema_file);
     Cursor execute (in Connection connection,
       in string command);
   };
```

Concurrency Control Service

The Concurrency Control Module

```
     #include <CosTransactions.idl>

     module CosConcurrencyControl {
       enum lock_mode {
         read,
         write,
         upgrade,
         intention_read,
         intention_write
       };

       exception LockNetHeld {};

       interface LockCoordinator {
         void drop_locks();
       };

       interface LockSet {
         void lock(in lock_mode mode);
         boolean try_lock (in lock_mode mode);
         void unlock(in lock_mode mode)
           raises(LockNotHeld);
         void change_mode (in lock_mode held_mode,
             in lock_mode new_mode)
           raises(LockNetHeld);
         LockCoordinator get_coordinator (
           in CosTransactions::Coordinator which);
       };
```

```
interfaceTransactionalLockSet {
  void lock (in CosTransactions::Coordinator current,
    in lock_mode mode);
  boolean try_lock (in CosTransactions::Coordinator current,
    in lock_mode mode);
  void unlock (in CosTransactions::Coordinator current,
      in lock_mode mode)
    raises(LockNotHeld);
  void change_mode (in CosTransactions::Coordinator current,
      in lock_mode held_mode,
      in lock_mode new_mode)
    raises(LockNotHeld);
  LockCoordinator get_coordinator (
    in CosTransactions::Coordinator which);
};

interface LockSetFactory {
  LockSet create();
  LockSet create_related (in LockSet which);
  TransactionalLockSet create_transactional();
  TransactionalLockSet create_transactional_related (
    in TransactionalLockSet which);
  };
};
```

Externalization Service

The Externalization Module

```
#include <LifeCycle.idl>
#include <Stream.idl>

module CosExternalization {
  exception InvalidFileNameError {};
  exception ContextAlreadyRegistered {};

  interface Stream: CosLifeCycle::LifeCycleObject {
    void externalize (
      in CosStream::Streamable theObject);
    CosStream::Streamable internalize (
        in CosLifeCycle::FactoryFinder there)
      raises(CosLifeCycle::NoFactory,
        CosStream::StreamDataFormatError);
```

```
    void begin_context()
      raises(ContextAlreadyRegistered);
    void end_context();
    void flush();
  };

  interface StreamFactory {
    Stream create (in string theFileName)
      raises(InvalidFormatNameError);
  };
};
```

The Stream Module

```
#include <LifeCycle.idl>
#include <ObjectIdentity.idl>
#include <CompoundExternalization.idl>
module CosStream {
  exception ObjectCreationError {};
  exception StreamDataFormatError {};
  interface StreamIO;

  interface Streamable:
      CosObjectIdentity::IdentifiableObject {
    readonly attribute CosLifeCycle::Key external_form_id;
    void externalize_to_stream (
      in StreamIO targetStreamIO);
    void internalize_to_stream (
        in StreamIO sourceStreamIO,
        in FactoryFinder there)
      raises(CosLifeCycle::NoFactory,
        ObjectCreationError,
        StreamDataFormatError);
  };

  interface StreamableFactory {
    Streamable create_uninitialized();
  };

  interface StreamIO {
    void write_string (in string aString);
    void write_char (in char aChar);
```

```
        void write_octet (in octet anOctet);
        void write_unsigned_long (in unsigned_long anUnsignedLong);
        void write_unsigned_short (in unsigned short anUnsignedShort);
        void write_long (in long aLong);
        void write_short (in short aShort);
        void write_float (in float aFloat);
        void write_double (in double aDouble);
        void write_boolean (in boolean aBoolean);
        void write_object (in Streamable aStreamable);
        void write_graph (in CosCompoundExternalization::Node aNode);
        string read_string()
          raises(StreamDataFormatError);
        char read_char()
          raises(StreamDataFormatError);
        octet read_octet()
          raises(StreamDataFormatError);
        unsigned long read_unsigned_long()
          raises(StreamDataFormatError);
        unsigned short read_unsigned_short()
          raises(StreamDataFormatError);
        long read_long()
          raises(StreamDataFormatError);
        short read_short()
          raises(StreamDataFormatError);
        float read_float()
          raises(StreamDataFormatError);
        double read_double()
          raises(StreamDataFormatError);
        boolean read_boolean()
          raises(StreamDataFormatError);
        Streamable read_object (
            in FactoryFinder there,
            in Streamable aStreamable)
          raises(StreamDataFormatError);
        void read_graph (
            in CosCompoundExternalization::Node
              starting_node,
            in FactoryFinder there)
          raises(StreamDataFormatError);
    };
  };
```

The Compound Externalization Module

```
#include <Graphs.idl>
#include <Stream.idl>

module CosCompoundExternalization {
  interface Node;
  interface Role;
  interface Relationship;
  interface PropagationCriteriaFactory;

  struct RelationshipHandle {
    Relationship theRelationship;
    ::CosObjectIdentity::ObjectIdentifier constantRandomId;
  };

  interface Node: ::CosGraphs::Node, ::CosStream::Streamable {
    void externalize_node (in ::CosStream::StreamIO sio);
    void internalize_node (in ::CosStream::StreamIO sio,
        in ::CosLifeCycle::FactoryFinder there,
        out Roles rolesOfNode)
      raises(::CosLifeCycle::NoFactory);
  };

  interface Role: ::CosGraphs::Role {
    void externalize_role (in ::CosStream::StreamIO sio);
    void internalize_role (in ::CosStream::StreamIO sio);
    ::CosGraphs::PropagationValue externalize_propagation (
      in RelationshipHandle rel,
      in ::CosRelationships::RoleName toRoleName,
      out boolean sameForAll);
  };

  interface Relationship:
      ::CosRelationships:Relationship {
    void externalize_relationship (in ::CosStream::StreamIO sio);
    void internalize_relationship (in ::CosStream::StreamIO sio,
      in ::CosGraphs::NamedRoles newRoles);
    ::CosGraphs::PropagationValue externalize_propagation (
      in ::CosRelationships::RoleName fromRoleName,
      in ::CosRelationships::RoleName toRoleName,
      out boolean sameForAll);
  };
```

```
      interface PropagationCriteriaFactory {
        ::CosGraphs::TraversalCriteria create_for_externalize();
      };
    };
```

The Externalization Containment Module

```
    #include <Containment.idl>
    #include <CompoundExternalization.idl>

    module CosExternalizationContainment {

      interface Relationship:
        ::CosCompoundExternalization::Relationship,
        ::CosContainment::Relationship {};

      interface ContainsRole:
        ::CosCompoundExternalization:Role,
        ::CosContainment::ContainsRole {};

      interface ContainedInRole:
        ::CosCompoundExternalization:Role,
        ::CosContainment::ContainedInRole {};
    };
```

The Externalization Reference Module

```
    #include <Reference.idl>
    #include <CompoundExternalization.idl>

    module CosExternalizationReference {

      interface Relationship:
        ::CosCompoundExternalization::Relationship,
        ::CosReference::Relationship {};

      interface ReferencesRole:
        ::CosCompoundExternalization:Role,
        ::CosReference::ReferencesRole {};

      interface ReferencedByRole:
        ::CosCompoundExternalization:Role,
        ::CosReference::ReferencedByRole {};
    };
```

Query Service

The CosQuery Module

```
module CosQuery {

    exception QueryInvalid {string why};
    exception QueryProcessingError {string why};
    exception QueryTypeInvalid {};

    enum QueryStatus {complete, incomplete};

    typedef CosQueryCollection::ParameterList ParameterList;
    typedef CORBA::InterfaceDef QLType;
    interface QueryLanguageType {};
    interface SQLQuery : QueryLanguageType {};
    interface SQL_92Query : SQLQuery {};
    interface OQL : QueryLanguageType {};
    interface OQLBasic : OQL {};
    interface OQL_93 : OQL {};
    interface OQL_93Basic : OQL_93, OQLBasic {};

    interface QueryEvaluator {
       readonly attribute sequence<QLType> ql_types;
       readonly attribute QLType default_ql_type;

        any evaluate (in string query, in QLType ql_type, in
ParameterList params) raises(QueryTypeInvalid, QueryInvalid,
QueryProcessingError);
      };

    interface QueryableCollection : QueryEvaluator, CosQuery
Collection::Collection {};

    interface QueryManager : QueryEvaluator {
       Query create (in string query, in QLType ql_type, in
ParameterList params) raises(QueryTypeInvalid, QueryInvalid);
      };

    interface Query {
       readonly attribute QueryManager query_mgr;

       void prepare (in ParameterList params) raises(QueryProcessingError);
       void execute (in ParameterList params) raises(QueryProcessingError);
```

```
         QueryStatus get_status ();
         any get_result ();
      };

   };
```

The CosQueryCollection Module

```
   module CosQueryCollection {

      exception ElementInvalid {};
      exception IteratorInvalid {};
      exception PositionInvalid {};


      enum ValueType {TypeBoolean, TypeChar, TypeOctet, TypeShort,
   TypeUShort, TypeLong, TypeULong, TypeFloat, TypeDouble, TypeString,
   TypeObject, TypeAny, TypeSmallInt, TypeInteger, TypeReal,
   TypeDoublePrecision, TypeCharacter, TypeDecimal, TypeNumeric};
      struct Decimal {long precision; long scale; sequence<octet> value;}
      union Value switch(ValueType) {
         case TypeBoolean: boolean b;
         case TypeChar: char c;
         case TypeOctet: octet o;
         case TypeShort : short s;
         case TypeUShort : unsigned short us;
         case TypeLong : long l;
         case TypeULong : unsigned long ul;
         case TypeFloat : float f;
         case TypeDouble : double d;
         case TypeString : string str;
         case TypeObject : Object obj;
         case TypeAny : any a;
         case TypeSmallInt : short si;
         case TypeInteger : long i;
         case TypeReal : float r;
         case TypeDoublePrecision : double dp;
         case TypeCharacter : string ch;
         case TypeDecimal : Decimal dec;
         case TypeNumeric : Decimal n;
      };
      typedef boolean Null;
      union FieldValue switch(Null) {
         case false : Value v;
```

```
    };
    typedef sequence<FieldValue> Record;
    typedef string Istring;
    struct NVPair {Istring name; any value;};
    typedef sequence<NVPair> ParameterList;

    interface Collection;
    interface Iterator;

    interface CollectionFactory {
      Collection create (in ParameterList params);
    };

    interface Collection {
      readonly attribute long cardinality;

      void add_element (in any element) raises(ElementInvalid);
      void add_all_elements (in Collection elements) raises(ElementInvalid);

      void insert_element_at (in any element, in Iterator where)
raises(IteratorInvalid, ElementInvalid);

      void replace_element_at (in any element, in Iterator where)
raises(IteratorInvalid, PositionInvalid, ElementInvalid);

      void remove_element_at (in Iterator where)
raises(IteratorInvalid, PositionInvalid);
      void remove_all_elements ();

      any retrieve_element_at (in Iterator where)
raises(IteratorInvalid, PositionInvalid);

      Iterator create_iterator ();
    };

    interface Iterator {
      any next () raises(IteratorInvalid, PositionInvalid);

      void reset ();
      boolean more ();
    };
};
```

Property Service

The Property Interface

Note that Istring is a place-holder, first used in the Naming service, for an internationalized string data type.

```
#include "Naming.idl"
module Property {

  struct Property {
    Istring property_name;
    any value;
  };

  typedef sequence<Istring> PropertyIDList;
  typedef sequence<Property> PropertyList;

  interface PropertyIDIterator {
    boolean first( out Istring property_name );
    boolean next_one( out Istring property_name );
    boolean next_n(
      inout unsigned long how_many,
      out PropertyIDList property_names );
  };

  interface PropertyIterator {
    boolean first( out Property property );
    boolean next_one( out Property property );
    boolean next_n(
      inout unsigned long how_many,
      out PropertyList properties );
  };
};
```

The Property Store Interface

```
#include "Naming.idl"
#include "Property.idl"
#include "Constraint.idl"

module PropertyStore {

  interface PropertyStore {
```

```
/* Exceptions */
exception InvalidPropertyName {
  Istring failing_property_name; };
exception ConflictingProperty {
  Istring failing_property_name; };
exception PropertyNotFound {
  Istring failing_property_name; };
enum NotSupportedReason {
  unsupported_Typecode,
  unsupported_property_name,
  properties_are_fixed,
  properties_are_read_only
};
exception NotSupported {
  NotSupportedReason why;
  Istring failing_property_name;
};
exception IllegalConstraintExpression {
  Istring failing_constraint_substring;
};

/* Administration */
attribute sequence<TypeCode> allowed_property_types;
attribute sequence<Istring> allowed_property_names;

/* Support for Adding and Setting Properties */
void add_property(
    in Property prop )
  raises( PropertyNotFound,
    InvalidPropertyName,
    ConflictingProperty,
    NotSupported );
void add_properties(
    in PropertyList properties )
  raises( InvalidPropertyName,
    ConflictingProperty,
    NotSupported );

/* Support for listing and getting properties */
unsigned long get_properties_count();
unsigned long get_properties_size();
```

```
void list_properties(
  in unsigned long how_many,
  out PropertyIDList pbl,
  out PropertyIterator rest );
void get_property(
    in Istring property_name,
    out any value )
  raises( PropertyNotFound,
    InvalidPropertyName );
void get_properties(
    in unsigned long how_many,
    in PropertyIDList properties,
    out PropertyList properties,
    out PropertyIterator rest)
  raises( PropertyNotFound,
    InvalidPropertyName );
void get_all_properties (
    in unsigned long how_many,
    out PropertyList properties,
    out PropertyIterator rest )
  raises( PropertyNotFound );

/* Support for removing properties */
void remove_property(
    in Istring property_name )
  raises( PropertyNotFound,
    InvalidPropertyName,
    NotSupported );
void remove_properties(
    in PropertyIDList property_names )
  raises( PropertyNotFound,
    InvalidPropertyName,
    NotSupported );
void remove_all_properties()
  raises( NotSupported );

/* Support for search */
boolean has_property(
    in Istring property_name )
  raises( InvalidPropertyName );
boolean satisfies_constraint(
```

```
        in Constraint::Cstring c )
      raises( IllegalConstraintExpression );
  };
};
```

The Constraint Interface

```
#include "Naming.idl"
module Constraint {
  typedef Naming::Istring Cstring;
};
```

Guide to CORBA Resources

The first rule of software engineering taught by instructor Dennis Allison at Stanford University is: "Don't re-invent it, steal it." Of course, there are legal limits to this approach, but you will find there is an amazing array of information and software resources that are freely available to OMG members and non-members.

OMG encourages the free use of its standards, regardless of membership. This includes all OMG IDL that appears in dozens of adopted OMG specifications.

Virtually all OMG documentation is also freely available (in some form) over the Internet. You may not get the prettiest or best organized versions (available as paid publications from OMG), but you can get accurate versions of adopted standards, as well as all proposed specifications, white papers, presentations, and meeting minutes.

D.1 Freeware

There are many freeware contributors of OMG technologies. These are listed below, as well.

D.1.1 Inter-Language Unification (ILU) Freeware ORB

The inter-language unification (ILU) object request broker (ORB) is a freeware software package with its own web page: http://www-diglib.stanford.edu/ilu

True to its name, ILU is a CORBA-compliant ORB with many programming language bindings. These bindings are implemented through ILU's OMG IDL compiler. Some of these bindings are unique to ILU (such as Modula), and some exist in other forms in other CORBA products, such as Lisp, C++, and SmallTalk.

D.1.2   Fresco Freeware Library ORB

Fresco is a technology created by the X Consortium as a future object-oriented replacement of X Windows. Fresco includes several major elements: an IDL compiler for C++, a scripting toolkit, a graphical embedding library, and a basic set of widgets. Fresco was architected by Mark Linton at Silicon Graphics. Much of the recent work on Fresco has been done by Steve Churchill and his colleagues at Fujitsu. Fujitsu has created a commercial version of the Fresco technology, which they support.

An interesting result of the Fresco research is experience with using OMG IDL in a nondistributed ORB environment. Mark Linton and his colleagues found that OMG IDL is a valuable addition to the programming environment even when C++ is the only language and the whole program is in the same address space. The key advantage is due to OMG IDL's clean separation of interface from implementation. Ordinary C++ class definitions contain implementation dependencies, such as their constructors, which lead to unwanted implementation dependencies. Similar benefits of OMG IDL have been encountered at Novell in the programming of real-time network operating systems. In that case, OMG IDL provided clean boundaries between parts of their operating system and helped Novell to avoid unwanted dependencies among subsystems even when they were in the same address space.

The freeware version of Fresco can be downloaded with the X Windows release X11R6. Note that the C++ language binding is not compliant with CORBA 2. This issue is resolved in the Fujitsu version of the ORB.

D.1.3   CORBUS Government-Furnished Software ORB

A free version of a CORBA is available to U.S. government contractors and other organizations (when approved). This ORB includes bindings to Common Lisp and C++. The maker is Bolt, Beranek, and Newman (BBN), the company that did much of the early work on the Internet's predecessor, ARPANET. For more information on CORBUS, visit: http://www.bbn.com/offerings/corbus.html

D.1.4   DISCUS Freeware Documentation
and Government-Furnished Software

The DISCUS project was the U.S. government's first CORBA-compliant application architecture. DISCUS has been widely reused on government software projects and is potentially applicable to commercial systems integration. An on-line address for electronic mail consulting is: discus@corba.mitre.org

DISCUS is described in detail in another book, *The Essential CORBA: Systems Integration Using Distributed Objects*, John Wiley & Sons, 1995. (ISBN 0-471-10611-9) For more information on DISCUS, visit: http://www.serve.com/mowbray/discus.html

D.2   Insider's Guide to the Object Management Group's Resources

The OMG and its many resources provide a source for much useful information, most of which is available free to members and nonmembers.

D.2.1   You May Already Be an OMG Member

OMG membership is available on an annual basis for a nominal fee. Since there are thousands of OMG members, it is possible that your organization is already a member. To determine this, call OMG or check a recent issue of *OMG First Class Magazine.*

A key benefit of membership is that you can get direct subscriptions to OMG's mailing lists. Every OMG subgroup has its own mailing list, including less-formal working groups. You must specifically request subscription to each list. Subscribe by sending an e-mail note to: request@omg.org

Ask for the particular subgroup that you wish to monitor. Electronic membership in subgroups is almost as good as being there because the minutes and electronic documents presented at the meeting are posted for most subgroups.

D.2.2   How to Get Invited to an OMG Meeting

OMG membership enables you to come to OMG meetings without an invitation. If you are not a member, you need two invitations, but that is generally not a problem. Almost anybody can get invited to an OMG meeting by contacting OMG directly; OMG can help you solicit the required invitations from two corporate members.

D.2.3   How to Contact OMG

The Object Management Group, Inc.
492 Old Connecticut Path
Framingham, MA 01701 U.S.A.
Phone: (508)820-4300
FAX: (508)820-4303
Electronic mail: request@omg.org
Internet: http://www.omg.org

D.2.4   OMG Documentation via E-mail

Believe it or not, OMG insiders use electronic mail retrieval more than any other form of access to OMG documentation. To obtain OMG's on-line documents through Internet electronic mail, send a one-line message containing the single word *help*, to: server@omg.org

The server will respond via electronic mail with further instructions.

Here's an example, using UNIX commands:
mail server@omg.org
Subject:
help
^D

D.2.5   OMG Information on World Wide Web

OMG's home page on the WWW contains general information about OMG and publications.

http://www.omg.org

D.2.6   Freeware OMG IDL Compiler Toolkit
and Interoperability Toolkit

Use the Internet file transfer protocol (ftp omg.org) and log in as anonymous; this log in is automatic for America Online users. Located on this FTP is the freeware OMG IDL compiler development toolkit and the freeware IIOP CORBA 2 interoperability toolkit and compiler toolkit. Almost everything is located in the /pub directory.

D.2.7   OMG Document Access via Internet File Transfer
Protocol (FTP)

FTP access to OMG documentation is available through anonymous file transfer protocol to the host ftp.omg.org. Currently, the documents are posted under the directory: /pub/archives/docs. Each subgroup has its own directory for documents dated 1996 or later. There are combined directories for all subgroups for documents dated 1995 and earlier.

Also available on the OMG's FTP site is a complete set of OMG briefings in editable form. Check the /pub/presentations directory. Note that the PostScript (.ps) versions are printable but not editable. The PowerPoint (.ppt) versions are both printable and editable using Microsoft Powerpoint (Windows format). Since these briefings are copyrighted, make sure you request their usage from the OMG before you adapt them to your own needs. One of the most useful of these briefings is the "overview.ppt," which contains the general introduction that the OMG uses for new audiences. This briefing contains useful background information on the "notes" pages. We often require our new technical staff to learn how to deliver this briefing because it contains the basics about the OMG and

CORBA technologies. I have given this briefing numerous times to audiences and it is amazingly self-explanatory and bulletproof.

D.2.8   OMG MARKETFAX

A convenient way to get free information about OMG is through their auto-mated fax service, called MARKETFAX. To automatically retrieve information about the Object Management Group (OMG) through fax, call (800)486-9808 or (508)820-0633 and dial the extension of the document you wish to retrieve. Samples from the MARKETFAX documents are:

Extension	Information
100	List of FAX Documents Available
102	Publication Order Form
105	Suggested Readings

D.2.9   CORBA Products Directory

The OMG publishes a list of CORBA technology sources. There is also a pay version of this information on CD-ROM, from Ovum Ltd. (Check with OMG, Ovum, or your library.)

D.2.10   OMG Object Technology White Paper

An executive level overview of object technology and the OMG. Available from the OMG.

D.2.11   OMG Membership Kit or Press Kit

This folder of information contains the OMG White Paper, membership appli-cation forms, and various other info. Contact OMG.

D.2.12   Object World Conference Series

This is a worldwide series of conferences and generally includes free access to the exhibits show floor along with many free lectures, panels, and social events. All major CORBA product announcements and demonstrations occur at these conferences and are a great source of up-to-date information about products, ser-vices, and the standards process. Annual conference locations include Boston, San Francisco, London, Sydney, Frankfurt, and Tokyo. Contact: Object World c/o COMDEX Corporation, 300 First Avenue, Needham, MA 02194-2722; Fax: (617)433-2814; Phone: (617)433-1500. Visit their Internet site at: http://www. ow.com

D.2.13   CORBA Academy

CORBA Academy is an OMG/COMDEX event targeted at programmers. This is a three- to four-day training event that usually includes social activities. Unique technical material is presented in the focus sessions on the final days of the conference. CORBA Academy provides initial training for people new to CORBA.

Contact: CORBA Academy c/o COMDEX Corporation, 300 First Avenue, Needham, MA 02194-2722; Fax: (617)433-2814; Phone: (617)433-1500. Visit their Internet site at: http://www.ow.com

D.2.14   OMG Social Opportunities

OMG events provide many excellent social opportunities. One of the best social events of the year is the ComputerWorld Object Application Awards Reception at Object World San Francisco. This event always occurs on Wednesday night during Object World and includes live music, food, refreshments, and an excellent gift.

At most Object World conferences, there are a number of free receptions, some publicly announced. Some receptions occur on the show floor. Check with the vendor booths for the availability of such events. The companies that hold particularly good events are: Apple, Digital Equipment Corp., Microsoft, NeXT, Oracle, Rational, and Sun Microsystems.

OMG meetings provide many opportunities to socialize with CORBA product developers. Attendees at OMG meetings include the top architects and developers from some of the world's most advanced object technology companies. OMG meetings are usually held at a select hotel with formal meetings Sundays through Fridays. Every evening during the week, OMG folks gather in the hotel lobby after the formal sessions, usually between 5:30 pm and 7 pm. One can easily join with these groups and enjoy some interesting technical and nontechnical discussions over dinner. The hotel bar is another meeting place for OMG meeting participants after hours. Some of the most valuable contacts are made in such informal environments.

D.3   Insider's Guide to CORBA-Related Publications

- Mowbray, T.J., and R. Zahavi, *The Essential CORBA: Systems Integration Using Distributed Objects.* New York: John Wiley, 1995. (ISBN 0-471-10611-9)

  The focus of this, my previous CORBA book, is on object-oriented software architecture. It provides much useful guidance on how to build successful systems using CORBA. This book is a must-have for all corporate developers and systems integrators.

For information: http://www.serve.com/mowbray/essential.html

- Mowbray, T.J., and R. Malveau, *CORBA Design Patterns*. New York: John Wiley, 1997. (ISBN 0-471-15882-8)

  This is the second book of the Mowbray/CORBA trilogy. Its focus is on object-oriented design patterns for use with distributed objects. The book combines and extends the best ideas from distributed objects, software architecture, and design patterns and provides systematic theory and guidance, including advanced programming tricks, advanced architecture techniques, and CORBA/Internet patterns. This is a must-have for experts and people needing systematic guidance for CORBA migration.

  For information: http://www.serve.com/mowbray/CDPflyer.html

- *Object Management Architecture Guide* (OMA Guide). Object Management Group, New York: John Wiley, 1995.

  This is the root node of OMG's standards documentation. It contains much useful, but general, information, including an explanation of the OMG architecture reference model, an explanation of the OMG process, a standard glossary of object technology terminology, and the core object model. This book is great for managers interested in OMG and is a must-have for people who want to understand the OMG process.

- *Common Object Request Broker Architecture and Specification (CORBA). Revision 2*, Object Management Group, August 1995.

  This is the official standards document describing CORBA. It is a must-have for all users and developers of CORBA ORBs. This specification is available on-line from the OMG site: http://www.omg.org

- *CORBAservices*. Object Management Group, OMG TC Document 95-3-31, 1995.

  This is the official standards document for all adopted CORBAservices (formerly Common Object Services Specifications). This is a must-have for all developers and architects using CORBAservices. This book is available on-line from the OMG site: http://www.omg.org

- *CORBAfacilities*. Object Management Group, OMG TC Document 95-1-2, 1995.

  This is the official standards document describing the CORBAfacilities architecture and the adopted CORBAfacilities. This is a must-have for everybody who wants to understand the CORBAfacilities or become involved in the OMG process for vertical markets. This publication is available on-line from the OMG site: http://www.omg.org (see the public documents section).

- Guttman, M., and J.R. Matthews, *The Object Technology Revolution*. New York: John Wiley, 1995.

    This is a nontechnical introduction to object technology and CORBA. It is a must-have for executives and other decision makers.

- Orfali, R., D. Harkey, D., and J. Edwards, *The Essential Distributed Object Survival Guide*. New York: John Wiley, 1995.

    This is an illustrated guide to popular object technologies: CORBA, OpenDoc, OLE, COM, CommonPoint, and so forth. This book is a must-have for people who need to be in the know about current technologies.

- Otte, R., P. Patrick, and M. Roy, *Understanding CORBA*. Upper Saddle River, NJ: Prentice Hall, 1995.

    This book is written by three developers of Digital Equipment Corp.'s ObjectBroker ORB. Mark Roy (currently at Semaphore, Inc.) is one of the most experienced consultants doing CORBA programming and programmer training. The book follows ObjectBroker product features closely. It covers many elements of OMG standards, except CORBAservices and CORBAfacilities, and contains many useful programming examples. This book is a must-have for users of DEC ObjectBroker.

- O'Calaghan, A. (Ed.), *Practical Experiences Of Object Technology*. London: Stanley Thornes Publishers, 1996.

    This book is a collection of papers on the topic of object technology development and migration. There is an entertaining chapter on CORBA migration, covering the IBM/Stanford Software Lego project.

- Brodie, M. and M. Stonebraker, *Migrating Legacy Systems*. New York: McGraw-Hill, 1995.

    This book describes the process of legacy system migration at a manager's level. The authors are database experts, so they focus on database migration as the core of the migration problem. The book has several cookbook listings of migration steps and advice that would be useful to managers. The book recommends that the target migration architecture follow the object management architecture reference model.

- *Distributed Object Computing* Magazine

    This new magazine published by the Object Management Group contains articles by CORBA developers, users, and researchers. *Distributed Object Computing* replaces the previous membership newsletter, *OMG First Class*. The magazine contains bi-monthly updates on OMG activities in its role as the newsletter's replacement. However, *Distributed Object Computing* has a broad perspective beyond OMG activities. Contact the Object Management Group for information.

- *Object Magazine*

    This magazine is devoted to object-oriented technology in general. It contains frequent articles on CORBA-related topics, including Tom Mowbray's bimonthly column on object-oriented architectures (ISSN 1055-3614). For information: http://www.sigs.com

Bibliography

Abnous, R., and S. Khoshafian, *Object Orientation: Concepts, Languages, Databases, User Interfaces*. New York: John Wiley, 1990.

Balda, D. M., and D. A. Gustafson, "Cost Estimation Models for the Reuse and Prototype Software Development Life-Cycles," *ACM SIGSOFT Software Engineering Notes*, Vol. 15, No. 3, July 1990.

Biggerstaff, T., and A. Perlis, *Software Reusability Vol. I, Concepts and Models*. Reading, MA: Addison-Wesley, 1989.

Biggerstaff, T., and A. Perlis, *Software Reusability Vol. II, Applications and Experience*. Reading, MA: Addison-Wesley, 1989.

Blaha, M., et al., *Object-Oriented Modeling and Design*. Englewood Cliffs, NJ: Prentice Hall, 1991.

Booch, G., *Object-Oriented Analysis and Design with Applications*. Reading, MA: Addison-Wesley, 1994.

Booch, G., *Object Solutions: Managing the Object-Oriented Project*. Reading, MA: Addison-Wesley, 1996.

Brando, T., "Comparing CORBA & DCE," *Object Magazine*, March 1996.

Brinch Hansen, P., *Operating Systems Principles*. Reading, MA: Addison-Wesley, 1976.

Brockschmidt, K., *Inside OLE*, Second Edition. Redmond, WA: Microsoft Press, 1995.

Brodie, M., and M. Stonebraker, *Migrating Legacy Systems*. New York, NY: McGraw-Hill, 1995.

Brooks, F. P., *The Mythical Man-Month: Essays on Software Engineering*. Reading, MA: Addison-Wesley, 1975.

Brooks, F. P., "No Silver Bullets: Essence and Accidents of Software Engineering," *IEEE Computer*, April 1987, pp. 10–19.

Cargill, C. F., *Information Technology Standardization: Theory, Process, and Organizations*. Bedford, MA: Digital Press, 1989.

Coad, P., and E. Yourdon, *Object-Oriented Analysis*. Englewood Cliffs, NJ: Prentice Hall, 1991.

Cornell, J. L., and L. B. Shafer, *Structured Rapid Prototyping: An Evolutionary Approach to Software Development*. Englewood Cliff, NJ: Yourdan Press/ Prentice Hall, 1989.

Demarco, T., and T. Lister, *Peopleware: Productive Projects and Teams*. New York, NY: Dorset House, 1987.

Demarco, T., and T. Lister, *Software State of the Art: Selected Papers*. New York, NY: Dorset House, 1990.

Dickman, A., "Race Between CORBA and ActiveX/DCOM," *Application Development*, January 20, 1997.

Dolberg, S. H., "Integrating Applications in the Real World," Open Information Systems: Guide to UNIX and Other Open Systems. Boston: Patricia Seybold Group, July 1992.

Fairthorne, B. (ed.), et al., "Security White Paper," OMG TC Document, 1994.

Gamma, E., R. Helm, R. Johnson, and J. Vlissides, *Design Patterns: Elements of Reusable Object-Oriented Software*. Reading, MA: Addison-Wesley, 1994.

Goldberg, A., and D. Robinson, *Smalltalk-80: The Language and Its Implementation*. Reading, MA: Addison-Wesley, 1983.

Goldberg, A., *Smalltalk-80: The Interactive Programming Environment*. Reading, MA: Addison-Wesley, 1984.

Guttman, M., and J. R. Matthews, *The Object Technology Revolution*. New York: John Wiley, 1995.

Hagmann, R., *Concurrency Within DOE Object Implementations*. SunSoft Microsystems, May 27, 1993.

Horowitz, B. M., *Strategic Buying for the Future*. Washington D.C.: Libey Publishing, 1993.

Humphrey, W., *Managing the Software Process*. Reading, MA: Addison-Wesley, 1989.

Hutt, A. (ed.), *Object-Oriented Analysis and Design*. New York: John Wiley, 1994.

IEEE, *Draft Guide to the POSIX Open System Environment*. IEEE P 1003.0, Institute of Electrical and Electronics Engineers, New York, 1993.

IEEE, POSIX Working Group P1003.4a/D6, "Threads Extension for Portable Operating Systems," Institute of Electrical and Electronics Engineers, 1993a.

Inmon, W. H., *Advanced Topics in Information Engineering*. Wellesley, MA: QED Information Sciences, 1989.

Johnson, J., "Creating Chaos," *American Programmer*, July 1995.

Katz, M., D. Cornwell, and T. J. Mowbray, "System Integration with Minimal Object Wrappers," Proceedings of TOOLS 93, August 1993.

Levy, L., *Taming the Tiger: Software Engineering and Software Economics*. New York, NY: Springer Verlag, 1987.

Linton, M., "An Introduction to Fresco," Tutorial W7, XWorld Conference, New York, June 1994.

Microsoft®, *A Strategic Look at the Business of Microsoft BackOffice*, Microsoft® Windows NT™ Server, 1996a.

Microsoft®, *Server Operating System*, Microsoft® Windows NT™ Server, 1996b.

Mills, H., *Software Productivity*. New York, NY: Dorset House, 1988.

Mowbray, T. J., and R. Malveau, *CORBA Design Patterns*, New York: John Wiley, 1997. (ISBN 0-471-15882-8)

Mowbray, T. J., and R. Zahavi, *The Essential CORBA: Systems Integration Using Distributed Objects*. New York: John Wiley, 1995. (ISBN 0-471-10611-9)

Mowbray, T. J., "Choosing between OLE/COM and CORBA," *Object Magazine*, November-December 1994c.

Mowbray, T. J., and R. Zahavi, "Distributed Processing with Object Management," *ConneXions—The Interoperability Report*, February 1994b.

Mowbray, T. J., "Distributed Objects Everywhere: An Early Assessment," *Object Magazine*, January 1994a.

Mowbray, T. J., and T. Brando, "Interoperability and CORBA-Based Open Systems," *Object Magazine*, September 1993.

Mullin, M., *Rapid Prototyping for Object-Oriented Systems*. Reading MA: Addison-Wesley, 1990.

Object Management Group, *Common Facilities Roadmap*, OMG Document 95.1.10, Framingham, MA: OMG, January 1995a.

Object Management Group, *Common Object Request Broker Architecture and Specification* (CORBA), Revision 2. New York: John Wiley, August 1995b.

Object Management Group, *CORBAfacilities*, (Interim OMG TC Document 95-1-2), New York: John Wiley, 1995c.

Object Management Group, *CORBAservices*, OMG TC Document 95-3-31, New York: John Wiley, 1995d.

Object Management Group, *Object Management Architecture Guide* (OMA Guide), New York: John Wiley, 1995e.

Object Management Group, *Object Services Architecture*, OMG Document 94.11.12, Framingham, MA: OMG, November 1994.

Object Management Group, *Object Services Roadmap*, OMG TC Document 92-09-05, Framingham, MA: OMG, 1992.

O'Calaghan, A. (ed.), *Practical Experiences Of Object Technology*. London: Stanley Thornes, 1996.

Open Software Foundation, *Introduction to OSF™ DCE*, Rev. 1.0, PTR. Englewood Cliffs, NJ: Prentice Hall, 1992.

Orfali, R., D. Harkey, and J. Edwards, *The Essential Distributed Objects Survival Guide*. New York: John Wiley, 1995.

Otte, R., P. Patrick, and M. Roy, *Understanding CORBA*. Upper Saddle River, NJ: Prentice Hall, 1995.

Roetzheim, W. H., *Developing Software to Government Standards*. Englewood Cliffs, NJ: Prentice Hall, 1991.

Roy, M., and A. Ewald, "Choosing Between CORBA and DCOM," *Distributed Objects*, October 1996b.

Roy, M., and A. Ewald, "Interworking COM with CORBA," *Distributed Objects*, May 1996a.

Roy, M., and A. Ewald, "Designing OMG IDL Interfaces," *Distributed Objects*, June 1995.

Rymer, J. et. al., "Microsoft OLE 2.0 and the Road to Cairo," *Distributed Computing Monitor*, Patricia Seybold Group, Vol. 9, No. 1, January 1994.

Shaw, M., and D. Garlan, *Software Architecture: Perspectives on an Emerging Discipline*. New York: Prentice Hall, 1996.

Shaw, M., "Software Architecture for Shared Information Systems," Carnegie Mellon University, Software Engineering Institute, Technical Report No. CMU/SEI-93-TR-3, ESC-TR-93-180, March 1993.

Sigel, J., "CORBA Getting to the Fundamentals: What is it and how it works," *Distributed Computing*, October 1996.

Taylor, D. A., *Object-Oriented Information Systems*. New York: John Wiley, 1992.

Taylor, D. A., *Business Engineering with Object Technology*. New York: John Wiley, 1995.

The Standish Group, "Charting the Seas of Information Technology: CHAOS," The Standish Group International, 1994.

Wiener, L., B. Wilkerson, and R. Wirfs-Brock, *Designing Object-Oriented Software*. Englewood Cliffs, NJ: Prentice Hall, 1990.

Acronyms

ACID	Atomic, consistent, isolated, durable
AI	Application interfaces
AKA	also known as
ANSI	American National Standards Institute
API	Application program interface
APM	Architecture projects management
APP	Application portability profile
BOA	Basic object adapter
CAD	Computer-aided design
CASE	Computer-aided software engineering
Cd	CORBAdomain
CDR	Common data representation
CD-ROM	Compact Disk Read Only Memory
Cf	CORBAfacility
CIO	Chief information officer
CMIP	Common management information protocol
CMU	Carnegie Mellon University
COM	Component object model
CORBA	Common object request broker architecture
Cos	Common object service (aka CORBAservice)
COSE	Common open software environment
COTS	Commercial off-the-shelf

CRC	Class-responsibility-collaborator
Cs	CORBAservice
CWC	Component-Ware Consortium
DEC	Digital Equipment Corporation
DCE	Distributed computing environment
DCOM	Distributed component object model
DDCF	Distributed document component facility
DDE	Dynamic data exchange
DDL	Data definition language
DII	CORBA dynamic invocation interface
DIN	German National Standards Organization
DISCUS	Data interchange and synergistic collateral usage study
DOM	Distributed object management
DSI	Dynamic skeleton interface
ECMA	European Computer Manufacturers Association
EDI	Electronic data interchange
ESIOP	Environment-specific inter-ORB protocol
FGDC	Federal Geographic Data Committee
FIPS	Federal information processing standard
FTP	File transfer protocol
GIF	Graphics interchange format
GIOP	General interoperability protocol
GIS	Geographic information systems
GOSIP	Government open systems interconnection profile
GOTS	Government off-the-shelf
GPL	Gamma pattern language
HTML	Hypertext markup language
HTTP	Hypertext transfer protocol
IBM	International Business Machines
ICD	Interface control document
IDL	Interface definition language

IEEE	Institute of Electrical and Electronics Engineers
IFR	CORBA interface repository
IIOP	Internet inter-ORB protocol
IOR	Interoperable object reference
IP	Internet protocol
ISO	International Standards Organization
IT	Information technology
LS-API	Licensing service-API
MOM	Message-oriented middleware
MQ	Message queue
NIH	National Institute of Health
NIST	National Institute of Standards and Technology
NITF	National imagery transmission format
O&M	Operations and maintenance
ODBC	Open database computing
ODMG	Object Database Management Group
ODP	Open distributed processing
OLE	Object linking and embedding
OLTP	On-line transaction processing
OMA	Object management architecture
OMG	Object Management Group
ONC	Open network computing
OO	Object-oriented
OOA	Object-oriented analysis
OOD	Object-oriented design
OODBMS	Object-oriented database management system
OOPL	Object-oriented programming languages
OPF	Opendoc parts framework
OQL	Object query language
ORB	Object request broker
ORBOS	ORB and object services task force at OMG

OSE	Open system environment
OSF	Open Software Foundation
PC	Personal computer
PCTE	Portable common tool environment
PID	Persistent identifier
PIDL	Pseudo-IDL
POSIX	Portable operating system interface for computer environments
RDA	Remote database access
RFC	Request for comment
RFI	Request for information
RFP	Request for proposal
RMI	Remote method invocation
RPC	Remote procedure call
SDTS	Spatial data transfer service
SEI	Software Engineering Institute
SII	CORBA static invocation interface
SNMP	Simple network management protocol
SOM	System object model
SPC	Software Productivity Consortium
SQL	Structured query language
STL	Standard template library
SYSMAN	X/Open system management
TC	TypeCode
TCP/IP	Transmission control protocol/Internet protocol
URL	Universal resource locator
VAN	Value added network
WAIS	Wide area information search
WWW	World Wide Web
XPG	X/Open portability guide

Index